Urbanisation at Risk in the Pacific and Asia

This book presents practical approaches for tackling the threats from climate change and disasters to urban growth in Pacific island countries and Asian nations.

With chapters written by leading scholars and practitioners, *Urbanisation at Risk* presents research and case studies from island countries across the Pacific, Cambodia, Nepal and the Philippines. The book explores and presents the theory, policy and practice of how governments, civil society, aid organisations and people themselves prepare for, withstand and recover better from urban disasters including windstorms, floods, earthquakes and fires, and the effects of climate change.

This book is written for urban policy makers, researchers, humanitarian aid and development workers, and anyone interested in urbanisation, participatory approaches, disasters, resilience and climate change adaptation.

David Sanderson is Professor and Inaugural Judith Neilson Chair in Architecture at the University of New South Wales (UNSW), Sydney. David has worked across the world in development and emergencies, both in practice, with NGOs and, latterly, in academia. In recent years, David is Editor of the 2016 IFRC World Disasters Report and the author of the ODI/ALNAP 2019 *Good Practice Review in Urban Humanitarian Response*.

Laura Bruce is Research Associate for the Inaugural Judith Neilson Chair in Architecture at UNSW, Sydney, where she is supporting research in urban resilience both internationally and in Australia. Laura has over 12 years' experience working for international NGOs in project management, advocacy and research for development and humanitarian programmes.

'An insightful read on the urgency for a critical understanding of cities in the Asia Pacific region with thoughtful analysis by leading experts. The combination of case-studies and interrogation of cross-cutting themes provides a concrete approach to address the pressing issues facing vulnerable populations with a focus on resilience'.
  —**Ronak B. Patel**, *Director of Urbanization and Resilience Program, Harvard Humanitarian Initiative*

'The rapid rate of urbanisation poses challenges in how humanitarian actors plan, prepare for and respond to disasters. The breath taking speed of change in the urban environment urgently requires adaptability and agility on the part of humanitarians. *Urbanisation at Risk* is a timely publication as it provides pragmatic advice to a policy makers and inspiring examples to practitioners. For the International Federation of Red Cross and Red Crescent Societies with its broad reach to communities through its 192 national societies around the world, this book is essential reading, not only to ensure engagement at the policy level, but also in the design of appropriate programmatic interventions in towns and cities where we work'.

—**Jemilah Mahmood,** *Under Secretary-General, Partnerships,*
International Federation of Red Cross and
Red Crescent Societies

Urbanisation at Risk in the Pacific and Asia

Disasters, Climate Change and Resilience in the Built Environment

Edited by David Sanderson and Laura Bruce

NEW YORK AND LONDON

First published 2020
by Routledge
52 Vanderbilt Avenue, New York, NY 10017

and by Routledge
2 Park Square, Milton Park, Abingdon, Oxon, OX14 4RN

Routledge is an imprint of the Taylor & Francis Group, an informa business

© 2020 Taylor & Francis

The right of David Sanderson and Laura Bruce to be identified
as authors of the editorial material, and of the authors for their
individual chapters, has been asserted by them in accordance with
sections 77 and 78 of the Copyright, Designs and Patents Act 1988.

All rights reserved. No part of this book may be reprinted or
reproduced or utilised in any form or by any electronic, mechanical,
or other means, now known or hereafter invented, including
photocopying and recording, or in any information storage or
retrieval system, without permission in writing from the publishers.

Trademark notice: Product or corporate names may be trademarks
or registered trademarks, and are used only for identification and
explanation without intent to infringe.

Library of Congress Cataloging-in-Publication Data
A catalog record for this title has been requested

ISBN: 978-0-367-25845-0 (hbk)
ISBN: 978-0-367-25847-4 (pbk)
ISBN: 978-0-429-29017-6 (ebk)

Typeset in Sabon
by Apex CoVantage, LLC

Contents

List of Contributors	vii
Foreword	xi
Preface	xiv
List of Abbreviations	xv

PART I
Pacific Island Countries   I

1 Urbanisation at Risk: Urban Resilience in Pacific
   Island Countries   3
   JOHN CONNELL AND MEG KEEN

2 Climate and Disaster Risks, Challenges and Opportunities
   for Resilient Pacific Towns and Cities   22
   DAVID SANDERSON, LAURA BRUCE AND PAMELA SITKO

3 The Humanitarian-Development Nexus in Pacific Urban
   Contexts: Lessons From Tropical Cyclone Winston in Fiji   34
   ANNA GERO AND KEREN WINTERFORD

4 Reflecting on a Journey From Climate Change Vulnerability
   Assessments to the Implementation of Climate Resilience
   Actions: Honiara, Solomon Islands   53
   DARRYN McEVOY, BERNHARD BARTH, ALEXEI TRUNDLE
   AND DAVID MITCHELL

5 What Does Neighbourhood-Level Urban Resilience Look
   Like in Honiara?   74
   LAURA BRUCE AND LEEANNE MARSHALL

vi Contents

6 Using a Systems Approach to Better Understand Urban
   Resilience in Port Vila, Vanuatu   89
   PAMELA SITKO, WALKER TOMA AND OLIVIA JOHNSON

7 'This Is Our Garden Now': Disasters and Belonging
   in an Urban Pacific   107
   JENNIFER DAY AND TOM BAMFORTH

8 Resilience in Pacific Towns and Cities: The Social
   Dimensions of Change   121
   MEG KEEN AND PAUL JONES

PART 2
Asia (and Beyond)   139

9 Planning for Climate Change: Adapting to a More
   Sustainable Urban Future   141
   BARBARA NORMAN

10 Community Resilience Through Self-Help Housing
   Adaptations: Examples From Nepal and the Philippines   152
   SANDRA CARRASCO AND NEERAJ DANGOL

11 The Discourse and Practice of Resilience Policy
   in Phnom Penh   171
   LAURA BECKWITH AND PISETH KEO

12 Are Children the Key to Designing Resilient Cities After a
   Disaster?   186
   ROBYN MANSFIELD

13 Identifying Resilience in Recovery—Complexity,
   Collaboration and Communication   206
   DAVID SANDERSON

   Index   220

Contributors

Editors

Laura Bruce is Research Associate for the Inaugural Judith Neilson Chair in Architecture at UNSW, Sydney, where she is supporting research in urban resilience both internationally and in Australia. Laura has over 12 years' experience working for international NGOs in project management, advocacy and research for development and humanitarian programmes.

David Sanderson is Professor and Inaugural Judith Neilson Chair in Architecture at UNSW, Sydney. David has worked across the world in development and emergencies, both in practice, with NGOs and, latterly, in academia. In recent years, David is Editor of the 2016 IFRC World Disasters Report and the author of the ODI/ALNAP 2019 *Good Practice Review in Urban Humanitarian Response*.

Chapter authors

Tom Bamforth is a writer and aid worker specialising in humanitarian shelter and settlements. He is currently the global focal point (coordination) for the IFRC Shelter Cluster. Tom has led disaster risk-reduction and response programmes in ten countries across the region for over a decade and is the author of *The Rising Tide: among the islands and atolls of the Pacific Ocean.*

Bernhard Barth is Human Settlements Officer at UN-Habitat's Regional Office for Asia and the Pacific, based in Fukuoka, Japan, where he oversees several country programmes including those in the Pacific island countries. Bernhard also oversees the UN-Habitat's Cities and Climate Change Initiative across the Asia and Pacific region.

Laura Beckwith is a PhD candidate in the School of International Development and Global Studies at the University of Ottawa. Laura's current research looks at the political ecology of urban resilience in Phnom Penh and has focused on the impact of urbanisation and environmental change on urban farmers.

viii Contributors

Sandra Carrasco is a McKenzie postdoctoral research fellow at the University of Melbourne. She holds masters and PhD degrees from Kyoto University, Japan. Sandra's research interests include post-disaster reconstruction and community resilience, the transformation of the built environment and the appropriateness of rebuilt settlements, incremental housing, informal settlements, governance and city planning.

John Connell is Professor of Geography in the School of Geosciences at the University of Sydney. John's research interests include rural development, migration and decolonisation, especially in the Pacific. He has written several books on the region, including *Urbanisation in the Island Pacific* (with John Lea, 2002), *Islands at Risk* (2013 and most recently edited *Change and Continuity in the Pacific*, with Helen Lee [2018]) and *Food Security in Small Island States* (with Kristen Lowitt, 2020).

Neeraj Dangol holds a PhD in Urban Planning from the University of Melbourne and has a master of urban and regional planning degree from the University of Hawaii at Manoa. Neeraj's research interests include informal settlements and housing, tenure security, risk perception, disaster risk reduction, community resilience and governance. His doctoral dissertation looks at factors affecting riverbank informal settlers' flood adaptation of housing.

Jennifer Day is Senior Lecturer in Urban Planning at the University of Melbourne. Jennifer is a lead organiser in the Regional Studies Association Research Network on Academic-Practitioner Collaboration for Urban Settlements, South Pacific (APCUS-SP), a network that unites academic knowledge and practitioner expertise towards better urban disaster response (http://apcus.cdmps.org.au).

Anna Gero is a climate change and disaster risk leader and specialist with over 10 years of experience in the Asia-Pacific region. Anna is an experienced project manager, and has led climate change and disaster resilience consultancies, evaluations and research projects since 2008 across 10 Pacific island countries. Anna has an applied understanding of the range of ways climate change and disasters influence development. She has published numerous research and evaluation reports.

Olivia Johnson is involved in the UN-Habitat's City Resilience Profiling Programme where she supports Port Vila's Municipal Council to develop resilience projects. Olivia has worked for international NGOs. Previous activities involve supporting the National Disaster Management Office (Vanuatu) with their community disaster climate change committee handbook and provincial-level disaster risk reduction and climate change adaptation emergency response plans.

Paul Jones is an Associate Professor in the School of Architecture, Design and Planning at the University of Sydney. Paul has extensive Asia and

Pacific island practice and research experience, having worked full-time for 18 years in urban development and management projects in the Pacific region for national governments, regional development agencies and partners such as the Asian Development Bank, UN-Habitat, UNES-CAP, PIFs and CLGF.

Meg Keen is Director of the Australia—Pacific Security College and Professor at the Crawford School of Public Policy at ANU, Canberra. Meg has conducted research projects across the Pacific islands, and was the project leader for the ANU's Urbanisation in Melanesia research programme (2015–19) while a Senior Policy Fellow at the Department of Pacific Affairs. Meg's current research focuses on regional security and resilience in the Pacific, with a focus on human, environmental and national security issues.

Piseth Keo is a researcher and practitioner in the field of environmental management and development. Piseth got his doctoral degree from the Joint-Doctoral Programme between National University of Singapore and Harvard-Yenching Institute in 2018. His doctoral dissertation was, 'Discourses, Institution, and Power: Political Ecology of Community-Based Natural Resource Management in Cambodia'.

Robyn Mansfield is a PhD candidate at Monash University. She is an international humanitarian design and consultation specialist. Robyn has an extensive background in local government, and has undertaken projects in Sri Lanka, Peru and Ecuador, and the Middle East. Robyn is a qualified landscape architect and holds master's degrees in international and community development, and disaster, design and development.

Leeanne Marshall is Shelter Technical Lead in the International Programs Department at Australian Red Cross where she supports the delivery of high-quality and inclusive shelter assistance to people affected by disaster and crises in the Asia Pacific region. She has field experience in both development and emergency contexts across the region and is particularly interested in investigating ways to support locally led preparedness, response and resilience.

Darryn McEvoy is a research professor in urban resilience and climate change adaptation in the School of Engineering, RMIT University. Darryn has extensive experience of research in the Asia Pacific region and currently leads the scientific component of the Climate Resilient Honiara project, funded by the UNFCCC Adaptation Fund and administered by UN-Habitat.

David Mitchell is Associate Professor with the School of Science, RMIT University. He holds a PhD from RMIT University, and his research focus is on the impact of climate change and naturally triggered disasters on land tenure, and how responsible land governance can help. He explores how securing and safeguarding land tenure rights, and effective land use planning, can enhance climate-resilient pathways.

Barbara Norman is Foundation Chair of Urban and Regional Planning and Director of Canberra Urban and Regional Futures (CURF) at the University of Canberra. Barbara is Honorary Professor at the University of Warwick, Visiting Fellow at ANU and is a past national president of the Planning Institute of Australia. She has a substantial professional background, having worked at all levels of government and running her own practice.

Pamela Sitko is an urban resilience specialist with a focus on people and the built environment. She holds a PhD in urban disaster resilience from Oxford Brookes University. Pamela has 14 years of experience consulting on projects in disaster, development and conflict settings in over 20 countries for UN-Habitat, the World Food Programme and various NGOs. She currently works in disaster recovery for the New South Wales Government Office of Emergency Management in Australia.

Walker Toma has worked for UN-Habitat's City Resilience Profiling Programme since 2017, focusing on making cities more resilient and sustainable. His current role involves supporting the municipality of Port Vila on new policy and government-led initiatives. Walker is currently pursuing a doctorate in architecture analysing the economic feasibility of current affordable housing policies in Barcelona.

Alexei Trundle is a PhD candidate at the University of Melbourne, based in the Australian-German Climate and Energy College. Alexei is the Future Cities research coordinator at the Melbourne Sustainable Society Institute and acts as a scientific advisor to the UN-Habitat Cities and Climate Change Initiative (CCCI) in the Pacific.

Keren Winterford has more than 20 years of experience working in the international development sector with NGOs, as a private consultant, and more recently in development research. Keren has extensive experience working in the Pacific on climate change-related research, evaluation and consultancy activities, many of which have included a focus on risk governance and gender and social inclusion.

Foreword

As with most of the rest of the world, Pacific island countries (PICs) and countries in Asia are experiencing high rates of urbanisation. Globally, Asia is predicted to experience the highest rate of urban growth, from the current level of 2.3 billion urban dwellers (as recorded in 2018) to an estimated 3.5 billion by 2050 (UNDESA, 2018). PICs were 23 percent urbanised by 2015 (Jones and Sanderson, 2017), a figure which is set to increase: predicted growth rates between 2013–23 see Suva (Fiji) growing from 20 percent to 31 percent, Port Moresby (Papua New Guinea) from 45 percent to 56 percent, and Honiara (Solomon Islands) from 35 percent to 64 percent (Pacific Region Infrastructure Facility, 2015).

Cities in PICs and Asia are also susceptible to sudden onset naturally triggered disasters, with climate change fuelling stronger windstorms, sea level rises and higher temperatures. Pacific islands such as Vanuatu are ranked as some of the most vulnerable nations on the planet. Tropical Cyclones Pam (2015), Winston (2016) and Gita (2018) that struck the Pacific islands of Vanuatu, Fiji and Tonga, respectively, caused widespread economic damage and loss of life. In Asia, Typhoon Haiyan tore through central Philippines in 2013 caused widespread damage and the loss of over 6,000 lives, while over one million people were evacuated into cyclone shelters in Bangladesh and India's Odisha State in the wake of 2019's Cyclone Fani. The evacuation dramatically reduced the death toll that would otherwise have occurred, but the cyclone's damage will take years to recover from. Elsewhere in Asia, many cities in India, Pakistan and Thailand are routinely flooded, causing huge economic losses, as well as large degrees of disruption.

Disasters of course are anything but natural—the term 'natural disaster' is an oxymoron—and rapid, sometimes unplanned urban growth is, often literally, building in vulnerabilities that make them more susceptible to sudden-onset disasters. The building of new settlements in flood-prone zones exacerbates risk needlessly. Buildings such as schools and hospitals made unsafe through corrupt building practices increases the risk of collapse in earthquakes (Ambrasays and Bilham, 2011). And, it is no coincidence that poorer people living in informal settlements within cities are

xii Foreword

among the most vulnerable, where those living in poorly constructed buildings with little protection from fires, windstorms and flooding are almost always going to suffer the most when disasters strike.

How can this dreadful confluence of urbanisation, disasters and vulnerability be fought? One approach that has widespread traction and appeal is the concept of resilience—efforts at a number of levels by differing groups to act before a disaster to reduce or prevent a catastrophic event; and, should one happen, to recover quickly and be stronger as a result. Resilience has found a home in a number of initiatives, including the Sustainable Development Goals (SDGs), and is used as the cornerstone for a wide range of policies and actions. Resilience, though, is not without its critics. Furthermore, it has to be very effective indeed if it is to square up to the challenges ahead.

How then does the concept of resilience apply to fast-urbanising cities in the Pacific and Asia in relation to climate change and disasters? This book seeks to explore this question. The book emerges from a conference, organised by the editors and held at the University of New South Wales (UNSW), Sydney in November 2018, in conjunction with Australian Red Cross, ARUP and the South Asia Institute at Harvard University. The conference, 'Urban Resilience Asia Pacific' was attended by around 200 researchers and practitioners from the Pacific, Asia and beyond. Presenters from the conference were invited to submit abstracts for this book. As a result, this publication comprises 13 chapters. Eight of the chapters focus on PICs, while a further five chapters explore resilience and climate change in Asia.

The title of the book, *Urbanisation at Risk* is taken from the opening chapter, written by John Connell and Meg Keen. The title is intended to be both a challenge and a provocation. Urbanisation is indeed at risk if it not managed sufficiently well, and if the threats of climate change and disasters are not taken into account sufficiently. 'Failed' urbanisation that succumbs to prevailing risks threatens the lives of countless people, as well as the very societies those people have created.

This book, while dealing with such issues, is not negative or defeatist; rather, it grapples with what can be done—by governments, aid organisations and most importantly, by people themselves—to use the concept of resilience to address current risks and those that lie ahead.

David Sanderson and Laura Bruce

References

Ambrasays, N. and Bilham, R. (2011). Corruption kills. *Nature*, 469. Available at: www.nature.com/articles/469153a.

Jones, P. and Sanderson, D. (2017). Urban resilience and informal and squatter settlements in the Pacific Region. *Development Bulletin*, 78, 11–16.

Pacific Region Infrastructure Facility (PRIF). (2015). *Unsettled: Water and Sanitation in Urban Settlement Communities in the Pacific*. Available at: www.theprif.org/documents/regional/water-sanitation/unsettled-water-sanitation-urban-settlement-communities-pacific.

UNDESA. (2018). *World Urbanization Prospects, the 2018 Revision*. UN. Available at: https://population.un.org/wup/Publications/Files/WUP2018-Report.pdf.

Preface

Pacific island countries (PICs) and Asian nations are at the forefront of experiencing the combination of rapid urbanisation and naturally triggered disasters, many of which are worsened by climate change. Urbanisation urgently needs to be understood and managed better if towns and cities are to avoid succumbing to the threats of stronger windstorms, floods and fires.

Urbanisation at Risk explores this challenge. Presenting research, case studies and lessons from a number of PICs, Cambodia, Nepal, the Philippines and elsewhere, the book explores both the policy and practice of how governments, civil society, aid organisations and, most important of all, people themselves can prepare for, withstand and recover better from disasters in towns and cities. In other words, how resilience is built. The book is particularly directed at those living in informal settlements, who are almost always the most vulnerable to natural hazards.

Edited by David Sanderson and Laura Bruce, *Urbanisation at Risk* comprises 13 chapters, eight concentrating on PICs, and five on Asia and beyond, written by leading researchers and practitioners. The book is a must-read for urban policy makers, researchers, humanitarian aid and development workers, and anyone interested in a safer world.

Abbreviations

ABA	Area-based Approach
ADB	Asian Development Bank
AIDS	Acquired Immune Deficiency Syndrome
ALNAP	Active Learning Network for Accountability and Performance
APCUS-SP	Academic-Practitioner Collaboration for Urban Settlements, South Pacific
ARC	Australian Red Cross
CCA	Climate Change Adaptation
CCCA	Cambodia Climate Change Alliance
CCCI	Cities and Climate Change Initiative
CDAC	Communication with Disaster Affected Communities
CDC	Council for the Development of Cambodia
CSO	Civil Society Organisation
CRI	City Resilience Index
CRPT	City Resilience Profiling Tool
CTP	Cash Transfer Programming
DFAT	Department of Foreign Affairs and Trade
DFID	Department for International Development
DRR	Disaster Risk Reduction
EECA	Elang Etas Community Association
EIA	Environmental Impact Assessment
FINPAC	Finnish Pacific Project
FRDP	Framework for Resilient Development in the Pacific
FTE	Fixed Term Estate
GAUC	Global Alliance for Urban Crises
GDP	Gross Domestic Product
GLTN	Global Land Tool Network
GPR	Good Practice Review
GRM	Grievance Redress Mechanism
HCC	Honiara City Council
HFA	Hyogo Framework for Action
HIV	Human Immunodeficiency Virus

xvi Abbreviations

HLP	Housing, Land and Property Rights
HURCAP	Honiara Urban Resilience and Climate Action Plan
IASC	Inter-Agency Standing Committee
ICESCR	International Covenant on Economic, Social and Cultural Rights
ICLEI	Local Governments for Sustainability
ICRC	International Committee of the Red Cross
IDP	Internally Displaced Person
IFRC	International Federation of Red Cross and Red Crescent Societies
IIED	International Institute for Environment and Development
ILO	International Labour Organization
INGO	International Non-governmental Organisation
IPCC	Intergovernmental Panel on Climate Change
IRC	International Rescue Committee
ISZ	Informal Settlement Zones
LiDAR	Light Detection and Ranging
LRRD	Linking relief, rehabilitation and development
MFAT	Ministry of Foreign Affairs and Trade
MoHMS	Ministry of Health and Medical Services
MLHS	Ministry of Lands Housing and Survey
MSM/TG	Men who have Sex with Men/Transgendered
NDMO	National Disaster Management Office
NGO	Non-governmental Organisation
NIDM	National Institute of Disaster Management
NIUA	National Institute of Urban Affairs
NIWA	National Institute of Water and Atmospheric Research
NRC	Norwegian Refugee Council
NUA	New Urban Agenda
ODI	Overseas Development Institute
OECD	Organisation for Economic Co-operation and Development
OHCHR	Office of the High Commissioner for Human Rights
P4CA	Planners 4 Climate Action
PCRAFI	Pacific Catastrophe Risk Assessment and Financing Initiative
PEBACC	Pacific Ecosystem-based Adaptation to Climate Change
PDNA	Post Disaster Needs Assessment
PHT	Pacific Humanitarian Team
PIC	Pacific Island Country
PIFS	Pacific Islands Forum Secretariat
PNG	Papua New Guinea
PUF	Pacific Urban Forum
PUMA	Planning and Urban Management Agency (Samoa)
PVMC	Port Vila Municipal Council
RAFT	Responsiveness, Adaptation, Facilitation and Transformation

RDI	Research for Development Impact
RMIT	Royal Melbourne Institute of Technology
SDG	Sustainable Development Goal
SIDS	Small Island Developing States
SIG	Solomon Islands Government
SINSO	Solomon Islands National Statistics Office
SIRCS	Solomon Islands Red Cross Society
SPC	the Pacific Community
SPCR	Strategic Program for Climate Resilience
SPREP	Secretariat of the Pacific Regional Environment Programme
STUMP	South Tarawa Urban Management Plan
TC	Tropical Cyclone
TCP	Tropical Cyclone Pam
TOL	Temporary Occupancy License
UCCRN	Urban Climate Change Research Network
UCLG	United Cities and Local Governments
UN	United Nations
UNDESA	United Nations Department of Economic and Social Affairs
UNDG	United Nations Sustainable Development Group
UNDP	United Nations Development Programme
UNDRR	United Nations office for Disaster Risk Reduction
UNECE	United Nations Economic Commission for Europe
UNESCAP	United Nations Economic and Social Commission for Asia and the Pacific
UNESCO	United Nations Educational, Scientific and Cultural Organization
UNFCCC	United Nations Framework Convention on Climate Change
UN-Habitat	United Nations Human Settlement Programme
UNHCR	United National High Commissioner for Refugees
UNICEF	United Nations International Children's Fund
UNISDR	United Nations office for Disaster Risk Reduction
UNOCHA	United Nations Office for the Coordination of Humanitarian Affairs
UNODC	United Nations Office on Drugs and Crime
UNSW	University of New South Wales
USAID	United States Agency for International Development
UTS-ISF	University of Technology Sydney, Institute for Sustainable Futures
WASH	Water, Sanitation and Hygiene
WHO	World Health Organization
WHS	World Humanitarian Summit
WMCCC	World Mayors Council on Climate Change
WUF	World Urban Forum

Part 1

Pacific Island Countries

Chapter 1

Urbanisation at Risk

Urban Resilience in Pacific Island Countries

John Connell and Meg Keen

Introduction

In small states, and especially the Pacific island countries (PICs), almost all towns and cities are coastal and at particular risk from environmental change and disasters (including sea level rise, cyclones, flooding and tsunamis). These 'ocean cities' (see Blaschke et al., 2019) are growing rapidly and consistently at rates beyond national population growth because of high rural-urban migration and fertility. In most PICs more than half the national population are now in urban areas. That has contributed to a 'coastal squeeze', where densely populated urban settlements can no longer fit into defined city boundaries and are expanding onto surrounding agricultural and customary land, causing social tensions.

Environmental challenges associated with water, energy and food security are escalating, with many Pacific cities becoming flood prone because of vegetation clearance, unmanaged settlement and blocked waterways. Mounting climate change pressures are adding to these challenges, with numerous examples of disasters indicating that urban communities and people are becoming less resilient to environmental hazards as the frequency and severity of weather-related events exceed adaptive capacity—and the situation is unlikely to improve without social, political and structural change.

Early warnings of the problems posed by urbanisation have occurred since the 1970s (Connell, 2011). Even so, it has proved difficult to establish an effective, integrated and comprehensive approach to urban management and resilience in circumstances where the dominant perception is that urbanisation is transient and to be discouraged. Political will, at any scale, has been largely elusive (Barbara and Keen, 2017). After half a century of these ocean cities growing, human and physical hazards and risks are becoming more pressing, and thus it is more crucial than ever that urban resilience and disaster risk reduction (DRR) move into the mainstream and gain significant local traction. In the Pacific islands, external multilateral and aid agencies have tended to be in advance of national governments (perhaps through the experience of Asian urbanisation), but inter-agency cooperation and coherence has not always been accomplished, despite the value of regional approaches (Keen and Connell, 2019). Valuable reports and recommendations have failed to get policies and practices rolling, and to generate support for national action. Similar circumstances confront other island regions, such as the Caribbean (Mycoo, 2018; Carby, 2018).

In most PICs, the domestic development focus has been centred on economic growth rather than welfare provision, even though there are well-known constraints to economic growth, including isolation, lack of natural resources, high transport and wage costs, and inequitable terms of trade (Connell, 2013). Development deficits have resulted in widespread rural-urban and international migration, contributing to a more deterritorialised form of development (Connell and Corbett, 2016), where remittances are significant both from internal and international migrants. Within PICs, many are moving to the cities to access jobs, education and services (Connell, 2019). There are costs of this development approach, such as the 'brain drain' that further depletes human resources from source areas.

Establishing an effective development strategy that combines sustainable development with urban resilience has been difficult in the dynamic and under-resourced circumstances of small states. Effective human, institutional and physical capacity building has been limited, while policy innovation and adaptation to address urban and climate change pressures are inadequate, leaving states—especially the smallest and most vulnerable—overwhelmed and reliant on donor-driven strategies and priorities that can be poorly tailored to local culture and place (Dean et al., 2017; Murray and Overton, 2011). In the face of these mounting pressures, Pacific regional agencies could provide valuable support and a mediating role between local and international interests, but to date have been missing in action.

The need for change is recognised, most recently at the Fifth Pacific Urban Forum, held in the Fijian city of Nadi in July 2019, which was the largest gathering of its type and had representation from all government levels. The dominant narrative currently driving action at the regional level, the 'Blue Pacific', has relevance to the pursuit of urban resilience. It calls for inspired leadership and policy commitment to act as one 'Blue Continent' to address pressing regional issues, share knowledge and learning, and strengthen connectivity to empower countries and people to act on development and sustainability issues (PIFS, 2017).

This chapter provides an overview of resilience and DRR issues in the urban areas of PICs, especially in the Melanesian states of Papua New Guinea (PNG), Solomon Islands and Vanuatu. This has particular contemporary resonance at a time of recurrent regional hazards (notably the recent sequence of Cyclones Pam, Winston, Maysak and Gita). In this disaster-affected part of the world, with Vanuatu being defined as the most risk-prone country globally (Edmonds and Noy, 2018), disaster risk is outpacing the ability to build resilience. As the challenges mount, we consider the potential for improved responsiveness at the community, state and regional levels. We conclude that in PICs with limited human, state and financial resources, community-based resources could be much better leveraged; and regional cooperation and support will also be essential for moving forward given weak urban governance. Disasters know no borders; vulnerabilities are shared and actions taken on a regional cooperative basis (such as knowledge sharing) can augment national and local actions to stimulate and enhance resilience. It is equally necessary to prioritise realistic and feasible sustainable development at all scales (beyond the wish lists, clichés and motherhood statements that exist).

Context, Challenges and Change in the Cities

Across the 12 independent PICs, but especially in socially diverse Melanesia, a considerable proportion of urban residents live in informal settlements (elsewhere referred to as 'squatter settlements'), where access to services (including water, waste disposal, sewerage and electricity) is inadequate, unemployment is high, and health, human and food security are problematic. Urban policy formation, environmental management and DRR have been neglected, despite intermittent interventions by various regional agencies. Even basic land use planning has been rare. The inability of Pacific states to match service provision in cities with their growing populations is a major challenge to resilience and the implementation of effective responses to disasters; it comes at considerable economic cost.

Rapid urban population growth is a product of high rural-urban migration and urban fertility. Internal migration has been particularly high in Melanesia and atoll states (such as Kiribati and Marshall Islands) creating some of the most densely populated cities globally, notably in South Tarawa and Majuro. Rapid and unmanaged urbanisation has put pressure on water resources, degraded coastal environments and fisheries, and polluted lagoons, urban ground water and rivers. As urban centres grow, new migrants are building their often informal homes in marginal sites that are vulnerable to hazards (well evident in the 2014 Mataniko river floods in Honiara, Solomon Islands, when more than 20 people died and hundreds lost homes). In the case of Honiara (but relevant elsewhere in the Pacific islands), cyclonic rain poses major problems. In 2014, an extreme weather event became a catastrophe not because of climate change but because settlements are in flood-prone areas (little choice existed), deforestation above the city added to water run-off, and obstructed city drainage resulted in storm water flooding—a combination of factors that might have been avoided with better land and infrastructure management.

Unregulated urban expansion has increased the costs of urbanisation and urban vulnerability. Policies that once had some ephemeral success have been overwhelmed by rapid population growth, bureaucratic inefficiency and land shortages (Jones and Lea, 2007; Storey and Hunter, 2010; Keen et al., 2017). Few effective housing policies exist, and state housing is undeveloped and beyond the reach of the poor, so that people have had little option but to provide for themselves. People are effectively urbanising and segregating areas of towns outside of any formal planning systems, often along kinship lines for social security and in response to institutional and political neglect. National attempts to manage urban development continue to be disappointing, a result of policy gaps, scarce capital and expertise, and competition among national authorities and power elites (for capital and primacy).

PICs face the same socioeconomic challenges as much larger countries, despite cities and towns being smaller than in many other parts of the world. But, in this area of the world, urban planning remains in its infancy (other than in Fiji). Thus, urban development has tended to serve narrow economic and sectoral interests, and problems are either left for external assistance, or blamed on external sources such as new migrants or climate change pressures. There is no doubt climate change and other external factors are exacerbating urban management challenges. Nonetheless, from an urban resilience perspective it is crucial to not allow this to distort the analyses of urban challenges and lend weight to views which see urban problems as externally driven, unpredictable and inevitable. Rather, many urban challenges in the Pacific islands, and further afield, emanate from a combination of local circumstances, policy neglect, and inadequate investment and thus are amenable to policy formation and more effective practice. A renewed urgency coupled with a greater appreciation of agency across scales and adaptive management can move Pacific island cities beyond inertia and reaction to proaction. The sections that follow examine some the challenges, but also the potential pathways to urban resilience.

Urban Citizenship and Informality

Rapid urban growth and the expansion of settlements has been particularly prevalent in Melanesia, but without integrated planning, let alone empathy, respect, and a sense of community and urban citizenship for the poor. In PNG's capital Port Moresby and Vanuatu's capital Port Vila, evictions, particularly on valuable land in the urban core, continue to occur. Bulldozing settlements has sometimes continued, for example the famous and contested case of Paga Point, Port Moresby, that became a cause célèbre (see next section). In Honiara, bulldozing and evictions are rare but neglect of most informal settlements remains a dominant, if unspoken, urban deterrence policy.

Many informal settlers are seen erroneously as temporary residents (despite being second, third or more generation urbanites), and policies and practices can be discriminatory, rather than inclusive. In reality, urban residents do not necessarily have rural homes to return to; indeed, longer-term returnees to villages can be resented because land is scarce, rural safety nets are strained, and urban migrants are valued more for their remittances and urban connections than their rural presence (Rasmussen, 2015). In the cities, urban safety nets are tenuous (Monsell-Davis, 1993), and urban and rural ties are fraying with infrequent contact. In Melanesian cities, a degree of self-organisation and care occurs based on urban cultural groups, partly differentiated by language and *wantok* ties, that settle together and include 'traditional leaders' with some residual authority. But urban-based informal safety nets—effectively indigenous forms of social protection—are being stretched as costs of living escalate, and many struggle to gain steady wage employment. Resilience becomes unusually difficult without effective government support or the ability of low-income residents to influence planning and resource allocations. As populations and settlements become more diverse via inter-marriage and new settlers, social cohesion is hard to maintain. Ocean cities are more tossed salads than melting pots. Like in ecosystems, that diversity can have its advantages as well as challenges.

Across the region, the number and variety of urban informal settlements and informal economies have proliferated. Street food and goods markets now contribute significantly to urban food security and household incomes, yet these activities remain outside formal planning regimes and are often discouraged by the government despite their major contribution to city life and economics (Keen and Ride, 2018; Kopel, 2017; Maebuta and Maebuta, 2009; Russell, 2009). Urban vitality and resilience could be enhanced with changes to the dominant urban policies that repress the poor and marginalised, force them out of prime urban areas and pursue a narrow development trajectory. Strengthened government-civil society partnerships with diverse community groups, churches and the private sector have the potential to bridge artificial formal-informal divides and contribute to urban inclusiveness and resilience (Koczberski et al., 2001; Connell, 2003). For example, at present the political and economic agency of market vendors—about 90 percent women—remains low and their policy exclusion high. Work under the UN Women Markets for Change programme is helping to improve vendor agency, organisation and economic empowerment (Keen and Ride, 2018). Improving the functionality and productivity of marketplaces through partnerships has positive flow-on effects for urban food supplies and rural-urban connectivity across sectors and communities. Investment in vendors' capacity, goods transport, and regional agricultural and fishery productivity can boost urban-rural livelihoods and the ability of the private sector to meet demand (Keen et al., 2017: 112).

Urban transformation in support of greater resilience requires changing mindsets. The 'informal' cannot be neatly categorised as unstructured, illegal or even corrupt, just as urban formal structures are certainly not the opposite. In some circumstances, settlements, markets and micro-enterprises are self-organising, and more effective and efficient than their government-run counterparts. Urban informality in the form of unsanctioned settlements and economic activities is not so much an urban transgression or premeditated breaking of laws, as it is often still described, but rather a survival strategy: an effort to re-create institutional arrangements in a way that facilitates greater opportunity, diversity and prosperity (Rubin, 2018). At the Solomon Islands Nation Urban Conference in 2016, informal settlements were referred to as 'affordable housing areas', without which housing would be beyond the reach of the average Honiara resident (Keen and Kiddle, 2016). Solomon Islands Home Finance Limited, an organisation charged with supplying affordable homes in Honiara, sells new houses at prices more than 50 times the annual median income of Solomon Islanders so that they are only able to be purchased by the government for public servants (Keen et al., 2017). Informality is quintessential and integral to PIC urban development.

Dealing With the Difficult: Land, Land and Land

Urban land has come under intense pressure, and is in short supply, and high population densities have followed. Land is ever more valuable as traditionally owned ancestral land is safeguarded for future generations against 'others' with different languages, cultures and ethnicities (Connell, 2012; Connell and Lutkehaus, 2016; Ha'apio et al., 2018; McDougall, 2016, 2017; Trundle et al., 2018). That has resulted in urban land being occupied under multiple-tenure regimes (government, private and customary) and with multiple uncertainties associated with unclear legal and social legitimacy. Agreements negotiated between landowners and tenants may be overturned and disregarded by another generation (Numbasa and Koczberski, 2012; Mecartney and Connell, 2017). Yet, some security of tenure is crucial for more resilient housing and livelihoods, and often for access to services and employment. Without recognised title to land, occupants cannot obtain loans (let alone mortgages), hence homes may be only partly built as settlers manage the slow process of income generation and capital formation. In turn, this structural inequality makes residents susceptible to hazards (McEvoy et al., 2019; Williams et al., 2019), while lack of resources makes their occupants less able to adapt and respond.

Tensions, disputes and violence over land in urban areas have occurred as people's traditional connections with rural villages diminish and landlessness becomes more common. Thus, in Honiara, disputes over land tenure in peri-urban areas were significant factors in the genesis of the 'tensions' that resulted in bitter and costly (of lives and economic growth) internecine violence for years. At Port Moresby's Paga Point redevelopment, one central urban area was particularly difficult, creating conflict among developers, the government and the residents because of the confusion over, and the complexity of, ownership and legal rights that are based upon combinations of oral histories, memories of memorandums of understanding, legal systems dating back to colonial times and post-colonial legal systems (Mecartney and Connell, 2017). At Paga Point, a highly desirable site for residential development, the dispute became both legal and political with court cases reaching the Crown Court, and prominent national politicians with land and political interests intervening to influence outcomes. Well-armed police enforced commercial interests and overseas investors advanced their interests. The hints of corruption, power and intrigue eventually inspired a documentary film. The lack of reliable records for reference and the multiple versions of the 'true' land tenure situation fuelled discontent.

The unspoken and poorly documented policies of the past and present in Pacific cities have not worked; a new approach is needed that, in part, recognises and contributes to socially acceptable urban development, community-supported governance and relationships, and greater inclusion of all in urban management and planning. Land access remains the overwhelming and persistent unresolved issue in Melanesian cities. There is an obvious need to mobilise customary land in the rapidly sprawling peri-urban areas. Mobilisation does not mean privatisation. Localised and culturally acceptable institutions need to evolve to mediate land access between state, landowner groups and buyers—or to navigate the often contentious issues of settlement upgrades. Some tentative first steps have been taken in Suva with state-supported alternative dispute-resolution processes, and NGO-community-government partnerships to share the burden of upgrades (Keen et al., 2017: 31–41). In Port Moresby, limited progress has been made towards improving the registration of land under customary tenure (most of the urban land) which allows more formal long-term leasing in what are effectively informal land markets (Chand and Yala, 2012; Chand, 2017; Walta, 2017). Presently, there is no mechanism through which such initiatives might be shared within the region, but greater clarity over regional responsibility for urban issues could better broker knowledge.

What also remains lacking are urban champions—those with strategic vision, ideas of social justice and a motive to advance urban agendas. With the partial exception of Suva, Melanesian local governments have neither the finances nor the capacity to manage their cities. Urban residents are poorly represented in national parliaments. Constituency Development Funds (as in PNG and Solomon Islands) and other government development programmes (as well as those of donors) continue to favour rural over urban development, although their bias has not slowed urbanisation. The urban labour force remains largely unorganised and citizen groups, if they exist, are still fragmented and in need of mechanisms to better boost agency. Urbanisation is yet to become a real driver of political, social or economic change.

Resilience Building: Strengthening Settlements and Services (From a Low Base)

A high proportion of people in Pacific island towns and cities, especially in Melanesia, live in informal settlements, crudely estimated at around 35 percent in Honiara, 35 percent in Port Moresby and 45 percent in Port Vila, with all such percentages growing (Kiddle et al., 2017). As noted previously, they are without security of tenure, and therefore secure housing and access to services. Since many have been constructed in marginal areas, and without any formal planning, they are particularly risk-prone, manifesting the worst aspects of the coastal squeeze. Ideally, new migrants and those in need would receive priority for public housing and services, but even if such policies existed, land tenure would constrain implementation. Development plans and policies in the region are not oriented to equity, and service delivery is limited everywhere.

Even efforts to secure basic urban rights to 'site and service', the simple schemes of the 1970s independence era, have not materialised. Most Melanesian cities continue to experience inadequate water, sanitation and waste-collection services. Water providers, usually state-owned enterprises, have limited finances to invest without expanding their client base and reducing the high levels of illegal (unpaid for) access. A recent study of water and sanitation services in urban settlements found that across the region, access to water and sanitation for settlements remains inadequate. Squatter settlements continue to be largely excluded from reticulated water and sewerage services. Other than in Fiji, fewer than 65 percent of Melanesian city settlements have access to reticulated water (Schrecongost and Wong, 2015). Other services (such as sewerage, waste disposal and electrification) are similarly thinly and inequitably distributed.

Adequate and equitable water, sanitation and hygiene (WASH) services are essential for upgrading informal settlements, especially in a context of DRR. In addition to providing a foundation for healthy and dignified lives, accessible and appropriately managed WASH services enable sustainable communities through control of pollution, development of local economies via a healthier workforce, and improved agency for women who are disproportionately affected by WASH services. There have been efforts to improve access to water supplies, such as recently in Port Moresby's urban village Hanuabada, where no households had individual access to water and 80 percent of households used the sea for sanitation. Success there proved elusive because of weak institutional arrangements and support.

What might have been a straightforward project to provide a more adequate water supply and sanitation to perhaps the most famous, and most visible, urban village in the Pacific, with considerable authority in the local Motu-Koitabu Assembly and powerful supporters in the national government, was unsuccessful, in part because of an unclear mandate to the providers, too many layers of decision-making, and a lack of community involvement and accountability. In microcosm, it typified problems elsewhere where top-down approaches undermine progress. Hanuabada should have been an easy urban upgrade success, but its failure holds insights into pathways forward—that is what must change to better engage communities.

Elsewhere, service provision is engaging communities more effectively. Water utilities have sought to improve services to settlements, including provision of community standpipes that allow communities and their existing governance structures to play a major role in service management. Special tariff arrangements for communities allow users to share a single meter, and placement of meters at the edge of settlements sidesteps land tenure constraints and provides an incentive for communities to self-organise to access and manage water services (Schrecongost and Wong, 2015). More participatory and community-based urban water service delivery suited to informal communities are being piloted in Honiara and Suva (Gooden, 2017; Phillips and Keen, 2016), drawing on African experiences with broader applicability. Key lessons from such water supply initiatives are: to ground service delivery in community needs and preferred governance arrangements, to tailor services to the limited resources of clients, to convey clear community messages on why and what water charges are necessary, and to work with communities and non-state actors to build relationships of trust and understanding between service providers and urban residents. This constitutes a particular example of how issues of urbanisation must be considered across sectors, social groups and scales, and how positive developments might be shared globally and regionally.

Urban Resilience: Elusive? Integrative? Innovative?

A broader understanding of what resilience might mean in the region stems from growing acceptance of the Rockefeller Foundation definition (whose broadness supports and emphasises a more integrative approach) and what amounts to its insistence on involving and developing the capacity of individuals, communities and systems. The Rockefeller Foundation (2015) defines resilience as 'the capacity of individuals, communities and systems to survive, adapt, and grow in the face of stress and shocks, and even transform when conditions require it.' Underlying this definition is an acknowledgement that achieving resilience, especially in the urban context, centres on sustainable development: it requires the integration of social, ecological and economic systems; it must be adaptive across scales and time; address equity; and, when necessary, be transformative.

True to sustainability approaches, the principle of subsidiarity applies, that action is best taken at the lowest scale possible. However, the multi-scalar nature of urbanisation drivers and impacts suggests that higher-order framing and action must complement and strengthen lower-level actions through the integration of efforts. Increasingly, urban issues are thus seen as more than a 'local problem' with recognition that a 'systems approach' is needed that spans local, regional and global scales, and that urban resilience is embedded within a political economy of urbanisation (Bai et al., 2016; Béné et al., 2018). Regional intervention offers the greatest possibility of mainstreaming new urban agendas, such as policies on basic needs, gender relations and anti-poverty strategies which are lacking in many PICs. It also allows for promoting the need for better linkages between humanitarian and development actors in their efforts to help affected communities and individuals reduce their vulnerability to multiple and interlocking disasters.

Resilience addresses the need to anticipate, absorb and adapt to destabilising pressures. It is centred on the capacity of households and communities to deal with external events emanating from social, political and ecological change, and the related ability to 'bounce back', ideally more successfully, from stresses and regain access to housing, services and livelihoods. Not surprisingly, therefore, resilience has increasingly appeared in humanitarian, development and climate change circles as an organising principle in relation to preventing, preparing for and responding to disasters at a regional level. Such statements themselves are complex enough; putting such notions into practice represents a challenge of a considerable order especially in PICs. In an ideal world,

> If managed well, cities can be engines of growth and provide workers and residents with quality job opportunities, better healthcare, improved housing, safety and social development. Cities can help contribute to national growth through increased revenue generation, political stability and post-conflict reconciliation. Opportunities do exist to harness the transformative potential of cities to promote development, implement effective disaster response systems and reduce violence.
>
> (de Boer, 2016: 114)

That is undeniable. But, few sustained examples exist where that has been achieved (at least in the cities of the global South), and the towns and cities of the Pacific are far from that. Moreover, much hangs on the phrase 'If managed well'.

Integration is crucial, beginning from the need to have relevant, functioning organisations and institutions. Planning and public policy, as important local resilience factors, involve the extent to which, firstly, communities (at different scales) have local emergency management plans, land use planning, development regulations and building standards; secondly, have integrated socioeconomic and environmental planning, at the core of which are land-use strategies and planning; and, thirdly, have plans that are valued,

Urbanisation at Risk 13

understood and supported by communities, and that are both ongoing and able to be implemented during emergencies. This is a considerable task for any urban centre, and a complex political and administrative problem—sharing learning across jurisdiction has obvious value.

The need for a transition to greater resilience through regionally supported frameworks has been addressed in the 'Framework for Resilient Development in the Pacific, 2017–2030' (SPC et al., 2016), but this says little about the need for urban resilience and the role and participation of urban communities, and focuses on recovery rather than ongoing resilience, thus ignoring the steps required to achieve resilience. Attempts to develop a 'Pacific Urban Agenda' (2015) have been stymied, and the UN's 'New Urban Agenda' (2016) has gained little traction in the region, although the recent 2019 Fifth Pacific Urban Forum, mentioned earlier, has, at least, focused attention. Practical measures consistently applied across the region are needed. For hazard events, preparation of local comprehensive plans can result in DRR, enhancing community resilience and sustainability, improving adaption to climate change and assisting with the rebuilding of communities after disasters. How to do this in practice is a complex social and political problem—especially with the lack of effective urban authorities. *Realpolitik* poses problems, which we explore in the following section, and map out some of the opportunities.

Politics and the Power of Information

Strengthening resilience in the face of climate change requires an integrated perspective that is multi-scalar and multi-sectoral, involves social and economic planning, and a participatory democracy that has hitherto been quite rare. Invaluable in normal times, it is essential in response to disasters, where local knowledge and experience is crucial (Gero et al., 2011, Rey et al., 2017; Le De et al., 2018). The widespread inability to develop effective urban policies in Pacific islands region is a function of several factors, underpinned by a 'shallow urban politics', arising from limited political representation of urban voters, and large and growing informal settlements, emphasising the lack of a political voice and legal recognition for most urban residents (ADB, 2016; Foukona, 2015). This 'shallow politics' is clientelistic rather than focused on ideology or policy, challenges inclusive engagement, and reduces the possibilities of achieving social and environmental justice, restricts movement towards SDGs and disables policies and practices other than those that are top-down and technocratic.

The urban authorities that have emerged have been limited in their ability to develop a differentiated and distinctive strategy for urban development and management. Ironically, where a sense of strength and authority has been effectively asserted by those in cities, it has been interpreted as challenging national authority (Jones and Lea, 2007). Equally significant is the shortfall in skilled human resources, with few trained in technical matters associated with urban planning and management (Corbett and Connell, 2015), creating a reluctance by urban managers to make critical decisions and implement policy. Indeed, even when bold moves are made, progress can be hindered by the protection of political and commercial interests, and the shortage of funds for the purchase and maintenance of infrastructure to deliver on upgrade initiatives.

Governance systems are inherently complex, involving multiple parties, and often require joint action (Andersson and Ostrom, 2008). Indeed, in the PICs, many NGOs, including churches, have an authority that may exceed that of the formal government. Deliberative and participatory processes, including those that can and must engage communities, are important in order to promote sustainability and social responsibility within place-based governance. Despite this need, many urban communities and NGOs are excluded from decision-making processes or 'included' in ways that do not reflect cultural values. Such structural injustices can be minimised with greater understanding across communication barriers existing at the 'boundaries' between groups (Zurba et al., 2019). Removing communication barriers and boundaries could do much to improve decision-making, agency and social justice, and this may require new platforms for dialogue that work across sectors and scales and generate shared knowledge sets.

In Pacific cities, important data deficiencies currently exist that impede evidence-based urban decision-making. Censuses can be as much as a decade or more apart, and are frequently inaccurate. Statistics (such as household income and expenditure surveys) are not necessarily rigorously or effectively produced, and usually neglect a spatial component. Ironically, in this data poor environment, grey literature and consultancy reports mount up, but are inaccessible and unread (some rendered useless by being commercial in confidence). In a large city such as Port Moresby, even the number of distinct informal settlements can only be guessed while information on the most basic characteristics of their occupants is unknown. Resilient cities that are proactively managed need an evidence base on which to act. Where nationally based capacity is limited, regional agencies could play a key role in information generation and dissemination.

New technologies and solutions are emerging that may prove useful in fragile cities. These include open data initiatives that can help cities and citizens monitor and evaluate interventions; real-time data collection and evaluation of critical infrastructure (electrical grids, water, telecommunication, banking and finance systems) with an embedded capacity to adapt and reconfigure in times of disaster; and, predictive modelling as a result of scalable 'smart' innovations (de Boer, 2016). NGOs, such as World Vision, are using mobile phone technology to survey and increase understanding of services and priorities within informal settlements in the region. Satellite imagery and drones are beginning to offer possibilities, with particular reference to participatory land-use mapping and catchment management, and more sophisticated hazard risk mapping (Hoque et al., 2018), thus the avoidance of development in hazard zones where socioeconomic data is absent (Hoover et al., 2017). However, data alone will not solve DRR and resilience problems; it will require sophisticated analytical skills and, in PICs, this will require investment in training and people, if the promise of these and other innovations is to deliver resilience results—an area where the University of the South Pacific is now playing an active role.

Mechanisms that generate data and apply it in practical ways exist, they just need to be more effectively shared and applied. Here there is a role for regional technical agencies, especially in the areas of evidence-based land use planning, vulnerability assessment and DRR responses, insurance schemes and community mobilisation for effective settlement upgrading. Many needed actions are not 'smart' or 'technological innovative', but they are invaluable. It remains true that basic data are presently missing in the prelude for progress to plan formation, public policy and implementation. Investing in cities means investing in people, capacity and processes, as well as bricks and mortar.

Conclusion: Beyond Motherhood, Towards Transformation

Change in Melanesian cities, and most other Pacific island cities, has been mostly related to population size rather than urban functionality. Too few politicians champion urban residents' needs, their livelihood aspirations and their welfare. Opposition to urbanisation from urban and national authorities and influential leaders occurs in the guise of achieving order and cleanliness, reducing crime, reserving land for business development, and demonstrating that the state is not weak and can control 'unmanaged urban settlements'. This approach to urban development derives from neo-liberal and neo-colonial development approaches that find little traction in contemporary cities with different cultural origins and mushrooming informal sectors. Top-down policies that focus on stopping or slowing urbanisation, decentralisation and regional development have been ineffective approaches of the past, as national governments exercise a weak role in policy formation. Without more effective development partnerships, knowledge brokering and community-based land management initiatives, resilient and sustainable urban development will be hard to secure.

To date, urban planning and management have proved unusually difficult in the Pacific because of limited resources, lack of appreciation of cities as economic drivers of growth, and reluctance to consider urban centres as deserving 'special' treatment. Within cities the diversity of urban populations, lack of skilled human resources, and competition rather than collaboration among national and local agencies retards progress. Achieving more effective urban governance and planning and moving towards resilience necessitates finding a constituency, a champion, and a link with appropriate local and regional agencies and initiatives (that have thus far been lacking). Limited progress towards urban resilience and DRR can be partially explained by external drivers such as climate change, uncoordinated donor assistance, and weak regional technical support and knowledge diffusion, but internal factors also play a role, not least of which are leadership and commitment by politicians, managers and technical staff, proactive planning, culturally appropriate urban dispute resolution, and local data creation and management. Within the ever-shifting urban trajectories of development change is not easy, but better performance is achievable.

Resilience in Pacific cities cannot be imposed from above. Instead it needs to be, and often is, found in the relationships that mediate people's everyday lives. Some of these capacities have emerged through informal networks, but *wantok* ties can exclude as much as they include. Some of the most resilient people and communities are those in places that have experienced the deepest challenges. These capacities have developed as a result of having overcome repeated disruptions and challenges to the point where a culture of resilience has emerged through informal networks rooted in trust and learned experience. Enhanced resilience needs to build on existing intrinsic qualities and assets within their unique local environments and create knowledge sharing mechanisms. That demands levels of trust, respect and cooperation (Sennett, 2012) that cannot be imposed and must first be achieved at a local level. Tuvalu's Prime Minister emphasised this point at the 2019 Fifth Pacific Urban Forum: 'there are no solutions that are not local solutions' (Keen and Kiddle, 2019).

Such solutions will involve NGOs, community groups and churches that have gained respect, usually more than governments. Thus, in urban Melanesia and especially PNG, most ordinary citizens will continue to rely on informal and hybrid arrangements in their communities for their security, which might include local *komitis*, church organisations and community leaders, extended families and, perhaps, the local Village Court magistrate. What is significant here is not merely that citizens can self-organise across many domains for survival—housing, access to water and jobs, security and so on—but that government services are often 'beyond the reach' of most in their current form, and hybrid forms of service delivery and even governance need to evolve to allow formal and informal urban governance to engage each other and create a more robust and resilient urban fabric. This raises basic questions about the positive role of the informal sector and informal relationships, the role of government as facilitator or otherwise, the nature of social justice and citizenship, and the significant tasks ahead.

Repeatedly, studies of urban management, often in response to or in the face of disasters, conclude along the lines of,

> At the level of community and from a policy and programme perspective, recovery processes are situated in a continuum of relief, rehabilitation

and development. They consist of continuous streams of activities, contestations, decisions and attitudes that inform and mediate the interplay of socio-spatial transformation, adaptation and persistence in disaster-affected communities . . . [that] determine who has access to resources, and how and where they can be used.

(Tafti and Tomlinson, 2019: 8)

Not surprisingly, calls for more effective integration and inclusion are commonplace, but they are rarely targeted or offer straightforward starting points or take note of scarce resources, information and skills in contexts that vary enormously across developing states. Transformations of planning processes will require long timeframes and sustained support from multiple stakeholders. Making sense of climate change and achieving greater resilience in urban communities demands attention to the cultural and political processes that shape how risks are conceived. Achieving multi-directional flows of information is a difficult and invariably key institutional challenge as it relates to the lack of coordination and communication between relevant actors (Middelbeek et al., 2014). Learning from the actions that people have taken based on local experience and knowledge may very well be more informative than those devolved from the government, especially during crises or social transformations.

Some barriers to urban resilience and DRR policymaking are related to discrepancies in problem framing (disaster response versus risk reduction, ambiguity regarding the notion of DRR) and hurdles to collaborative governance (lack of coordination, inadequate information-sharing, unclear roles and mandates). These challenges emphasise the need to develop strategies supporting inter-organisational collaboration and closer stakeholder dialogue regarding policy and planning priorities. Integration is important for critical preventive measures in climatic risk-prone areas and for the coordination of disaster responses. Obvious preventive measures include risk assessments, early warning systems, flood management systems and multi-scale risk and hazard mapping that can contribute to climate change adaptation, DRR and resilience—but getting from paper to action is difficult. Risk reduction is embedded within multiple policy areas, in particular those of agriculture, water resources, health, land use, environment, finances and planning, and multiple agencies, even discounting NGOs and the private sector. Thus 'facilitating integrative risk [reduction] by enhanced multi-stakeholder collaboration' sounds, and is, impressive, but it is not easy to translate into practice (Gerkensmeier and Ratter, 2018). Even the UN's Sustainable Development Goal (SDG) 11, which calls for sustainable settlements, has lofty goals but only ill-formed visions of how to actually achieve success. Rationalising and localising targets and actions will be a valuable starting point.

Ultimately PICs, with their limited resources, can learn from regional (and global) experience and partnerships, for there are linkages and comparisons across ocean realms, where ocean cities experience similar problems. Global evidence clearly shows that steadily increasing inequality (as is occurring in Pacific island cities) is bad for almost everything—economic growth, social well-being, crime, stability and environmental health. It is time to critically reflect on current models of urban governance, and create new and contextual solutions and approaches to urbanisation in Melanesia. Pressures are mounting from social and demographic change as well as rising environmental pressures on the predominantly low-lying coastal cities of this region. In the words of one of the early scholars of urban Melanesia: 'In conditions of rapid change, there is no safety in standing still' (Oram, 1976: 259). Much has subsequently stood still. Policies and practices that involve and integrate communities with the wider context of urban service provision are long overdue for a sustainable urbanisation that involves and supports all national citizens. Time is short. The climate is changing and human needs in the cities must be addressed. A resilient future for Pacific cities is possible, if there is the will to create it.

References

Andersson, K. and Ostrom, E. (2008). Analyzing decentralized resource regimes from a polycentric perspective. *Policy Sciences*, 41, 71–93.

Asian Development Bank (ADB). (2016). *The Emergence of Pacific Urban Villages: Urbanization Trends in the Pacific Islands*. Pacific Studies Series. Manila: Asian Development Bank.

Bai, S., Surveyer, A., Elmqvist, T., et al. (2016). Defining and advancing a systems approach for sustainable cities. *Current Opinion in Environmental Sustainability*, 23, 69–78.

Barbara, J. and Keen, M. (2017). Urbanisation in Melanesia: The politics of change. *Development Bulletin*, 78, 16–19.

Béné, C., Mehta, L., McGranahan, G., Cannon, T., Gupte, J. and Tanner, T. (2018). Resilience as a policy narrative: Potentials and limits in the context of urban planning. *Climate and Development*, 10(2), 116–133.

Blaschke, P., Gawler, S., Kiddle, L., Loubser, D. and Zari, M. (2019). *Ocean Cities: Regional Policy Guide—Delivering Resilient Solutions in Pacific Island Settlements*. Bangkok: UN ESCAP.

Carby, B. (2018). Integrating disaster risk reduction in national development planning: Experience and challenges of Jamaica. *Environmental Hazards*, 17(3), 219–233.

Chand, S. (2017). Registration and release of customary-land for private enterprise: Lessons from Papua New Guinea. *Land Use Policy*, 61, 413–419.

Chand, S. and Yala, C. (2012). Institutions for improving access to land for settler-housing: Evidence from Papua New Guinea. *Land Use Policy*, 29, 143–153.

Connell, J. (2003). Regulation of space in the contemporary postcolonial Pacific city: Port Moresby and Suva. *Asia Pacific Viewpoint*, 44, 243–258.

Connell, J. (2011). Elephants in the Pacific? Pacific urbanisation and its discontents. *Asia Pacific Viewpoint*, 52(2), 121–135.

Connell, J. (2012). Population resettlement in the Pacific: Lessons from a hazardous history. *Australian Geographer*, 43(2), 127–142.

Connell, J. (2013). *Islands at Risk*. Cheltenham: Edward Elgar.

Connell, J. (2019). Contracting margins? Liquid international migration in the Pacific. *Revue Europeénne des Migrations Internationales*, in press.

Connell, J. and Corbett, J. (2016). Deterritorialisation. Reconceptualising development in the Pacific Islands. *Global Society*, 30(4), 583–604.

Connell, J. and Lutkehaus, N. (2016). *Another Manam? The Forced Migration of the Population of Manam Island*. Geneva: IOM.

Corbett, J. and Connell, J. (2015). All the world is a stage: Global governance, human resources and the 'problem' of smallness. *The Pacific Review*, 28(3), 435–459.

Dean, A., Green, D. and Nunn, P. (2017). Too much sail for a small craft? Donor requirements, scale and capacity discourses in Kiribati. In E. Stratford (ed.), *Island Geographies: Essays and Conversations*. London: Routledge, 54–77.

De Boer, J. (2016). Risk, resilience and the fragile city. In D. Sanderson, J. Kayden and J. Leis (eds.), *Urban Disaster Resilience: New Dimensions from International Practice in the Built Environment*. London: Routledge, 113–127.

Edmonds, C. and Noy, I. (2018). The economics of disaster risks and impacts in the Pacific. *Disaster Prevention and Management*, 27(5), 478–494.

Foukona, J. (2015). Urban land in Honiara: Strategies and rights to the city. *The Journal of Pacific History*, 50(4), 504–518.

Gerkensmeier, B and Ratter, B. (2018). Governing coastal risk as a social process: Facilitating integrative risk management by enhanced multi-stakeholder collaboration. *Environmental Science and Policy*, 80, 144–151.

Gero, A., Méheux, K. and Dominey-Howes, D. (2011). Integrating community based disaster risk reduction and climate change adaptation: Examples from the Pacific. *Natural Hazards and Earth System Sciences*, 11, 101–113.

Gooden, I. (2017). Water supply to informal settlements in Honiara. *Development Bulletin*, 78, 87–90.

Ha'apio, M., Morrison, K., Gonzalez, R., Wairiu, M. and Holland, E. (2018). Limits and barriers to transformation: A case study of april ridge relocation initiative, East Honiara, Solomon Islands. In W.L. Filho (ed.), *Climate Change Impacts and Adaptation Strategies for Coastal Communities*. Springer: Dordrecht, 455–470.

Hoover, J., Leisz, S. and Laituri, M. (2017). Comparing and combining Landsat Satellite imagery and participatory data to assess land-use and land-cover changes in a coastal village in Papua New Guinea. *Human Ecology*, 45, 251–264.

Hoque, M., Phinn, S., Roelfsemaa, C. and Childs, I. (2018). Assessing tropical cyclone risks using geospatial techniques. *Applied Geography*, 98, 22–33.

Jones, P. and Lea, J. (2007). What has happened to urban reform in the Island Pacific? Some lessons from Kiribati and Samoa. *Pacific Affairs*, 80, 473–491.

Keen, M., Barbara, J., Carpenter, J., Evans, D. and Foukona, J. (2017). *Urban Development in Honiara: Harnessing Opportunities, Embracing Change*. Canberra: State, Society and Governance in Melanesia Research Report. Canberra: ANU.

Keen, M. and Connell, J. (2019). From risk to resilience? Urban transitions and regional challenges in the Pacific Islands. *Urban Policy and Research*, vol. 37, no. 3, pp. 324–337.

Keen, M. and Kiddle, L. (2016). *Priced Out of the Market: Informal Settlements in Honiara, Solomon Islands*. In Brief 2016/28, Department of Pacific Affairs. Canberra: ANU.

Keen, M. and Kiddle, L. (2019). *A PUF of Fresh Air? Pacific Urban Forum 2019*. In Brief 2019/15, Department of Pacific Affairs. Canberra: ANU.

Keen, M. and Ride, A. (2018). *Markets Matter: Enhancing Livelihoods and Localities*. In Brief 2018/10, Department of Pacific Affairs. Canberra: ANU.

Kiddle, L., McEvoy, D., Mitchell, D., Jones, P. and Mecartney, S. (2017). Unpacking the Pacific urban agenda: Resilience challenges and opportunities. *Sustainability*, 9(10), 1878.

Koczberski, G., Curry, G. and Connell, J. (2001). Full circle or spiralling out of control? State violence and the control of urbanisation in Papua New Guinea. *Urban Studies*, 38, 2017–2036.

Kopel, E. (2017). *Understanding Gender Dynamics of the Informal Economy: The Case of Open Markets in NCD*. PNG NRI Discussion Paper, Port Moresby.

Le De, L., Rey, T., Leone, F. and Gilbert, D. (2018). Sustainable livelihoods and effectiveness of disaster responses: A case study of tropical cyclone Pam in Vanuatu. *Natural Hazards*, 91, 1203–1221.

Maebuta, H. and Maebuta, J. (2009). Generating livelihoods: A study of urban squatter settlements in Solomon Islands. *Pacific Economic Bulletin*, 24(3), 118–131.

McDougall, D. (2016). *Engaging with Strangers: Love and Violence in the Rural Solomon Islands*. New York: Berghahn.

McDougall, D. (2017). Lost passports? Disconnection/immobility in the rural and urban Solomon Islands. *Journal de la Société des Océanistes*, 144–145, 63–76.

McEvoy, D., Mitchell, D. and Trundle, A. (2019). Land tenure and urban climate resilience in the South Pacific. *Climate and Development*, in press.

Mecartney, S. and Connell, J. (2017). Urban Melanesia: The challenges of managing land, modernity and tradition. In S. McDonnell, M. Allen and C. Filer (eds.), *Kastom, Property and Ideology: Land Transformations in Melanesia*. Canberra: ANU, 57–84.

Middelbeek, L., Kolle, K. and Verrest, H. (2014). Built to last? Local climate change adaptation and governance in the Caribbean: The case of an informal urban settlement in Trinidad and Tobago. *Urban Climate*, 8, 138–154.

Monsell-Davis, M. (1993). Urban exchange: Safety net or disincentive? Wantoks and relatives in the urban Pacific. *Canberra Anthropology*, 16(2), 45–66.

Murray, W. and Overton, J. (2011). The inverse sovereignty effect: Aid, scale and neostructuralism in Oceania. *Asia Pacific Viewpoint*, 52(3), 272–284.

Mycoo, M. (2018). Urban sustainability in Caribbean Small Island Developing States: A conceptual framework for urban planning using a case study of Trinidad. *International Development Planning Review*, 40(2), 143–174.

Numbasa, G. and Koczberski, G. (2012). Migration, informal urban settlements and non-market land transactions: A case study of Wewak, East Sepik Province, Papua New Guinea. *Australian Geographer*, 43(2), 143–161.

Oram, N. (1976). *From Colonial Town to Melanesian City: Port Moresby 1884–1974*. Canberra: ANU.

Pacific Community (SPC), Secretariat of the Pacific Regional Environment Programme (SPREP), Pacific Islands Forum Secretariat (PIFS), United Nations Development Programme (UNDP), United Nations Office for Disaster Risk Reduction

(UNISDR) and University of the South Pacific (USP). (2016). *Framework for the Resilient Development of the Pacific (FRDP) 2017–2030.*

Pacific Islands Forum Secretariat (PIFS). (2017). *Forty-Eighth Pacific Island Forum Communique*, 5–8 September 2017.

Phillips, T. and Keen, M. (2016). *Sharing the City: Urban Growth and Governance in Suva, Fiji.* Discussion Paper 2016/6. Canberra: ANU State, Society and Governance in Melanesia.

Rasmussen, A. (2015). *In the Absence of the Gift: New Forms of Value and Personhood in a Papua New Guinea Community.* New York: Berghahn.

Rey, T., Le De, L., Leone, F. and Gilbert, D. (2017). An integrative approach to understand vulnerability and resilience post-disaster. The 2015 Cyclone Pam in urban Vanuatu as case study. *Disaster Prevention and Management*, 26(3), 259–275.

Rubin, M. (2018). At the borderlands of informal practices of the state: Negotiability, porosity and exceptionality. *Journal of Development Studies*, 54(12), 2227–2242.

Russell, L. (2009). *Stayin' Alive: A Report on Urban Livelihoods in Honiara, Solomon Islands.* Sydney: APHEDA.

Schrecongost, A. and Wong, K. (2015). *Unsettled: Water and Sanitation in Urban Settlements Communities of the Pacific.* Sydney: Pacific Regional Infrastructure Facility.

Sennett, R. (2012). *Together. The Rituals and Pleasures of Cooperation.* New Haven: Yale University Press.

Storey, D. and Hunter, S. (2010). Kiribati: An environmental perfect storm. *Australian Geographer*, 41, 167–181.

Tafti, M. and Tomlinson, R. (2019). Theorizing distributive justice and the practice of post-disaster housing recovery. *Environmental Hazards*, 18(1), 7–25.

Trundle, A., Barth, B. and McEvoy, D. (2018). Leveraging endogenous climate resilience: Urban adaptation in Pacific Small Island Developing States. *Environment and Urbanization*, 31(1), 53–74.

Walta, M. (2017). Transition to modernity: Migrant settlements and customary land issues in Port Moresby. *Development Bulletin*, 78, 39–43.

Williams, D., Costa, M., Sutherland, C., Cellers, L. and Scheffran, J. (2019). Vulnerability of informal settlements in the context of rapid urbanization and climate change. *Environment and Urbanization*, 31(1), 157–176.

Zurba, M., Maclean, K., Woodward, E. and Islam, D. (2019). Amplifying Indigenous community participation in place-based research through boundary work. *Progress in Human Geography*, in press.

Chapter 2

Climate and Disaster Risks, Challenges and Opportunities for Resilient Pacific Towns and Cities

David Sanderson, Laura Bruce and Pamela Sitko

Introduction

Pacific island countries (PICs) are among the most vulnerable in the world to natural hazards, and increasingly to those exacerbated by climate change, which is set to increase dramatically over the next 30 years, if unchecked (IPCC, 2019). Twenty-three percent of Pacific Islanders live in Pacific towns and cities (Jones, 2016). Urban growth rates exceed national population growth rates, and as a result, the urban population within the Pacific is expected to double within the next 25 years (Keen and Barbara, 2016). Many urban areas of PICs are located on the coast, making them especially vulnerable to climate-induced hazards.

Much of this urban growth is taking place in informal, low-income settlements, many of which lack adequate access to basic services such as water, electricity, sewage management and rubbish collection. People living in urban informal settlements who have little or no ability to fall back on subsistence farming tend to have lower levels of livelihood and food security (Manley et al., 2016). Poorer urban dwellers, often living on poor-quality land, are almost always the most vulnerable to disasters, and can be overlooked by rurally biased planning policies and humanitarian actors (Gero and Winterford, 2020; Day and Bamforth, 2020).

This chapter outlines the hazard threats facing urban areas, in particular those fueled by climate change. It discusses urban management and planning in PICs and reviews current limitations in planning practices. It then presents opportunities in policy and practice to contribute to more resilient urban areas, in particular relating to the *Framework for Resilient Development in the Pacific (FRDP), 2017–30* (Pacific Community, 2016), using references to other chapters in this book.

Climate and Disaster Risks in Urban PICs

PICs are particularly vulnerable to the impact of natural hazards, including cyclones and sea surges. Pacific islands are ranked among some of the highest-risk countries on the planet. One recent UN index ranks Vanuatu as the most disaster-prone country in the world, with Tonga not far behind (UNU-EHS, 2018).

Such hazards, however, are set to increase dramatically with the worsening effects of climate change. The IPCC's 2019 report *The Ocean and Cryosphere in a Changing Climate* presents bleak predictions on the impacts of climate change. This includes 'Many . . . small islands . . . are projected to experience historical centennial events at least annually by 2050' (IPCC, 2019: 32). Concerning urban atoll islands,

> High to very high risks are approached for vulnerable communities in coral reef environments, urban atoll islands . . . from sea level rise well before the end of this century in case of high emissions scenarios. . . . Some island nations are likely to become uninhabitable due to climate-related ocean and cryosphere change.
>
> (IPCC, 2019: 32)

Most Pacific island towns and cities are located on the coast and are therefore particularly vulnerable. Those living in poorer settlements in cities tend to be those worst affected by disasters. As one study notes, 'Inevitably, people living in low-income settlements are least equipped to deal with climate change' (Sanderson, 2019: 38). In addition to rapid-onset disasters, heat is also an increasing threat. The same study reports that, on a global scale, 'by 2050, some 215 million people will be living in poverty in 495 cities that have a regular three-month average temperature of over 35°C—which is eight times the current number' (Sanderson, 2019: 38, citing UCCRN, 2018). In low-income settlements, often characterised as dense settlements with poor quality, often poorly ventilated housing, sometimes with a tin roof and without air conditioning, the effects of heat can be extreme.

Figure 2.1 Informal Housing in Lautoka, Nadi, Fiji.

Source: David Sanderson (2019)

Figure 2.2 Informal Housing, Suva, Fiji.

Source: David Sanderson (2019)

In urban PICs a large number of people live in informal settlements. One paper reports that,

> The largest numbers of informal and squatter settlements are in the Melanesian capital cities—Port Moresby, Honiara, Port Vila, and Suva—and smaller towns of Micronesia, such as South Tarawa and Majuro. The recurring pattern in Pacific towns and cities is that they all contain a proportion of informal and squatter settlements to varying degrees, with the largest numbers being in Port Moresby, the biggest city in the Pacific region.
>
> (Jones and Sanderson, 2017: 11)

Urban Management and Planning

One recent review on urbanisation in the Pacific notes that, 'Throughout the Pacific islands, urban planning and management remain largely neglected' (Keen and Barbara, 2016). Keen and Kiddle (2019) note, 'Urban planners are rare in the Pacific, not surprising given there is no regional tertiary degree programme to train Pacific planners in a context-relevant manner. Some city councils do not even have one trained urban planner'. The following section discusses a number of issues relating to urban management and planning.

Migration

Urbanisation in PICs, as with other parts of the world, is of course dynamic: people living in cities may live there only part of the year, having established homes and communities in rural areas. Movement between rural and urban areas in PICs is a long-standing practice. Pacific island towns and cities offer a concentration of jobs, health services, education, and access to technology and the global economy. These factors are particularly appealing to younger people, who make up large numbers of PIC populations. ADB states, however, that this 'will increase the rates of . . . urban unemployment, and youth vulnerability" (ADB, 2012: 29).

Informality and 'Urban Villages'

Linked to rural-urban migration, Jones (2016: xiii) notes that 'urban villages' within the Pacific are 'a consequence of informal urbanisation' whereby traditional village-like settlements are spreading to high-risk, marginalised land deemed unsuitable for habitation by the formal planning system. The highest numbers of urban villages are in the Melanesian capitals of Honiara, Port Moresby, Port Vila, Suva and in Micronesian towns such as South Tarawa (Jones, 2016). Built on the edges of rivers and estuaries, ocean and lagoon foreshores, mangrove wetlands and swamps, waste disposal sites and electricity easements, urban villages place large populations of people at increased risk. Often tied to kinship and ethnicity, such urban villages are likely to use a kin-based governance structure, follow a mix of custom and colonial-based land tenure, and employ subsistence-based activities such as urban gardening (Jones, 2016). The literature on urbanisation in the Pacific has yet to define what the acceptable minimum standard for essential public services and infrastructure provided in all urban villages should be and the types of urban governance required to adequately deal with chronic stresses and shocks in an equitable way (Jones, 2016).

The informal economy has an important role in Pacific urban centres due to limited formal employment and a large unskilled workforce. One report states that most informal settlements are not included in health, demographic and socioeconomic surveys (Sitko and Goudswaard, 2019). ADB observes that 'the employment and income generating capacity of the informal sector will need to be recognised and supported if urbanisation is to be efficient' (ADB, 2012: 97).

Spatial Analysis and Change Over Time

Spatial analysis offers insight into how the built environment creates or averts climate and disaster risk in towns and cities, and conversely, how people create risk within the design of built environment. The built environment comprises physical infrastructure such as housing, roads, sanitation systems, and public buildings such as hospitals and schools. Connell (2003) details how sand mining for accelerated construction in Tuvalu has eroded the beach, while Campbell (2014) concludes that much environmental degradation can be attributed to population density, especially in urban areas.

In order to better understand the links between vulnerability, topography and urban form in Fongafale Islet (Tuvalu), Yamano et al. (2007) studied the changes in buildings, plots, open spaces, and roads between 1896 and 2004. In this study, historical reconstruction using topographical and geological maps (modern and historical), aerial photos, census data, satellite imagery and topographical profiles gave the authors granular detail about environmental, economic, and social characteristics that contribute to and create vulnerability. In Fongafale Islet, vulnerability relates to the original landform. The central part of the island was land reclaimed during World War Two from swampland, which is still prone to flooding during spring high tides. Following independence, migration, centralisation and economic growth led to the expansion of the built environment into swampland areas, deepening vulnerability to flooding (Yamano et al., 2007).

Challenges in Enacting Urban Policy

As noted, urban planning has not been high on the agenda in PICs—though that may be changing (this is discussed further in the following sections). Currently, there are challenges. One is rural bias. As Barbara and Keen

26 David Sanderson et al.

note, a 'strong rural bias has dominated Melanesian politics since pre-independence days, consistently prioritising provincial representation and programmes' (Barbara and Keen, 2017: 16). A second challenge is that urbanisation issues are rarely addressed explicitly in national climate adaptation or disaster risk-reduction plans (Kuruppu and Willie, 2015). Only a limited number of countries have national urban policies to guide governance, economic growth, environmental impact and social change. Samoa, Papua New Guinea and the Solomon Islands are among some of the few examples (Jones, 2017).

A third challenge concerns practical barriers to operationalising regional frameworks (Keweloh, 2015). While not impossible, integrating disaster risk reduction and climate change adaptation at a national, municipal and local level in the interest of reducing operational 'silos' is difficult to do well. Other practical challenges include agreeing on and maintaining a regional strategy and standards, maintaining a continued commitment to a regional framework as national and municipal governments change, and strengthening bottom-up approaches for long-term ownership of initiatives (Keweloh, 2015).

Opportunities for Resilient Pacific Towns and Cities

As discussed, the challenges facing rapidly urbanising PICs are substantial. Concerning climate change and disasters, the latest IPCC predictions present, at worst case, an existential threat to urban atolls, and severe disruption to other coastal urban areas of all low-lying islands. This is not new (although the rate of climate change is faster than previously thought), and globally the pressure for more climate change mitigation through, for instance, carbon emissions reductions is increasing. PICs already suffer frequent disasters, and the threat of more of these and at a greater intensity (in particular tropical cyclones) underlines the vital need for a focus on building resilience to these threats.

With greater concentrations of people and as places of economic generation, cities need particular attention (this of course does not mean at the cost of rural areas, which is discussed later). As also noted, there is an opportunity to engage more in urban planning and management.

There is evidence that this may be gaining momentum. The Fifth Pacific Urban Forum (PUF), held in Nadi in July 2019, was the largest PUF held to date, with attendance of senior leaders and some heads of state from across the PICs. The PUF5 Declaration provided 28 outcomes and recommendations. Concerning climate change, the Declaration

> Re-emphasize[s] that climate change is a crisis for the Pacific region and the world, representing a significant threat for sustainable development, and that reducing the vulnerability and contribution of Pacific cities

and human settlements to climate change and natural hazards calls for a reconsideration of the way cities are planned and transformed and the way infrastructure is developed.

(UN, 2019: 2)

A review of PUF5 notes that, 'for practitioners, securing transformational change in cities means changing the dominant narratives from dichotomous urban versus rural to ones which see connectivity and pathways for balance and complementarity'. This point was also made by Fiji's Prime Minister, who called for 'a systemic approach to governance that did not treat urban and rural separately, as if unconnected' (Keen and Kiddle, 2019). A way to support this view is to recast how cities are seen, and to go beyond the physicality and density differences that exist between rural and urban. An approach that achieves this is to see cities as a series of systems. One study describes this as follows:

A systems-based approach describes how different elements, aspects or functions of a city work together. Systems can be defined as 'an interconnected collection of things (for example people, institutions, infrastructure, societal norms, economy or ecosystems), organised in a pattern or structure that changes frequently'.

(Sanderson, 2019: 7)

With this perspective, looking, for example, at fishing as a livelihood system, a link can readily be made between catching the fish in the sea to immediate processing on boats and on the coastline, to their transport and selling at markets in cities. This 'fishing system' cuts across and clearly links rural and urban boundaries. A systems approach to understanding cities is explored in some depth in Sitko et al.'s chapter, 'Using a Systems Approach to Better Understand Urban Resilience in Port Vila, Vanuatu' in this book.

Another approach is that of 'ocean cities' and 'nature-based solutions' to urbanisation, developed by ESCAP, which relies on 'the recognition of the deeper links between Ocean Cities and ecosystems—both landscapes and seascapes—to guide future policy in integrated, climate resilient sustainable urban planning in the Pacific island region' (ESCAP, nd).

Urbanising the Framework for Resilient Development in the Pacific (FRDP)

A further opportunity could be a greater exploration of the application of urban contexts within the *Framework for Resilient Development in the Pacific (FRDP), 2017–30* (Pacific Community, 2016), which is acknowledged in the PUF Declaration. The FRDP is thin on its recognition of urbanisation. The words 'urban' and 'urbanisation' combined appear only three times in the 31-page report, most notably on page 22: 'There is a need to build awareness and capacity within the disaster management community at regional, national and local level, to broaden its practices, and to pay special attention to the resilience of urban spaces' ('city' appears once as a footnote on page 18, in relation to the Philippines).

This, however, does not mean that the FRDP is not relevant to urban issues—indeed, the reverse is true. The FRDP's guiding principles include, among other things, integrated climate change and disaster risk management, stakeholder engagement, strengthening partnerships, prioritising the most vulnerable and directing resilience-building measures towards poverty alleviation (Pacific Community, 2016: 6). Such an approach chimes in with approaches embodied, for instance, in the *New Urban Agenda* (which is discussed in Norman's chapter, 'Planning for Climate Change: Adapting to a More Sustainable Urban Future' in this book). The following section discusses each of the three goals of the FRDP from an urban perspective.

Goal One. Strengthened Integrated Risk Reduction and Adaptation to Enhance Climate Change and Disaster Resilience

A raft of measures can be enacted in cities to contribute to this goal. One example of far-reaching activities concerns the expansive work of the Rockefeller Foundation's *100 Resilient Cities* programme (which ended in July 2019), wherein 100 cities across the world supported a 'Chief Resilience Officer' to drive, convene and build partnerships across multiple actors towards building urban resilience initiatives (Rockefeller Foundation, nd). Concerning other resilience-related examples, this book addresses the issue in a number of chapters. For instance, McEvoy et al.'s chapter 'Reflecting on a Journey From Climate Change Vulnerability Assessments to the Implementation of Climate Resilience Actions: Honiara, Solomon Islands' describes 'a series of discrete steps that have taken place to identify local climate vulnerabilities and community priorities for action, as well as multi-stakeholder engagement processes which have been critical to the operationalisation of a climate action implementation programme' (McEvoy et al., 2020).

Addressing the intersection between urbanisation, climate change, and disaster risk through planning and policy activities provides an opportunity to prioritise, plan for and coordinate with responsible departments, urban-development interventions such as safer, low-income housing, clean water, solid waste management and sanitation, for example (UN-Habitat, 2018). Such examples include a number of projects resulting in the *South Tarawa Urban Management Plan* (STUMP), developed between 1995 and 2000, and the establishment of the Planning and Urban Management Agency (PUMA) in Samoa, from 2001 to 2003 (Jones and Lea, 2007). Lessons learned about urban reform from the two initiatives include the need for political will, an ability to attract urban development assistance, and the achievement of some degree of economic growth and environmental management (Jones and Lea, 2007).

Goal Two. Low Carbon Development

FRDP's second Goal, 'Low carbon development', provides a strong rationale for effective city planning. Well-run public transport and planning that provides density and prevents urban sprawl contributes to lower emissions. Also, the enacting building codes for new buildings and retrofitting existing built infrastructure can substantially improve energy efficiency. This includes the need to integrate informal settlements into formal planning processes. Designing urban infrastructure for a hotter future climate to reduce 'urban heat island' effects can reduce the need for energy-consuming air conditioning. As referred to earlier, ESCAP's 'nature-based solutions' to urban growth provide pointers for reducing carbon emissions.

Goal Three. Strengthened Disaster Preparedness, Response and Recovery

FRDP's third goal is 'Strengthened disaster preparedness, response and recovery', whose strategic objective is the 'Improved capacity of [PICs] to prepare for emergencies and disasters, thereby ensuring timely and effective response and recovery, and to ensure future risk is reduced, in relation to both rapid and slow onset disasters' (Pacific Community, 2016: 22). The goal also emphasises the need for improved coordination and capacity building, especially within government. In towns and cities this is especially resonant—coordination between actors in urban disaster response is a well-recognised opportunity, and challenge. This is because cities have diverse groups of actors that not only include government and its respective departments and levels, but also civil society organisations and businesses, who are increasingly recognised as key actors in urban disaster response (Sanderson, 2019).

Businesses range from formal businesses, who may have headquarters in capital cities, to small- and medium-size businesses. And, as noted earlier, the informal economy, home to large numbers of petty traders, is a vital part of many cities. Research concerning the contributions (formal) businesses can make in disaster recovery includes,

> new technologies and other innovations and the sharing of technical capacities in areas such as logistics, telecommunications and cash transfers. In addition, businesses, as seen in the growth of social enterprises, are increasingly developing models which are commercial in nature but

which ultimately help to meet humanitarian needs and reduce vulnerability to future disasters.

(Zyck and Kent, 2014)

Concerning informal markets, these are often up and running immediately after a disaster, and can be capitalised on in a response (Clermont et al., 2011).

Recent research has also identified a particular grouping, emergent groups, 'who come together, often spontaneously, immediately after a disaster to perform first aid and provide water, food, warmth and shelter. Emergent groups may themselves be affected by disaster. Such groups may disappear as spontaneously as they appear' (Sanderson, 2019: 55, citing Twigg and Mosel, 2017). Emergent groups are made up of voluntary groups of people who aim to assist after a disaster.

A further urban-specific group to engage in includes gangs. Long-standing urban gang culture is well documented in Port Moresby (Dupont, 2012). Post-disaster, engagement with gangs by external humanitarian actors is inevitable:

> Any work carried out by humanitarian players in a city neighbour-hood, or in an area within a prison, that is controlled by a gang will be subject to discussion or authorisation by the gang, whether one is aware of it or not.
>
> (Sanderson and Knox Clarke, 2012: 19)

Research by Ferris (2012, cited in Sanderson, 2019: 63) notes the need to 'gain acceptance from gang leaders, given that many gangs are hierarchically organised; also that gang leaders need to perceive some benefit from the organisation's operation'.

Urban disaster response and recovery is discussed in a number of chapters in this book. Day and Bamforth's chapter, '"This is Our Garden Now": Disasters and Belonging in an Urban Pacific', discusses how a low-income settlement in Vanuatu was largely ignored by humanitarian response following Tropical Cyclone Pam. The authors attribute this to 'an unfortunate confluence of a rural bias within humanitarian aid, an intentional direction of resources by government away from these particular peri-urban settlements, and a feeling by members of the community that they did not *belong* to the city' (Day and Bamforth, 2020).

Concerning the links of response to longer-term recovery, Gero and Winterford's chapter in this book, 'The Humanitarian-Development Nexus in Pacific Urban Contexts: Lessons From Tropical Cyclone Winston in Fiji', explores how an urban response to a disaster connected with longer-term development—an area referred to by some as 'the nexus'. The chapter ends with recommendations for improved future urban disaster response, including a need for better coordination ('a fit-for-purpose subnational cluster system') and the enacting of subnational development plans that would include informal settlements (who are often omitted from formal plans) that would be made available to humanitarian actors after a disaster.

In a similar vein to Gero and Winterford's chapter, Sanderson's chapter in this book, 'Identifying Resilience in Recovery—Complexity, Collaboration and Communication', takes an essentially developmental approach to disaster recovery. Among other things, two particular urban-oriented recovery approaches gaining traction are the use of cash in recovery, and area-based approaches. Taking cash first, the premise is that cities contain the goods necessary (with the important caveat of when markets are functioning) to allow people to source the goods they need themselves. The chapter gives examples of successful cash-based programmes enacted following Tropical Cyclone Winston in Fiji and for people relocated from Vanuatu's Ambae following volcanic activity. Area-based approaches, or ABAs, are a developmental, people-centred approach to post-disaster recovery, which draws from participatory urban planning principles. ABAs have been shown to work well in a number of post-disaster urban contexts.

Concluding Comments

In summary, managed urbanisation is a prerequisite if the future challenges of climate change and worsening climate-fuelled disasters are to be prepared for and mitigated against. Existing frameworks such as the FRDP provide a valuable set of lessons for enacting such approaches, while there is an opportunity to 'embrace' urbanisation and its implicit links to rural Pacific identities in order to ultimately contribute to more resilient PICs.

References

ADB (Asian Development Bank). (2012). *The State of Pacific Towns and Cities: Urbanization in ADB's Pacific Developing Member Countries*. Pacific Studies Series. Manila: Asian Development Bank.

Barbara, J. and Keen, M. (2017). *Urbanisation in Melanesia: The Politics of Change.* Development Bulletin No. 78, 16–19.

Campbell, J.R. (2014). Climate-change migration in the Pacific. *Contemporary Pacific*, 26, 1–29.

Clermont, C., Sanderson, D., Spraos, H. and Sharma, A. (2011). *Urban Disasters— Lessons from Haiti*. Study of Member Agencies' Responses to the Earthquake in Port au Prince, Haiti, January 2010. London: Disasters Emergency Committee (DEC).

Connell, J. (2003). Losing ground? Tuvalu, the greenhouse effect and the garbage can. *Asia Pacific Viewpoint*, 44, 89–107.

Day, J. and Bamforth, T. (2020). 'This is our garden now': Disasters and belonging in an urban Pacific. In D. Sanderson and L. Bruce (eds.), *Urbanisation at Risk: Pacific and Asia*. New York: Routledge.

Dupont, S. (2012). *Raskols: The Gangs of Papua New Guinea*. New York: power-House Books.

ESCAP. (nd). *Ocean Cities of the Pacific Islands*. Policy Brief No. 3, Renaturing Urbanisation. Available at: www.unescap.org/sites/default/files/Ocean%20 Cities%20of%20the%20Pacific%20Islands_PB3_UNESCAP_USP_0.pdf.

Ferris, E. (2012). *Urban Disasters, Conflict and Violence: Implications for Humanitarian Work*. Washington, DC: Brookings Institution. Available at: www.brook ings.edu/on-the-record/urban-disasters-conflict-and-violence-implications-for-humanitarian-work/.

IPCC. (2019). *The Ocean and Cryosphere in a Changing Climate*. Available at: www.ipcc.ch/srocc/home/.

Jones, P. (2016). *The Emergence of Pacific Urban Villages: Urbanization Trends in the Pacific Islands*. Mandaluyong City: Asian Development Bank.

Jones, P. (2017). *Informal and Squatter Settlements: The Self-made Urban Order Shaping Pacific Towns and Cities*. Available at: https://crawford.anu.edu.au/rmap/ devnet/devnet/db-78.pdf.

Jones, P. and Lea, J. (2007). What has happened to urban reform in the Island Pacific? Some lessons from Kiribati and Samoa. *Pacific Affairs*, 80, 473–491.

Jones, P. and Sanderson, D. (2017). Urban resilience and informal and squatter settlements in the Pacific region. *Development Bulletin*, 78, 11–16.

Keen, M. and Barbara, J. (2016). *Pacific Urbanisation: Changing Times*. Devpolicyblog. Available at: www.devpolicy.org/pacific-urbanisation-changing-times-20160225/.

Keen, M. and Kiddle, L. (2019). *A PUF of Fresh Air? Pacific Urban Forum 2019*. Department of Pacific Affairs. Available at: http://dpa.bellschool.anu.edu.au/sites/ default/files/publications/attachments/2019-07/dpa_ib_2019_15_in_brief_keen_ kiddle_final_0.pdf.

Keweloh, R. (2015). *Integrating Disaster Risk Reduction and Climate Change Adaptation in Theory and Practice: A Case Study of the Red Cross and Red Crescent Movement in Asia*. Working Paper, Vol. 5, No. 3, Rurh-Universitat Bachum.

Kuruppu, N. and Willie, R. (2015). Barriers to reducing climate enhanced disaster risks in least developed country: Small islands through anticipatory adaptation. *Weather and Climate Extremes*, 7, 72–83.

Manley, M., et al. (2016). *Research and Analysis on Climate Change and Disaster Risk Reduction*. Working Paper 1: Needs, Priorities and Opportunities Related to Climate Change Adaptation and Disaster Risk Reduction. Report to the New Zealand Ministry of Foreign Affairs and Trade, Wellington.

McEvoy, D., et al. (2020). Reflecting on a journey from climate change vulnerability assessments to the implementation of climate resilience actions: Honiara, Solomon Islands. In D. Sanderson and L. Bruce (eds.), *Urbanisation at Risk: Pacific and Asia*. New York: Routledge.

Pacific Community. (2016). *Framework for Resilient Development in the Pacific. An Integrated Approach to Address Climate Change and Disaster Risk Management (FRDP), 2017–2030*. Available at: http://gsd.spc.int/frdp/assets/FRDP_2016_ Resilient_Dev_pacific.pdf.

Rockefeller Foundation. (nd). Available at: www.100resilientcities.org/.

Sanderson, D. (2019). Urban humanitarian response. *Good Practice Review*, No. 12. London: ODI/ALNAP. Available at: https://odihpn.org/wp-content/uploads/2019/ 03/GPR-12-2019-001-244-web4_FINAL.pdf.

Sanderson, D. and Knox Clarke, P. (2012). *Responding to Urban Disasters: Learning from Previous Relief and Recovery Operations*. London: ALNAP. Available at: www.alnap.org/system/files/content/resource/files/main/alnap-lessons-urban-web. pdf.

Sitko, P. and Goudswaard, S. (2019). *Development in the Urban Era: Six Strategies for Better Managing Urbanisation in Asia and the Pacific*. RDI Network. Canberra: ACFID

Twigg, J. and Mosel, I. (2017). Emergent groups and spontaneous volunteers in urban disaster response. *Environment and Urbanization*, 29(2), 443–458. Available at: http://journals.sagepub.com/doi/abs/10.1177/0956247817721413.

UCCRN. (2018). *The Future We Don't Want: How Climate Change Could Impact the World's Greatest Cities*. UCCRN Technical Report. Available at: https://c40-production-images.s3.amazonaws.com/other_uploads/images/1789_Future_We_Don't_Want_Report_1.4_hi-res_120618.original.pdf.

UN-Habitat. (2018). *National Urban Policies*. Online: UN-Habitat. Available at: https://unhabitat.org/urban-initiatives/initiatives-programmes/national-urban-policies/.

UN-Habitat. (2019). *Fifth Pacific Urban Forum Declaration*. Available at: www.fukuoka.unhabitat.org/info/news/puf.html.

UNU-EHS. (2018). *World Risk Report*. Available at: https://reliefweb.int/sites/reliefweb.int/files/resources/WorldRiskReport-2018.pdf.

Yamano, H., et al. (2007). Atoll island vulnerability to flooding and inundation revealed by historical reconstruction: Fongafale Islet, Funafuti Atoll, Tuvalu. *Global and Planetary Change*, 57(3–4), 407–416.

Zyck, S. and Kent, R. (2014). *Humanitarian Crises, Emergency Preparedness and Response: The Role of Business and the Private Sector*. London: ODI. Available at: www.odi.org/publications/8534-humanitarian-crises-emergency-preparedness-and-response-role-business-and-private-sector-final.

Chapter 3

The Humanitarian-Development Nexus in Pacific Urban Contexts

Lessons From Tropical Cyclone Winston in Fiji

Anna Gero and Keren Winterford

Introduction

This chapter explores disaster response in an urbanising setting in the Pacific. We present empirical research from Fiji—a Pacific island country highly exposed to natural hazards and climate change, and also experiencing rapid urbanisation—providing an example of the humanitarian-development nexus[1] in action. Our research draws on the response to Tropical Cyclone (TC) Winston in Fiji's Western Division, and we unpack the concept of the humanitarian-development divide and relevant issues such as urban disaster policy and localisation of response in the Fiji context. Our findings point to several ways in which urban response policy in the Pacific can better align with development planning going forward.

The remainder of the Introduction provides research background, including a brief historical reflection of the humanitarian-development nexus. The Introduction is followed by a description of the research context and our research approach. We then outline two main findings and reflections from the research: 1) the policy lag in terms of urban development and disaster response in the Pacific; 2) evidence of bridging the humanitarian-development divide from the TC Winston response in Fiji through a) subnational governance and b) the emerging 'cluster system'.[2] Our results provide examples of localisation of disaster response in action and we conclude by providing critical reflections and suggested avenues to further overcome the challenges associated with the humanitarian-development divide.

Research Background

Humanitarian action and development approaches both seek to improve conditions for people in need but operate through different systems in terms of policy, stakeholder groups, budgets, terminology, timescales, principles and practice (Stamnes, 2016). The clear distinction between humanitarian action (responding to acute crises) and development (addressing chronic poverty) has led actors on both sides to acknowledge the existence of a divide, despite humanitarian response, recovery and development occurring along a continuum with no clear delineation of where response stops and where development begins. Bridging the divide between the humanitarian and development practices (inclusive of key stakeholder groups and their ways of working) has been a goal of key actors across both domains for decades. The gap between humanitarian assistance and development activities was first identified in the 1980s through responses to the African food crises, and was first conceptualised as 'Linking Relief, Rehabilitation and Development' (LRRD). LRRD was thought of as a continuum model, where a linear and sequential transition progressed from the disaster relief phase to the development phase (Mosel and Levine, 2014).

Various authors began to critique the LRRD continuum model (e.g. Buchanan-Smith and Maxwell, 1994; Longhurst, 1994), as it assumed a continuum model where disaster response interventions were short-term, and that development was insensitive to the impact of humanitarian crises (Mosel and Levine, 2014). In reality this is not the case, with disaster response and development often occurring simultaneously. The continuum model was therefore replaced with an updated model that allowed for the application of concurrent instruments and approaches—termed a contiguum model (Mosel and Levine, 2014).

Recognition of the importance of linking humanitarian response with development through the concept of LRRD occurred with the informal donor forum called the Good Humanitarian Donorship initiative (European Union, 2008). Seventeen donors endorsed good practice principles at a meeting in Sweden in 2003. Since then, membership has increased to 42 and there is increasing recognition that humanitarian response can potentially have negative effects on development. This increased recognition is reflected in global policy frameworks including the Sendai Framework for Disaster Risk Reduction 2015–2030 (UNISDR, 2015), which includes mention of 'build back better' as part of disaster recovery. The Sustainable Development Goals, or SDGs, also aim to reduce risk and vulnerability from both humanitarian and development perspectives, with the notion of 'leave no-one behind' common to both stakeholder groups.

Contemporary dialogue on the humanitarian-development nexus culminated at the 2016 World Humanitarian Summit (WHS) in Turkey, where a shared Agenda for Humanity (UN, 2016) was agreed upon. This included a core responsibility to 'deliver collective outcomes: transcend humanitarian development divides', and to

> Commit to the following elements in order to move beyond traditional silos, and work across mandates, sectors and institutional boundaries, with a greater diversity of partners, towards ending need and reducing risk and vulnerability in support of national and local capacities and the achievement of the 2030 Agenda.
>
> (UN, 2016: 58)

United Nations (UN) agencies and other development stakeholders at global, regional, national and subnational levels have since progressed on agreed actions from the WHS. For example, the UN Office for the Coordination of Humanitarian Affairs (UNOCHA)'s 'New way of working' report (UNOCHA, 2017) further developed the ideas from the Agenda for Humanity and describes the need to overcome the barriers that exist between humanitarian and development workers. The notion of 'localisation' within humanitarian response was also a key theme at the WHS, which provides means to overcome the humanitarian-development divide through local leadership. Since then, commitments to improve localisation of humanitarian response have gained traction, for example the adoption of the 'Grand Bargain' (Metcalfe-Hough et al., 2018) by a number of key donors and the Charter For Change,[3] which is a non-government commitment to support localisation of humanitarian response. While these commitments are commendable, a clearer articulation of what 'localisation' means (for example, led at national or subnational level) and how it enables the humanitarian-development nexus is still needed.

Within regional forums in the Pacific, for example the Pacific Islands Forum Secretariat (PIFS), humanitarian and development actors have also been discussing the need to think of humanitarian response and development as a continuum, rather than as separate fields of work. The Pacific's Framework for Resilient Development in the Pacific (PIFS et al., 2016) notes that: 'Knowledge brokering, communication and access to meteorological, climate, geological and other relevant information and tools are essential to effectively address key risks across the humanitarian-development continuum' (PIFS et al., 2016: 29).

The Pacific Humanitarian Partnership (a collaboration between the UN, Pacific Island country representatives, NGOs, donors and private-sector actors) has also made efforts to overcome the traditional divide between humanitarian and development work. At the Pacific Humanitarian Team's 2016 meeting, it was noted that transformative change in the traditional ways of working were needed, and this included changes to governance structures to support the humanitarian-development nexus (UNOCHA, 2016a). Examples of such transformation were echoed in our research findings (e.g., 'evergreen clusters'—see our section on Bridging the Divide).

In Fiji, progress is also being made to address the divide between humanitarian response and development. In 2015, the Commissioner of Fiji's Western Division demonstrated his leadership on this issue, preparing a communiqué which provides guidance that all planning and sectoral programming in the Western Division integrates considerations of risk in order to reduce and/or mitigate the impact of climate change and disaster (Western Division Government of Fiji, 2015). Within this context, this chapter explores the interface between humanitarian response and long-term development in relation to TC Winston in the Western Division of Fiji, which struck in February 2016.

Urbanisation and Development in the Pacific

Within conversations on bridging humanitarian response and development, urban issues remain largely absent. Some authors have acknowledged this gap, highlighting that while humanitarian response has provided much-needed immediate post-disaster assistance, it has done so (and continues to do so) with no regard for local development needs (Tag-Eldeen, 2017). This is particularly true in the Pacific, in part because urban planning challenges are a new and emerging issue. The complex dynamics present in any urban setting are acknowledged to be a challenge in humanitarian response (Dodman et al., 2013), and the Fiji example certainly highlights this to be the case. This research aims to bring some new thinking to the topic of linking humanitarian response and development in urban contexts.

The rates of rural-to-urban migration across the Pacific are increasing. Values and social norms of Pacific Islanders are shifting in line with the influence of Western culture and capitalism. The result has meant shifts away from the communal village lifestyles to those more focused on individual wealth (Mecartney and Connell, 2017). Consequently, many Pacific Islanders are turning from traditional subsistence lifestyles to cash economies, drawn to urban centres seeking paid employment, education and health-related opportunities. Climate change and disasters are also key forces driving rates of urbanisation in the Pacific. Subsistence livelihoods are becoming more difficult as climate change renders land unproductive as a result of sea level rise, salination of soil and coastal erosion (Connell, 2013). This is contributing to high rates of urbanisation in the Pacific, providing a catalyst for migration to urban centres (Connell, 2017).

Urbanisation and urban policy issues are relatively new in the Pacific. Given the rural-to-urban migration trends observed across the region, urban development and urban disaster response are critical policy areas requiring attention. Despite the clear need for urban policy development, authors report a strong 'anti-urban bias' among Pacific governments, where little priority is placed on developing appropriate urban policies or appropriately resourcing urban administrations (Butcher-Gollach, 2015). This lack of focus on—and resourcing of—urban areas reflects the legacy of rural development and corresponding governance arrangements, as well as a lack of appreciation and value of the urban economy (Butcher-Gollach, 2015).

Research Context

The research presented in this chapter focuses on Fiji, a Pacific Island nation with a population of 892,000 (World Bank, 2015a), almost 54 percent of which live in urban areas (World Bank, 2015b). The Fiji Pacific Islands are highly exposed to natural hazards, particularly tropical cyclones and floods, with climate change heightening these risks (Government of Fiji et al., 2017). Furthermore, Fiji is experiencing rapid urbanisation. Therefore, Fiji provided a good location for addressing questions around disaster response and development challenges in urban contexts.

Fiji's subnational government is divided into four divisions: Northern, Eastern, Western and Central, with Divisional Commissioners responsible for coordinating government services and development activities (Rahman and Singh, 2011). This research focused on Western Division (see Figure 3.1), and specifically in and around the city of Lautoka. With a population of 52,000, Lautoka is the second-largest city in Fiji (after Suva, the capital, with a population of 88,000). Lautoka is a low-lying coastal city, vulnerable to flooding, storm surges, coastal erosion and sea level rise.

Our research focused on a major extreme weather event, and explored if and how the response to the disaster that ensued linked to longer-term development planning. TC Winston struck Fiji in February 2016 as the most severe cyclone on record to affect Fiji, making landfall as a Category 5 storm: the highest intensity of tropical cyclones (Joint Typhoon Warning Center, 2016).

TC Winston had one-minute sustained wind speeds of 285 km/h, recorded prior to landfall. Wind gusts peaked at around 306 km/hour. Forty-four

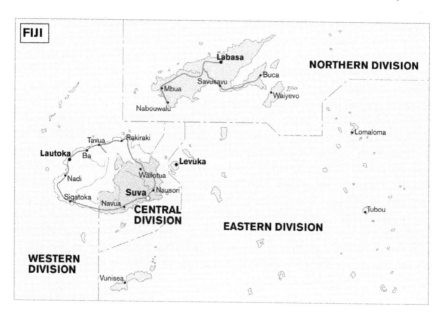

Figure 3.1 Divisional Structure of Fiji Highlighting Western Division.
Source: Netmaps

people were killed as a result of TC Winston (21 in the Western Division, 15 in the Eastern Division, six in the Central Division and two in the Northern Division). An estimated 126 people were injured and approximately 540,400 people (equivalent to 62 percent of the country's total population) were affected by the storm (Government of Fiji, 2016). Twenty-four thousand homes were destroyed, while 30,369 houses, 495 schools, and 88 health clinics and medical facilities were damaged or destroyed. Approximately 80 percent of the population lost power, including the whole of Vanu Levu Island.

TC Winston was the highest-cost cyclone to affect the South Pacific, costing Fiji approximately US$500 million or 10 percent of Fiji's gross domestic product (GDP) (Government of Fiji, 2016). The storm partly damaged 12,421, while 6,660 were completely destroyed. More than 30,000 people were made homeless and most school buildings were severely damaged, delaying classes for more than a month while some were temporarily closed due to the extent of damages sustained.

The government of Fiji declared a State of Natural Disaster and led the disaster response, which was supported by the Fijian Military Services as well as national and international donors, non-government organisations, UN agencies, the Red Cross and the private sector. Jointly with the United Nations, the Fijian government launched a three-month US$38.8M flash appeal, of which 51% was funded (UNOCHA, 2016b). Bilateral donors also pledged assistance to the value of US$66M, comprising cash and in-kind support (Ministry of Economy, 2016). During the response phase, the main humanitarian needs included emergency shelter and support to evacuation centres, access to health services, water, sanitation and hygiene, food and protection, and support to vulnerable communities (UNOCHA, 2016b). The response to the cyclone involved the distribution of cash vouchers for food and rebuilding materials, which was a new approach to humanitarian response in the Pacific. The education and health sectors were able to reopen and resume operations relatively quickly with the use of temporary learning spaces and immediate repairs to health facilities (UNOCHA, 2016b). Within the shelter sector, much emphasis was placed on 'Build Back Safer' for improved future resilience, providing an example of the humanitarian-development nexus, which will be discussed later.

Research Approach

This research was undertaken by the University of Technology Sydney, Institute for Sustainable Futures (UTS-ISF) and funded by the International Institute for Environment and Development's (IIED's) Urban Crises Learning Fund. Fieldwork was undertaken in 2017. The aim of the research was to explore how the humanitarian-development divide was revealed in the response to TC Winston in Western Division, Fiji, with a particular focus on the governance arrangements for both development and humanitarian response. The research approach was informed by a case-study methodology, focusing on the experience of the TC Winston response in the Western Division, Fiji. The design of the research recognised the leadership of the Western Division subnational government in relation to the nexus of humanitarian response and development planning.

Primary data was collected using key informant interviews and a multi-stakeholder workshop. The key informant interviews were undertaken at both national (Suva) and subnational levels (Western Division). Twenty-eight interviews were conducted (seven female, 21 male). The gender representation of interview participants is indicative of broader trends of men and women in senior government roles in Fiji. The multi-stakeholder participatory workshop was held with 34 participants attending (11 female, 23 male) representing government sectors and the Commissioner's Office from Western Division, and locally based NGOs, for example the Red Cross, Viseisei Sai Health Centre and Empower Pacific.

At the national level and based in Suva, key stakeholders relevant to the TC Winston response were also consulted during the research, and included:

- Fiji National Disaster Management Office (NDMO);
- Donors, including Australia's Department of Foreign Affairs and Trade (DFAT) and New Zealand's Ministry of Foreign Affairs and Trade (MFAT);
- United National agencies including UNOCHA, UNDP, UNICEF;
- Humanitarian response agencies (based in Suva) including Save the Children and International Federation of the Red Cross and Red Crescent Societies (IFRC).

Primary data was supplemented by a document review which focused on generating insight from the TC Winston response and revealing opportunities to strengthen the nexus between humanitarian response and development goals. Data analysis of both primary and secondary data was conducted using the qualitative software NVivo. Inductive thematic analysis was undertaken where areas of inquiry framed by research questions formed the basis of the coding and analysis structure. The research was carried out with ethics approval from the University of Technology Sydney. Informed consent was obtained from all research participants and consideration was made to ensure privacy and protocols for secure data storage were in place.

Findings

Findings across two main areas are presented in the following sections—these relate to the urban policy lag and bridging the humanitarian-development divide.

Urban Policy Lag

The legacy, familiarity and focus on the rural development agenda, and its overriding of urban issues as described earlier in the chapter, clearly emerged in our research findings. Our research found a disconnect and an imbalance between rural and urban policy and planning, where urban issues were absent in broader response and development planning. Policy around urban development (including informal settlements and urban disaster response) was limited and did not reflect the increasing trends regarding the rapid urban-population growth occurring in Fiji. This finding became clear as our research approach sought to focus on urban dimensions of development and humanitarian response, but primary (interview and workshop responses) and available secondary (relevant documentation we gathered and analysed) data focused on rural situations. There was a clear focus on disaster response for rural areas, and urban humanitarian responses were not well integrated within the broader humanitarian response discussions or documentation. This finding is not altogether surprising, as other authors have commented that development initiatives across the Pacific (and indeed elsewhere) have tended to focus on rural issues including infrastructure, access to services and maintaining healthy ecosystems (Jones, 2012). Furthermore, the focus on rural contexts is echoed across other small-island developing states, including in the Caribbean (Butcher-Gollach, 2015). Given the high rates of urbanisation across the Pacific, and increasing populations within informal settlements in urban and peri-urban areas, urban development and response policy needs consideration as part of national and subnational policy frameworks. This is particularly pertinent given the higher levels of exposure and vulnerability faced by people living in informal settlements.

An example of the lag in urban development policy can be seen in relation to people living in informal settlements and access to services. In Lautoka, approximately 20,000 people reside in informal settlements, many of whom have migrated from rural areas across Fiji's islands (UN-Habitat, 2012). The rate of change in urban population growth has outstripped the ability of subnational governments to adequately respond to ensure services and adequate housing and health provisions. The research team was told the city boundary was to be amended (through the Ministry of Local Government and Housing) to include informal settlements on the periphery of the Lautoka city boundary to enable the local government to legally to provide water, sanitation and electricity services. Such amendments would also ensure that residents have formal tenure of their property. It was unclear whether or not these services and rights had been passed on to residents. By definition, residents of informal settlements lack formal land leases. Accessing financing and credit through financial institutions requires a land lease. While Fiji's National Housing Policy includes significant mention of the need to address issues relating to informal settlements, in practice, this issue remains a gap in policy and practice, as evidenced in the Western Division. It also points to the need for improved institutional capacity around urban policy—a need repeated in other Pacific countries (Keen and McNeil, 2016).

We also found a lack of policy focus around urban disaster response, from both government and donor perspectives. Disaster response policy had a clear rural focus, and research participants were more familiar with rural response mechanisms than those that existed, or were required, for urban settings. This, too, is reported among others in the humanitarian and development sectors, recognising that disaster risk reduction and response in urban areas are often adopted directly from rural experiences (Rey et al., 2017). Analysis of past disaster responses in the Pacific (e.g., April 2014 floods in Solomon Islands) point to the political, institutional and cultural challenges around urban disaster response policy (see Discussion section, as well as Keen and McNeil, 2016). Given the different disaster and humanitarian impacts sustained in urban setting as compared to rural settings, this points to a gap in disaster response policy and the specific response mechanisms and frameworks required for urban settings. Some progress has been made, e.g., the Pacific Catastrophe Risk Assessment and Financing Initiative (PCRAFI, led by the Pacific Community [SPC], World Bank and the Asian Development Bank) is a large collection of geospatial information on disaster risks and risk assessment tools for 15 PICs focused on urban locations.[4] However, what is missing is a translation of such disaster risk information to national and subnational disaster response policy. Fiji's disaster response policy framework also contains a lack of urban focus. For example, the only mention of 'urban' in the National Disaster Management Plan (NDMO) Plan (1995) is that the Permanent Secretary for Urban Development sits on the National Disaster Management Council and various committees. The NDMO Act (1998) notes that 'The Ministry responsible for the rural housing programme will be responsible for the rehabilitation of urban and rural housing' (Government of Fiji, 1998: 16), highlighting again the dominance of rural over urban focus. Improved institutional capacity around urban disaster policy is therefore needed to meet this shortcoming—as well as a recognition of the potential positive contributions of urban areas for development and economic growth (Phillips and Keen, 2016).

Despite these challenges and limitations, we observed evidence of how the urban policy lag regarding development and disaster response may be (and was) overcome in the case of TC Winston in the Western Division, Fiji.

Bridging the Divide

The foundations for bridging the divide between humanitarian response and development were present in the Western Division of Fiji. Research findings point to two main approaches that helped to bridge the divide: subnational governance structures and the emerging cluster system. These are described in the following paragraphs.

Subnational Governance as a Means to Overcome the Divide

The research found different governance arrangements for development, response and recovery at the time of TC Winston. Humanitarian response and development planning at the subnational level were informed by different governance and institutional arrangements. Governance arrangements for the recovery period, post-TC Winston, were also different to those for longer-term development and humanitarian response. Figure 3.2 provides a simplified illustration of the institutional arrangements for development planning (left) and humanitarian response (right) in the Western Division.

Government officials acknowledged that humanitarian response and development planning at the subnational level were informed by different governance and institutional arrangements. However, research participants from government and civil society preferred the governance and institutional arrangements they worked within during the humanitarian response to those in place for long-term development. Furthermore, they expressed a strong appetite for stronger coordination that stretched across this divide, a recognition of the value of integrating principles such as 'risk integration' and 'build back better'. Balancing the immediacy of humanitarian response with other goals (e.g., long-term development goals, local ownership and transparency; see DFAT, 2017) is a challenge. However, meeting urgent humanitarian needs in post-disaster settings need not compromise longer-term development goals if risk integration principles are carefully built into response and recovery efforts. These issues are discussed further in the next paragraphs.

The governance structures defined line ministry departments (e.g., education, health, housing) who reported to their Ministers and were responsible for development planning in the Western Division. There were separate governance arrangements for designated urban centres such as Lautoka, who reported through the Ministry of Local Government and Urban Development similarly at the national level. There were also institutional arrangements for rural village-level governance, who reported to Indigenous Affairs (iTaukei Affairs). The Divisional Commissioner coordinated and consulted with heads of departments across these different ministries, but the staff were accountable to their designated ministers at the national level. And while there were a variety of meetings at the divisional level, such as the heads of department meetings which the Commissioner chaired, these were primarily for sharing of information only. The institutional structures and lines of reporting within the multiple institutional fragments meant that whilst the Commissioner could call multiple agencies together for sharing, he was not mandated to coordinate development planning and implementation at the

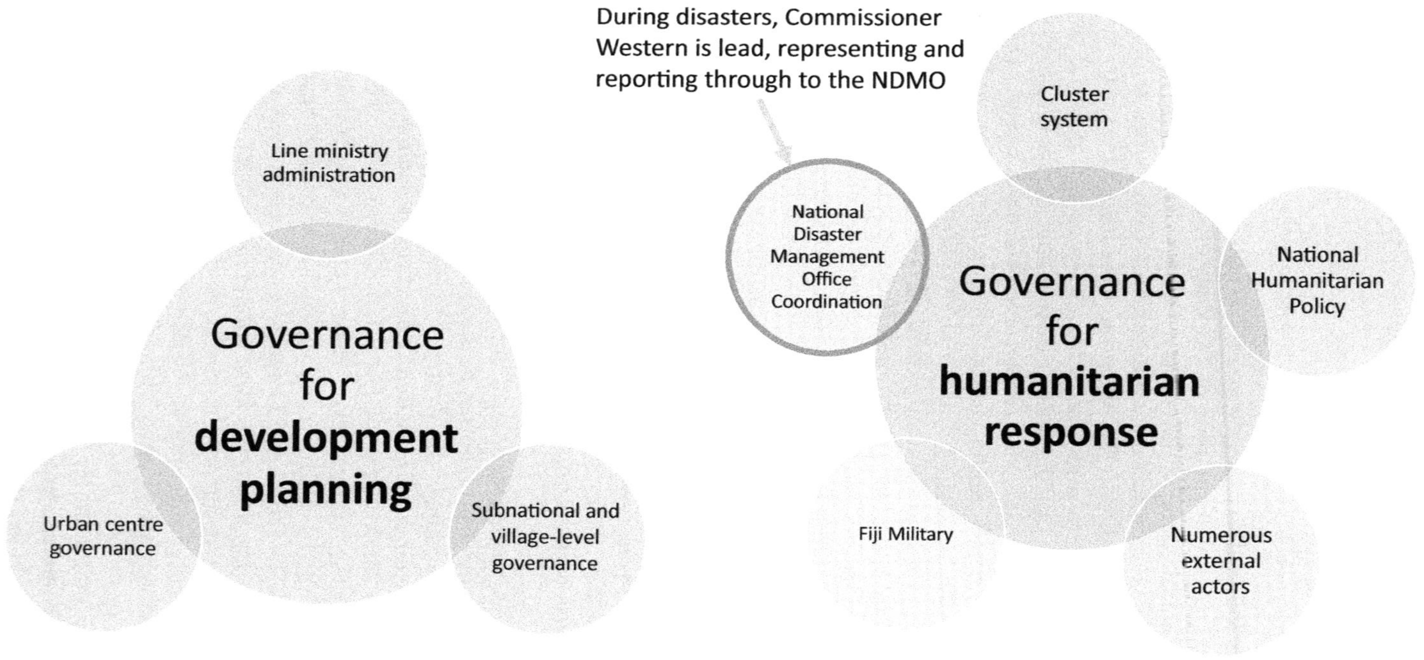

Figure 3.2 Institutional Arrangements for Development Planning (left) and Humanitarian Response (right).

Source: Anna Gero

subnational level. The fragmentation of governance in Lautoka also links to earlier findings regarding the urban policy lag.

During disasters and humanitarian response, this governance structure changes as the National Disaster Management Act delegates authority from the NDMO to coordinate the response at divisional levels to the divisional commissioners. In the case of this research, the (then) Commissioner for the Western Division was vested with authority for the TC Winston disaster response. In practice, this meant that line ministry administration, urban centre governance, and subnational and village-level governance (i.e., all divisional government staff) all reported to Commissioner for the Western Division. As noted by a divisional staff member, 'The Ministry of Public Service Commission, they send out a memo to the departments, telling them to release the public servants for disaster operations' (Government staff, research participant).

This governance arrangement provided the practical experience of bridging the humanitarian-development divide. Divisional staff, whose day-to-day work outside times of disaster was development planning and reporting to multiple departments, particularly at national level, now reported to the delegated NDMO representative at the divisional level (Commissioner Western). However, what was missing was an explicit effort or process to ensure response efforts linked to local development plans. Divisional staff were not encouraged to connect their disaster response activities to their longer-term development planning objectives or plans. This is an opportunity for future response efforts elsewhere, and will be further discussed later.

Our research found that Western Division government officials and civil society representatives preferred the governance and institutional arrangements they worked within during the humanitarian response to those in place for long-term development. They found benefit in working together towards a common goal, and all reporting to one central place (i.e., the divisional head, Commissioner Western). One workshop participant said, 'In "peace times" we have our own sector plans. We have Head of Department meetings but we don't have a combined plan. It would be good to have one'.

The Emerging Cluster System as a Means to Overcome the Divide

Another example of overcoming the humanitarian-development divide was through Fiji's emerging 'cluster system'. The cluster system, which is modelled on the global cluster system (IASC, 2006), provides governance and institutional arrangements that link the humanitarian responses and the development agenda. At the time of our research, Fiji was developing its national cluster system within its National Humanitarian Policy. Since then, the Humanitarian Policy has been endorsed by the National Disaster Management Council. The policy endorses and supports a national, government-led cluster system and contains considerable mention of the role of subnational leadership in times of disaster (see next section, Localisation in Action). However, it does not specifically prioritise ongoing activities within or between clusters outside of times of disaster response. Our research found stakeholders at both national and subnational levels expressing strong endorsement for 'evergreen clusters' (i.e., maintaining ongoing, continuous activities outside times of humanitarian response) that reach down to the divisional level while also connecting to the national level. By operating outside of times of disasters, clusters can engage in activities that integrate risk and promote resilience whilst building relationships across government and non-government stakeholders.

We found some evidence of some clusters operating in an 'evergreen' approach at the national level. An example was the Water, Sanitation and Hygiene (WASH) Cluster. The WASH Cluster is led by the Ministry of Health and Medical Services (MoHMS), and the Cluster's Terms of Reference note that clusters are expected to operate continuously, however, this is not mentioned in the National Humanitarian Policy. Documentation from the WASH Cluster indicated ongoing, continuous coordination between the cluster lead, MoHMS, and UNICEF and WHO, and also included membership lists within the cluster. Research participants commented on the WASH Cluster's effectiveness, noting that UNICEF's co-funding of some activities also helped with its ongoing activities. For example, one Suva based stakeholder commented,

> They [the WASH Cluster] are using the forums to discuss longer term issues. They are updating of contact details and doing site assessments, they know who are in the positions. They are comfortable with the [development] partners. The partners also know the ministries.

Discussions at the Pacific Humanitarian Partnership Meeting in 2016 also recognised how 'evergreen clusters' provide a means to overcome the humanitarian-development divide (see PHT, 2016). Our research further supports this notion, particularly if the clusters are extended, or linked to, local-level governance (see next section).

The examples mentioned highlight that shared experiences of humanitarian response and its impact on development goals provides an entry point for overcoming the humanitarian-development divide. What is still missing from this picture is explicit linkages and alignment with local development plans during times of disaster response. There is a clear need to make local development plans (at both the sector and divisional level) available, for these to highlight the key priorities for development in that sector, and, importantly, for these plans to guide the disaster response. Doing so would further contribute to bridging the humanitarian-development divide in practice at the local level.

Discussion

Findings from this research provide insights into ways to further overcome the humanitarian-development divide in Pacific urban settings, including examples of localisation in action. The World Humanitarian Summit called for a change in the way humanitarian aid was delivered, with localisation of aid providing an approach that respects local leadership—both in terms of government and civil society actors. While most definitions of 'localisation' refer to the leadership of national actors (e.g., ARC, 2017), some actors have recognised that a common understanding of localisation in post-disaster settings is needed (e.g., see DFAT, 2017, which includes a specific recommendation for defining 'localisation' in a disaster response review of TC Pam, which struck Vanuatu in 2015). Our reflections of localisation in the context of the TC Winston response go further and provide evidence of how Fiji's disaster response arrangements allowed for leadership at the subnational level. This approach helped to overcome the humanitarian-development divide in the case of the TC Winston response in Western Division.

Fiji has a clear policy, planning and operational framework for disaster preparedness and response, and part of this policy involves decentralisation of authority during times of disaster from the central government (the NDMO) to divisional levels. Humanitarian response is informed by the government of Fiji's National Disaster Management Plan (1995), the National Disaster Management Act (1998) and the National Emergency Operation Centre's standard operating procedures (2010). As noted in the previous section, the National Disaster Management Act delegates authority to coordinate disaster response at divisional levels to the divisional commissioners. For TC Winston, this meant Commissioner Western had authority over all divisional government staff. And, as described in the previous section, this governance structure was valued by local government actors.

Localisation, through Commissioner Western's leadership, allowed for a bridging of the humanitarian-development divide because it was the same government staff leading the TC Winston response as were leading development planning outside of times of disaster. This had two benefits to bridging the divide: 1) During the TC Winston response, staff understood the development needs and priorities in the communities in which they were providing emergency relief; and 2) outside of the TC Winston response, integrating risk into development planning was something many subnational government staff in Western Division could speak about with confidence and experience. Research participants could describe numerous examples of how their everyday work incorporated disaster risk, e.g., Environmental Impact Assessments (EIAs), risk screening tools, agricultural practices incorporating risk management and through implementing risk response training for village communities. Their understanding of risk integration into development planning was grounded in their experiences in responding to TC

Winston. Our research therefore highlights how supporting local leadership in disaster response provides the means to help to bridge the humanitarian-development divide and, importantly, ensure localisation.

Finally, research participants raised the idea around subnational localisation of the cluster approach. The National Humanitarian Policy is clear around the need for a national cluster system and includes mention of subnational arrangements. However, our research revealed the desire among some stakeholders to implement the cluster approach at the subnational level, as described by a research participant: 'The mechanism of clusters should go down to divisional [level] but also connect to the national level as well'.

Subnational government stakeholders had limited exposure to the national cluster system, given it was new and primarily operated at the national level. As such, research participants in Western Division and Suva both commented that the cluster system was not visible at the local level. Despite the lack of a formalised cluster system, some research participants reported that government sectors and NGOs worked well together in Western Division during the TC Winston response. Formalising these relationships through a fit-for-purpose subnational cluster system could further progress efforts of localisation of disaster response. Actions to implement such a mechanism at the local level should consider lessons from other countries, as the cluster approach has not always been regarded as the most appropriate approach (DFAT, 2017).

The research presented in this chapter resonates with findings from other post-disaster reviews in Pacific countries. For example, Rey et al. (2017) highlight the lack of focus on urban disaster response policy in the context of TC Pam in Vanuatu (a 2015 category 5 storm). These authors also found that the negative impacts of TC Pam were amplified by urban growth, given the higher levels of baseline vulnerability faced by those living in tenuous urban situations (e.g., informal settlements). Findings from our research also align with lessons from the April 2014 floods in Solomon Islands, which highlight the gaps in institutional capacity for developing responses to the needs of residents of informal settlements (Keen and McNeil, 2016).

Conclusion

This research explored ways in which the humanitarian-development divide was revealed through the experience of the TC Winston response. While based in and around the urban centre of Lautoka in Fiji's Western Division, and during a period of rapid urban population growth, we found very little focus on, or prioritisation of, urban disaster response issues or challenges. What we did find was evidence of ways in which the humanitarian-development divide was overcome, primarily through the governance structures that require local and divisional-level government staff and NGOs to report to the Divisional Commissioner. We also found that the notion of localisation of humanitarian response was present during TC Winston, with the delegation of authority to Commissioner Western allowing for local leadership and coordination.

Our research also revealed several opportunities to more effectively overcome the humanitarian-development divide in the future, and for responses to disasters elsewhere. As such, we propose the following recommendations.

Firstly, development planning should more effectively focus on and prioritise key concepts that strengthen the humanitarian-development nexus. Concepts like 'build back better' and 'risk integration' within long-term development planning that reduce risk while building resilience are widely endorsed by government, civil society and communities. Focusing on such concepts can help anchor governance and institutional arrangements within a coordinated humanitarian-development nexus.

Secondly, and linked to the previous recommendation, is the need to develop subnational development plans (e.g., for Western Division, specific sectors and including an urban focus, inclusive of informal settlements), and to make these widely available. Development agendas can enable the humanitarian-development nexus. The longer-term development agenda can support and create the enabling environment needed for efficient humanitarian response and recovery, which in turn can feed back into and support longer-term development. To practically achieve this nexus, local development plans could be made available to multiple stakeholders, including humanitarian responders, so they can be considered during times of disaster response.

Finally, we recommend a fit-for-purpose subnational cluster system, linked to the national system, that operates in an ongoing, continuous manner. Such a decentralised cluster system could acknowledge subnational development priorities within its preparedness and mitigation activities and ensure these same priorities flow through into humanitarian response and recovery. Decentralised clusters could be led by senior subnational government officials (e.g., Divisional Commissioners) with responsibility for both development and humanitarian response, and could develop standard operating procedures that support better integration.

Notes

1. The humanitarian-development nexus refers to better connectivity between humanitarian and development efforts, and ensuring no one is left behind in development and humanitarian response efforts. See www.unocha.org/es/themes/humanitarian-development-nexus
2. The dominant global approach for coordinated humanitarian response to promote predictability, accountability and partnership is called the cluster approach: www.humanitarianresponse.info/en/about-clusters/what-is-the-cluster-approach
3. http://charter4change.org/
4. http://pcrafi.spc.int/

References

Australian Red Cross (ARC). (2017). *Going Local: Achieving a More Appropriate and Fit-for-Purpose Humanitarian Ecosystem in the Pacific.* Carlton, Australia: Australian Red Cross, Centre for Humanitarian Leadership, Fiji National University, Humanitarian Advisory Group.

Buchanan-Smith, M. and Maxwell, S. (1994). Linking relief and development: An introduction and overview. *IDS Bulletin, 25,* 4.

Butcher-Gollach, C. (2015). Planning, the urban poor and climate change in Small Island Developing States (SIDS). *International Development Planning Review,* 37(2), 225–248.

Connell, J. (2013). Soothing breezes? Island perspectives on climate change and migration. *Australian Geographer,* 44(4), 465–480.

Connell, J. (2017). The urban Pacific: A tale of new cities. *Development Bulletin,* 78, 5–10.

Department of Foreign Affairs and Trade (DFAT). (2017). *Humanitarian Assistance in the Pacific: An Evaluation of the Effectiveness of Australia's Response to Cyclone Pam.* Canberra: DFAT.

Dodman, D., et al. (2013). *Understanding the Nature and Scale of Urban Risk in Low- and Middle-Income Countries and Its Implications for Humanitarian Preparedness, Planning and Response.* London: IIED. Available at: http://pubs.iied.org/10624IIED.

European Union (EU). (2008). *Joint Statement by the Council and the Representatives of the Governments of the Member States Meeting within the Council.* The European Parliament and the European Commission, Joint Declarations Council (2008/C 25/01).

Government of Fiji. (1998). *National Disaster Management Act.* Available at: http://www.ndmo.gov.fj/images/Legislature/NDM_ACT.pdf.

Government of Fiji. (2016). *Post-Disaster Needs Assessment: Tropical Cyclone Winston,* February 20, 2016.

Government of Fiji, World Bank, and Global Facility for Disaster Reduction and Recovery. (2017). *Fiji 2017: Climate Vulnerability Assessment—Making Fiji Climate Resilient.* Washington, DC: World Bank.

Inter-Agency Standing Committee (IASC). (2006). *Guidance Note on Using the Cluster Approach to Strengthen Humanitarian Response.* Available at: https://interagencystandingcommittee.org/node/7059.

Joint Typhoon Warning Center. (2016). *Tropical Cyclone 11P (Winston) Rolling Best Track.* US Naval Research Laboratory, Marine Meteorology, 20 February 2016. Available at: www.nrlmry.navy.mil/tcdat/tc16/SHEM/11P.WINSTON/trackfile.txt.

Jones, P. (2012). Searching for a little bit of utopia: Understanding the growth of squatter and informal settlements in Pacific towns and cities. *Australian Planner,* 49(4), 327–338.

Keen, M. and McNeil, A. (2016). *After the Floods: Urban Displacement, Lessons from Solomon Islands. State, Society and Governance in Melanesia.* In Brief 2016/13. Canberra: Australian National University Press.

Longhurst, R. (1994). Conceptual frameworks for linking relief and development. *IDS Bulletin, 25,* 4.

Mecartney, S. and Connell, J. (2017). Urban Melanesia: The challenges of managing land, modernity and tradition. In S. Mcdonnell, M.G. Allen and C. Filer (eds.), *Kastom, Property and Ideology Land Transformations in Melanesia*. Canberra: Australian National University Press.

Metcalfe-Hough, V., Poole. L., Bailey, S. and Belanger, J. (2018). *Grand Bargain Annual Independent Report (2018)*. Humanitarian Policy Group, ODI.

Ministry of Economy. (2016). *Disaster Recovery Framework, Tropical Cyclone Winston, 20th February 2016*. Report prepared in coordination with The World Bank, United Nations, European Union, Asian Development Bank and the Pacific Community.

Mosel, I. and Levine, S. (2014). *Remaking the Case for Linking Relief, Rehabilitation and Development: How LRRD Can Become a Practically Useful Concept for Assistance in Difficult Places*. Humanitarian Policy Group, ODI. Available at: www.odi.org/sites/odi.org.uk/files/odi-assets/publications-opinion-files/8882. pdf.

Phillips, T. and Keen, M. (2016). *Sharing the City: Urban Growth and Governance in Suva, Fiji. State, Society and Governance in Melanesia*. In Brief 2016/6. Canberra: Australian National University.

PHT. (2016). *After Action Review Report: Tropical Cyclone Winston*. Pacific Humanitarian Team.

PIFs, et al. (2016). *Framework for Resilient Development in the Pacific: An Integrated Approach to Address Climate Change and Disaster Risk Management (FRDP) 2017–2030*. Available at: http://bit.ly/2HmCsnw.

Rahman, M.H. and Singh, S. (2011). Towards strong local governance: Current reform scenario in Fiji. *International Journal of Public Administration*, 34(10), 674–681.

Rey, T., Le De, L., Leone, F. and Gilbert, D. (2017). An integrative approach to understand vulnerability and resilience post-disaster: The 2015 cyclone Pam in urban Vanuatu as case study. *Disaster Prevention and Management*, 26(3), 259–275.

Stamnes, E. (2016). *Rethinking the Humanitarian-Development Nexus*. Norwegian Institute of International Affairs, Policy Brief, 24/2016.

Tag-Eldeen, Z.N. (2017). Bridging urban planning knowledge into post-disaster response: Early recovery road map within the International Humanitarian Cluster System. *International Journal of Disaster Risk Reduction*, 24, 399–410. https://doi.org/10.1016/j.ijdrr.2017.05.023.

UN-Habitat. (2012). *Lautoka City Urban Profile*. United Nations Human Settlements Programme, Kenya.

United Nations (UN). (2016). *One Humanity: Shared Responsibility*. Report of the Secretary General for the World Humanitarian Summit. Available at: http://sgreport.worldhumanitariansummit.org.

United Nations Office for Disaster Risk Reduction (UNISDR). (2015). *Sendai Framework for Disaster Risk Reduction 2015–2030*. Geneva, Switzerland.

UNOCHA. (2016a). *Pacific Humanitarian Partnership Meeting Report*. 19–21 October 2016, Holiday Inn Suva, Fiji.

UNOCHA. (2016b). *Tropical Cyclone Winston Response and Flash Appeal Final Summary*, 13 June 2016.

UNOCHA. (2017). *New Way of Working*. UNOCHA Policy Development and Studies Branch (PDSB). Available at: www.unocha.org/story/new-way-working.

Western Division. (2015). *Communiqué on Disaster and Climate Risk Integration into Development Planning*. Government of Fiji

World Bank (WB). (2015a). *World Bank Fiji Data*. Available at: http://data.world bank.org/country/fiji.

World Bank (WB). (2015b). *World Bank Urban Population Data*. Available at: http://data.worldbank.org/indicator/SP.URB.TOTL.IN.ZS.

Chapter 4

Reflecting on a Journey From Climate Change Vulnerability Assessments to the Implementation of Climate Resilience Actions

Honiara, Solomon Islands

Darryn McEvoy, Bernhard Barth, Alexei Trundle and David Mitchell

Introduction

A combination of urbanisation and climate change is undermining the resilience of many towns and cities throughout the Asia-Pacific region. Indeed, the sheer scale and pace of rural-to-urban migration (UN ESCAP and UN-Habitat, 2015; Kiddle et al., 2017) is not only exaggerating existing climate vulnerabilities, it is also introducing new risks within urban environments (Friend and Moench, 2013). This is being witnessed in the case of informal settlers living in hazard-prone areas, with inadequate housing and infrastructure, and limited adaptive capacity (Satterthwaite, 2013; McEvoy et al., 2019). The challenges are particularly acute in the context of Small Island Developing States (SIDS) in the South Pacific (Jones, 2012). Not only are they highly exposed to natural and climate-related hazards, their primary cities are also growing at a rapid rate (Keen and Barbara, 2015; McEvoy and Mitchell, 2019). Added to this, SIDS are geographically isolated, have small economies, possess inadequate urban infrastructure and have limited institutional capacity (Gero et al., 2011).

In response to the many contemporary challenges arising from the interaction of urbanisation and global environmental change drivers, research, policy and practitioner agendas are co-creating approaches with the aim of improving the resilience of urban systems to current and future impacts (Leichenko, 2011; Tyler and Moench, 2012; UN-Habitat and EcoPlan International, 2014). However, despite the increased attention on assessing urban vulnerabilities to climate-related impacts there are a number of identified barriers—typically either socioeconomic or institutional in nature—to the implementation of climate adaptation measures (Biesbroek et al., 2013; Eisenack et al., 2014; Betzold, 2015).

To showcase a successful journey from an initial vulnerability assessment through the implementation of urban resilience and climate actions, this chapter focuses on Honiara, Solomon Islands' capital in the Melanesian region of the South Pacific (see Figure 4.1). It reflects on the programme of work that has been ongoing since 2012 under UN-Habitat's 'Cities and Climate Change Initiative', culminating in the 'Climate Resilient Honiara' project funded by the UNFCCC Adaptation Fund in 2018. The narrative of this journey involves a series of discrete steps that have taken place to identify local climate vulnerabilities and community priorities for action, as well as multi-stakeholder engagement processes which have been critical to the operationalisation of a climate action implementation programme. This narrative also involves ongoing scientific support from a multidisciplinary team of academics from Australia. While not a directly transferable 'blueprint' to enable climate actions elsewhere, by charting the journey travelled—and some of the key lessons learned—this chapter highlights some of the important factors that may help to bridge the vulnerability assessment/climate adaptation divide that is all too common in practice.

Planning for Climate Change

While cities and local governments had engaged on climate change issues before the 13th session of the UNFCCC Conference of the Parties in Bali (known as COP13) which took place in 2007, it was at this event that a local climate road map was first framed.[1] Key urban networks such as ICLEI-Local Governments for Sustainability, World Mayors Council on Climate Change (WMCCC), United Cities and Local Governments (UCLG), Metropolis, C40 and CITYNET—supported by international organisations such as UN-Habitat as well as national governments—agreed to collectively address urban climate change challenges.[2]

In support of this agenda, UN-Habitat launched a Cities and Climate Change Initiative (CCCI) in 2008, with a new emphasis on climate change adaptation. In addition to global and national policy advocacy and capacity building, four pilot cities—Esmeraldas (Ecuador), Kampala (Uganda), Saint Louis (Senegal) and Sorsogon (Philippines)—were chosen for the development of comprehensive climate change vulnerability assessments and climate action plans. In 2010, UN-Habitat published a participatory climate change assessment toolkit based on the Sorsogon experience (UN-Habitat, 2010), which was then expanded on to develop a climate change guide for urban planners, titled 'Planning for Climate Change'. An internal version of this guide, finalised in 2011, was tested in cities throughout Asia-Pacific (including Honiara) over a three-year period, before being published in 2014 (UN-Habitat and EcoPlan International, 2014).

While the approach was intended to assist urban professionals in the development of city-wide vulnerability assessments and action plans (as well as integrating climate change considerations into statutory plans by focusing on vulnerable people, places and institutions), each case study pointed

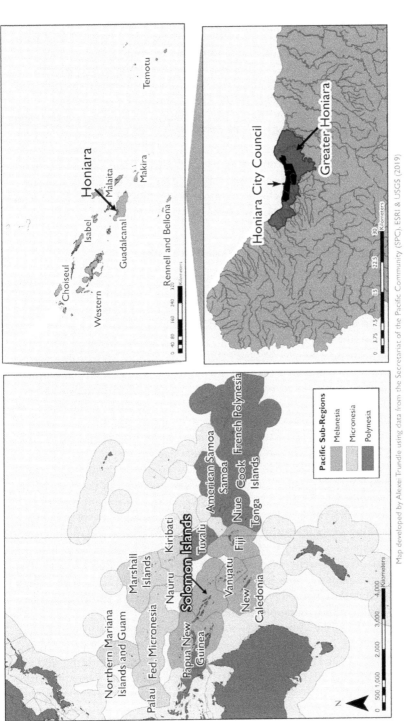

Figure 4.1 Honiara, as Situated With the Pacific Group of SIDS (left), Solomon Islands Provinces (top right) and the Island of Guadalcanal (bottom right).

Source: Authors' own

to informal settlements being vulnerability 'hotspots'. Time and time again, these urban poor communities proved to be those most exposed to climate hazards, with impacts aggravated by local socioeconomic and environmental/spatial sensitivities, as well as relatively low levels of adaptive capacity.

The CCCI has evolved over the years but still remains true to its founding core principles. The four pillars of the CCCI approach are now framed as: (i) Climate-Proof Urban and Regional Planning, (ii) Low Carbon Resilient Basic Services and Buildings, (iii) Pro Poor Approaches to Climate Action, and (iv) Multi-Level Governance of Climate Action.[3] In the Solomon Islands, this evolution of this programmatic approach is also reflected in UN-Habitat's long-term partnerships with multiple stakeholders in an effort to more effectively mainstream climate change considerations into informal settlement upgrading and the Solomon Island National Urban Policy.[4]

Assessing Climate Change Vulnerabilities

UN-Habitat supported the development of the Honiara Climate Change Vulnerability and Adaptation Assessment in 2012, and published the full report in early 2013. An abridged report was later published in early 2014 and reissued later that year with the added endorsement of the Lord Mayor; the Minister for Lands, Housing and Survey; and the Minister for Environment, Climate Change, Disaster Management and Meteorology (UN-Habitat, 2014). The high-level recognition of the vulnerability assessment can be partially attributed to its accuracy, which unfortunately was verified by the devastating floods of April 2014 that resulted in the deaths of 22 people. After the Mataniko River burst its banks, houses were washed away and critical infrastructure was damaged, with an estimated 12,000 people affected. The vulnerability assessment had identified Koa Hill informal settlement as particularly flood prone, with floods predicted to reach 2.5 metres. It was this settlement that was worst impacted by the flood event. Besides serving as a baseline for the physical characteristics of the affected communities, the vulnerability assessment also provided a comprehensive understanding of the exposure of communities to climate-related hazards and highlighted a wide range of socioeconomic pre-conditions, as well as the limited adaptive capacity of communities to climate-related impacts. The complex interplay of these factors resulted in the identification of a high degree of climate vulnerability across a number of informal settlements (identified as 'vulnerability hotspots' in the report).

Later in 2014, the vulnerability assessment was updated in partnership with academics from Royal Melbourne Institute of Technology University (RMIT) at the request of the Honiara City Council, with the updates published as part of the Honiara Urban Resilience and Climate Action Plan (HURCAP) (SIG, 2016). In addition to better understanding current and future exposure to climatic events, further investigations of the socioeconomic sensitivity and critical infrastructure in the context of the urban growth dynamics were undertaken for the second-generation vulnerability assessment (definitions are shown in Box 1).

Box 1   Vulnerability Assessment Definitions

Vulnerability Assessment

'Exposure' refers to the extent, frequency, and severity of the climate-related shocks and stresses that the city faces, such as the low-lying areas likely to be inundated by sea level rise or the chance of a category 5 cyclone hitting the city in any given year.

'Sensitivity' is defined as the factors that determine how affected the city will be when such an event hits; for instance, the young, sick and elderly are more at risk during a heat wave, while weaker buildings are more likely to collapse during a severe storm event.

'Adaptive capacity' relates to the ability of the city, its institutions and its citizens to respond to such an event, whether through formal disaster response arrangements (such as National Disaster Management Office [NDMO] evacuation centres), or through social, traditional or informal means (for example, relying on relatives and kinship for temporary housing and support following the April 2014 floods).

Source: HURCAP

Initially, sensitivity was assessed across the city. The spatial analysis of Honiara included the mapping of informal settlements, population densities and household attributes such as access to improved sanitation, metered water, electricity, as well as makeshift, improvised or traditional roofing (as a proxy-indicator for the structural integrity of housing). In parallel to the spatial analysis, based on existing government data, numerous community workshops ensured that local realities across the city were also accounted for in detail. Furthermore, stakeholder consultations across sectors and government agencies provided valuable additional information to the analysis. In this case, the value of a participatory approach to assessing vulnerabilities, and better understanding the local context and institutions, cannot be overemphasised.

Adaptive capacity was assessed using proxies from available government data such as mobile phone ownership rates and internet access, and then presented spatially. In addition, autonomous, collective and institutional adaptive capacities were assessed based on 16 indicators across five categories: economic wealth, technology, infrastructure, information and skills, and institutions and social capital. Here again, inputs from participatory exercises with communities were used to inform the assessment (interestingly, social and cultural networks were considered strong but under-used; see the later section that discusses endogenous resilience).

An overlay of exposure, sensitivity and adaptive capacity data led to the identification of five vulnerability hotspots covering three major informal settlements as well as two coastal villages: Gilbert Camp, Aekefo-Feraladoa, White River, Ontong Java and Kukum Fishing Village; totalling a population of approximately 9,400 or 11 percent of the urban population (as of 2015) (see Figure 4.2). Koa Hill, despite the intent of the Honiara City Council not to allow resettlement due to the high-risk of repeat flooding, has already been re-occupied by informal settlers (as of Feb 2019). Thus, Koa Hill can be considered a sixth vulnerability hotspot, having been identified as such in the initial vulnerability report.

In order to successfully strengthen resilience, underlying vulnerabilities need to be understood, as well as emerging and longer-term risks. At the community-level, the multitude of complex and inter-related vulnerabilities, for example water and sanitation needs, require responses that are targeted to the most vulnerable households and individuals (female-headed households, people with disabilities and elderly people). Moreover, an integrated approach is needed to build long-term sustainability of actions. This involves addressing urban sectoral priorities such as housing while ensuring that local human capacities are developed, initiatives are financed, and governance systems and coordination between government agencies are improved—from the community development councils to the ward development councils, Honiara City Council and national government.

The Honiara Urban Resilience and Climate Action Plan (HURCAP)

The HURCAP was developed by RMIT University on behalf of UN-Habitat, with the plan being taken up and endorsed by both the city council and the national government and published in 2016 (SIG, 2016). The process to develop the plan was framed by the 'Planning for Climate Change' guidelines described earlier in this paper (UN-Habitat and EcoPlan International, 2014), however refinements were necessary to make it fit for local purposes (which are discussed later in this section).

From the outset, the process of developing the action plan was designed to be stakeholder-led. This approach enabled local people to take part in group discussions about their perceived vulnerabilities to a changing climate, the priority needs in their respective communities, and to be directly involved in the identification and co-design of potential climate actions. Adopting a highly participatory process also enabled traditional knowledge, approaches, and social and cultural structures to be adequately accounted for in the action plan. This is critically important in the Solomon Islands

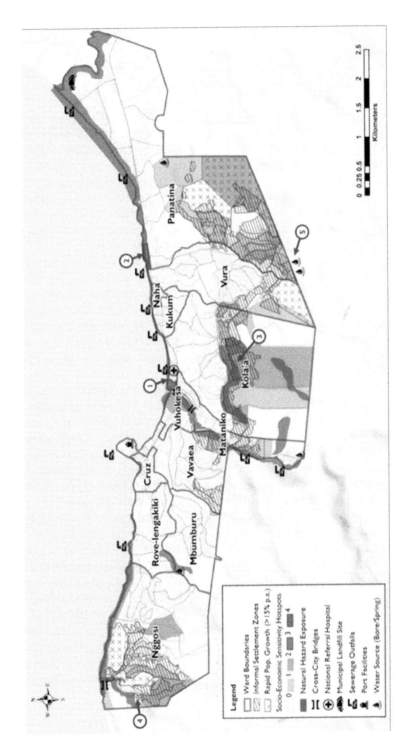

Figure 4.2 Location of the Five Main Vulnerability Hotspots.
Source: Authors' own

context, as elsewhere in the Pacific region, where shared traditions (known locally as *kastom*) continue to play an important role in day-to-day lives, even in the fast-growing capital city. Indeed, the majority of residents continue to refer to themselves as being from their 'home' island rather than from Honiara (Trundle et al., 2018).

A second important feature of the research approach, strongly influenced by its participatory nature, was the need—as the project evolved—to expand the focus beyond looking at climate-related drivers only and to formulate an action plan that accounted for multiple external and internal shocks and stresses that are adversely affecting urban resilience. These include all natural hazards (e.g., earthquakes and tsunamis), not just those that are climate-related. Perhaps even more critical are the substantial development deficits which are being exaggerated by rapid urbanisation pressures that are leading to increases in current-day vulnerabilities (particularly in informal settlements).

Figure 4.3 illustrates the priority issues that were identified by members of the vulnerability hotspot settlements in community workshops. The most important issues for local people were sanitation, population growth and overcrowding, and waste. Flooding and water security and quality were the highest-ranked of the hazard-based issues. The findings of this bottom-up assessment provided clear indications that communities prioritised short-term development and flooding issues over longer-term climate change impacts. This had implications for the structure and content of the action plan for Honiara, which evolved to consider both urban resilience and climate actions (SIG, 2016). In essence, a shift of focus to current-day vulnerabilities (and consideration of a range of different drivers) moved the action plan from its original starting point of 'planning for climate change' to one that embraced a broader urban resilience theme. This required an integration of climate change adaptation, disaster risk reduction, and development agendas and goals. The authors argue that such an integrated approach provides a more solid socioeconomic foundation that will not only enhance current levels of urban resilience, but also better support more effective longer-term climate adaptation planning.

Translating issues into urban resilience and climate objectives took place during a series of participatory workshops in 2014. In total over 180 individual stakeholders, representative of a broad cross-section of the community, government decision-makers and NGOs, were directly involved in objective-setting and planning activities. Five councillors and 10 local government department heads also took part in a Honiara City Council workshop. Objectives were developed by breakout groups on the basis of the issues that they had previously identified, and were subsequently grouped and categorised by the RMIT project team. Ten thematic areas emerged from this participatory process:

1. Urban planning and land development
2. Housing

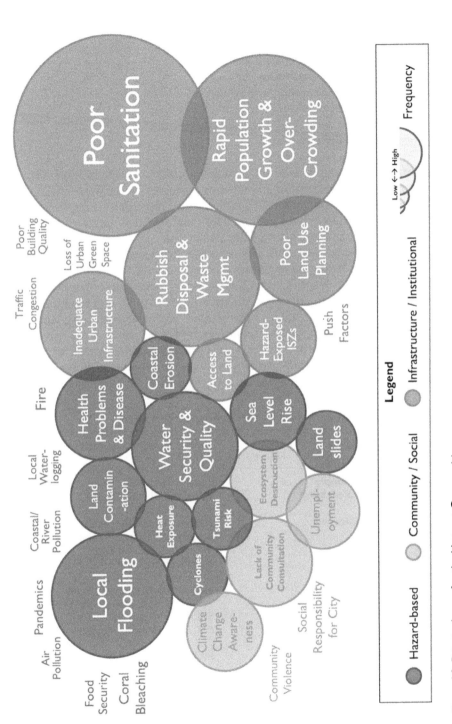

Figure 4.3 Priority Issues for the Hotspot Communities.
Source: SIG (2016)

3. Infrastructure
4. Water, sanitation and waste
5. Ecosystem services and coastal processes
6. Human health and well-being
7. Communication: awareness and education
8. Livelihoods and behaviour change
9. Disaster preparedness and response
10. Governance and partnerships

As shown in the urban planning and land development example in Table 4.1, each thematic area consisted of a number of objectives which were labelled according to the level of climate influence and also the proposed implementation partners for any related actions. This then provided the overarching framework for urban resilience and climate actions.

A portfolio of specific actions was subsequently identified through various local stakeholder engagement processes and grouped according to the high-level thematic categories, as well as linked to specific objectives where relevant. Actions relating to urban planning, water, waste and sanitation, and governance processes emerged as the most prevalent at the city-scale. Proposed city-wide actions were subject to further scrutiny at an expert workshop held in Honiara in 2016. This workshop involved many of the proposed lead implementing partners, allowing for potential actions to be debated and confirmed, implementation leaders to be agreed, and any

Table 4.1 City-Wide Urban Planning and Land Development Objectives.

1. Urban Planning and Land Development	Climate Related (1–4)	Stakeholder-proposed Implementation Partners
1.1 Adequate land supply and land release strategy	0	**Land Board**, HCC, MLHS, MID, MECCDM, MHMS, Chiefs, Chinese Assn, WDCs, GPG
1.2 Reduction in informal settlements	1	**Ministry of Lands, Housing and Survey (MLHS)**, UN-Habitat, Chiefs, WDCs, CDCs, Land Board
1.3 Effective land use planning scheme	1	**MLHS**, Police Force, HCC, MID, SIEA, SIWA
1.4 Zoning of landslide and flood-prone areas	4	**Honiara City Council**, MLHS, WB-REP, Chiefs, Elders, MID, WHO
1.5 Protection of water easements and catchment areas	3	**Solomon Water**, MLHS, HCC, MECCDM, Community Leaders, MID
1.6 Relocation strategy for at-risk households	4	**MLHS**, Land Board, HCC, SIRC, MHA
1.7 Reduced water-logging	3	**Ministry of Infrastructure and Development**, MLHS, HCC, I/NGOs

Source: SIG (2016)

additional actions put forward for inclusion in the action plan. The final listing of actions included consideration of timing, priority, cost and the lead implementation organisations (as an example, see: Table 4.2). Similar tables of actions were also developed for ward and community levels (see SIG, 2016).

HURCAP collated a portfolio of multi-level actions for the city. It could, however, also be used to provide a useful overarching governance framework or a coordinating mechanism for multiple, previously discrete, projects in Honiara. Each individual project could potentially add value to Honiara's goal of increased resilience and could be mapped and integrated with the HURCAP framework where possible and relevant. For instance, given the city's continuing development needs, water, sanitation and hygiene (WASH) programmes and projects implemented by NGOs (e.g., Live and Learn's M-Wash initiative, World Vision's programme of water tank installation in informal settlements) can be referred to in the context of HURCAP's 'water, sanitation and waste' theme. Ongoing work by UN-Habitat as part of the Participatory Slum Upgrade Program (PSUP)[5] seeks to strengthen community, city and national key stakeholders' capacities in participatory slum upgrading, and can make valuable contributions to the 'urban planning and land development' theme. 'Pacific Ecosystem-based Adaptation to Climate Change' (PEBACC), a five-year programme implemented by the Secretariat of the Pacific Regional Environment Programme (SPREP), has Honiara as a case study, and can also contribute to resilience responses under the 'Ecosystem Services' theme. These provide examples of where a collaborative approach between different Honiara programmes would reap mutual benefits for a coherent forward plan.

During the HURCAP learning process it was found that there are two important factors that need to be taken into consideration when assessing vulnerabilities. These are looking at ways to reinforce local adaptive capacity, and promoting the effective implementation and sustainability of urban resilience and climate actions in the context of Honiara (and other Pacific cities). These two factors—endogenous (or local, informally derived) resilience and land tenure security—are worthy of specific mention, given their importance in the South Pacific.

Building on Informal Resilience

The share of Honiara's population living in government-classified 'Informal Settlement Zones' is estimated to be approximately a third of the city and is continuing to grow. A further unknown proportion of the urban populous live through a range of other informal tenure arrangements, from squatting on leased or zoned land and roadsides to customarily arranged occupancy of peri-urban domains (for further exploration of these tenure types, see McEvoy et al., 2019). As discussed previously, these settlement areas tend to

Table 4.2 City-Level Disaster Risk Reduction and Management Actions.

9. City-Wide Disaster Risk Reduction and Management Actions	Objective(s)	Resilience Area(s)			Implementation Factors			
		Climate	DRR	Urban	Timing	Priority	Cost	Lead
HCA9.1 Update the HCC Disaster Operation Plan based on the outcomes of the UNISDR Resilience Toolkit and ICLEI capacity-building programme	9.1, 10.3, 10.4	✗	✗	✗	Med. Term	High	$$$$	Honiara City Council
HCA9.2 Develop the digitisation of hazard maps for the city for landslide, flood, tsunami, coastal erosion and storm surge risks, and collate in one accessible location	1.4, 1.6, 7.1, 9.1	✗	✗	✗	Short Term	Med	$$$$	Ministry of Envt, Climate Change, and Disaster Management
HCA9.3 Create an at-risk household rapid response taskforce for assisting hazard-prone communities located in the areas identified in HCA8.2, linked to CDCs and WDCs	7.4, 9.2, 10.3, 10.4, 10.7		✗	✗	Med. Term	High	$$$$	National Disaster Management Office
HCA9.4 Assess the coverage of emergency shelters across the Greater Honiara area and identify additional shelter sites required to cover 100% of the city's residents	7.1, 9.3, 10.4	✗	✗		Short Term	High	$$$$	Ministry of Lands, Housing and Survey
HCA9.5 Integrate HCA8.3's taskforce with early warning systems, built in all at-risk communities for relevant hazards (with a coordinator for each ward)	9.2, 10.2, 10.3, 10.4	✗	✗	✗	Med. Term	High	$$$$	National Disaster Management Office
HCA9.6 Embed DRR personnel within all major ministries at a national level, contact points across departments within HCC and conduct NDMO-led training with WDCs	9.1, 10.2, 10.4	✗	✗	✗	Med. Term	High	$$$$	Office of the Prime Minister and Cabinet
HCA9.7 Initiate a DRR awareness programme in schools	7.7, 9.1, 9.2	✗	✗	✗	Med. Term	High	$$$$	Honiara City Council
HCA9.8 Set aside a day for Honiara-wide disaster response exercises	9.3, 9.5, 9.6, 7.2	✗	✗	✗	Med. Term	High	$$$$	Honiara City Council

Source: SIG (2016)

correlate with the most climate-vulnerable areas of cities; a product of their unsanctioned occupancy of high-exposure, 'left-over' hazard areas, heightened sensitivity of their often improvised built form, a lack of infrastructure to cope with climate-related shocks and stressors, and poor government connectivity (reducing their adaptive capacity).

Despite this, it was noted during the HURCAP's development that the capacity of these informal populations to 'bounce back' from recent climate-related events was higher than would otherwise be expected based on the vulnerability outputs resulting from the 'Planning for Climate Change' spatial assessment framework. This was all the more remarkable given the limited government support and institutional capacity at a whole-of-city level, as observed in the HURCAP's stakeholder-based assessment of adaptive capacity (reflected on previously). As a result, further investigations were conducted into these informal areas to identify the sources of resilience that were not effectively being taken into account through the vulnerability framework.

Community-level consultations revealed that although surveyed adaptive capacity did reflect aspects of heightened vulnerability to climate change relevant to the informal settlement areas, additional capacities were in play that not only operated outside of formal institutional structures, but often played a substitutive role in supporting the adaptive capacity of the informal settlements themselves. These were either overlooked or unable to be measured through quantitative assessments and institutional mechanisms. For instance, city-based governance frameworks were not reflective of codified community organisational systems derived from either church or island-based chiefly structures. Similarly, state-run utility network maps and access levels did not account for the use of natural springs and other ecosystem services, which prevail in informal areas. These revelations further demonstrated the importance of taking a participatory approach to climate action planning, which not only empowered local communities but was also shown to highlight potential shortcomings in relying on 'top-down' government or scientific data alone.

Many of these endogenous, informal capacities were codified through customary laws either brought in from migrants' home islands, or hybridised with other urban systems or the surrounding customs of the Guadalcanal traditional population. For instance, along the city outskirts, extensive 'bush gardens' occupy extensive areas of both customary and government-owned land (occupation that is overlooked or accepted by government institutions and customary landowners). These unofficial land uses provided both subsistence food supplies and a secondary income to many of the inhabitants of the city's informal settlements that they could draw upon following natural hazard events (Keen et al., 2017). Other observed capacities included women's savings groups, cost-sharing through use of communal infrastructure (such as water tanks and washing areas), and semi-institutional social support frameworks operated through churches and community social structures.

Despite the obvious potential for building on these endogenous modes of climate resilience, many were in direct conflict with formal governance frameworks and planning initiatives, or were being undermined through officially sanctioned commercial activities (such as logging or coastal development). Such conflicts risk undermining the resilience of the city as a whole, as was demonstrated in the 'ethnic tensions' that led to armed conflict between the local Guale population and Malaitan migrants between 1998 and 2003 (Ride and Bretherton, 2011). Driven by a lack of national government engagement with customary land-owner groups over encroachment, resource rights and employment opportunities, the ethnic tensions demonstrated the potential negative consequences of failing to reconcile external state-based development efforts with informal capacities and structures at a community level.

While these observations were highly localised, there is evidence of other endogenous resilience capacities across the South Pacific, and similar capacities have also been observed in informal settlement settings elsewhere. Ziervogel et al., for example, identify the use of 'informal networks', linked with deep, locally derived experiential knowledge, as key mechanisms for poor African urban dwellers to cope with shocks and stressors in lieu of formal urban governance (2017: 11). Within the Pacific region, Vanuatu's capital city, Port Vila, demonstrated the enactment of similar endogenous resilience strengths within peri-urban communities following Tropical Cyclone Pam, which destroyed much of the city in March 2015 (Trundle, 2017). In this instance, the use of *wantok* social networks both during the disaster (assisting with evacuation and shelter) and in reconstruction was demonstrated to be critical to the recovery of the city, while informally established bush gardens in the city periphery were quickly replanted to avoid inflated purchasable food costs (Rey et al., 2017). A study into ecosystem-based adaptation options that built on a parallel UN-Habitat vulnerability assessment further quantified extensive informal ecosystem resource use by Port Vila's inhabitants (McEvoy et al., 2017). The interface between these endogenous local contributors to resilience, and exogenous state- and donor-led resilience-building efforts, is therefore a critical area for further research (Trundle et al., 2018).

Land Tenure Security and Climate Vulnerability

An important part of the HURCAP journey towards the implementation of climate resilience actions is the recognition of the strong inter-linkages between climate vulnerability and security of land tenure in both the city and peri-urban areas. This observation showed that beyond informality, the insecurity of differing forms of both formal and informal tenure could be a potential barrier to climate actions (McEvoy et al., 2019).

Within wider groupings of 'informality' is a complex array of land occupancy arrangements, with differing levels of tenure security. 'Temporary Occupancy Licenses' (TOLs), for instance, were established in the 1950s to cope with growing informal populations by the then British Protectorate government (Foukona, 2015). Originally intended to be renewed annually, a 2006 household survey reported that only three out of 3,000 household TOLs had not expired, despite many informal settlement representatives not being aware of their licenses having lapsed (McEvoy et al., 2019). Amendments to legislation just prior to independence in 1978 allowed freehold and longer leases to be converted into fixed-term estate (FTE) leases of 75 years. The creation of FTE land, along with state land (perpetual estate), meant there was a pool of land that could be used for housing through leases (Foukona, 2017). However, urbanisation has increased rapidly in recent times, with the Honiara rate of urbanisation one of the highest in the Pacific region. Indeed, the urban population of the Solomon Islands is increasing at almost twice the rate of national population growth, and is likely to double in 17 years (Keen and Barbara, 2015).

While a planning scheme exists for much of the currently settled areas, enforcement of the planning control has been ineffective, as evidenced by settlements and land reclamation that does not comply with the planning scheme requirements—as well as being increasingly in hazard-prone areas (Foukona, 2017). Furthermore, as urban areas expand beyond the municipal boundary into customary areas in Guadalcanal Province other governance challenges arise, with households no longer falling under the jurisdiction of the Honiara City Council. Customary law allows land owners in these areas to reach agreements with settlers on the occupation of their land, subject to conditions—and this is a common practice (Foukona, 2017).

In order to identify where land tenure conflicts and issues could impact the implementation of climate resilience measures, it is important to understand the land tenure context at the settlement and household level. To this end, community workshops were held in 2017 in Aekefo informal settlement (inland) and Kukum Fishing Village (coastal) as part of a project funded by the Global Land Tool Network (GLTN, UN-Habitat) on land tenure and climate vulnerability (McEvoy et al., 2019). These workshops were designed to elicit information on land tenure arrangements, the relationship between land tenure and climate vulnerability, how adaptation measures may impact local tenure security and how land tenure issues could influence the implementation of resilience actions in their settlement (also see: McEvoy and Mitchell, 2019).

Many of the Aekefo households have TOLs that were granted in the 1970s but have now lapsed. Participants indicated that upgrading to FTE was a priority, as this provides a higher level of certainty for households; allows connection to formal electricity, water and sanitation services; and is an important factor in decisions to build community-level infrastructure in the area. The Ministry of Lands, Housing and Survey (MLHS) is systematically issuing households letters with an offer to upgrade to FTE upon payment of a fee. At present, however, the uptake is low and the fee appears to be a strong deterrent. Meanwhile, houses continue to be built, with many situated in hazardous locations along the river edge or in areas subject to landslide. The increase in housing density, and location near water sources, is contributing to reduced water quality; exacerbated by poor household waste disposal and sanitation practices.

While Kukum Fishing Village has individual FTEs, there are many more houses than titles as a consequence of extended family members (known locally as *Wantok*) migrating to the settlement. Much of the unauthorised housing is on the coastal margins and sometimes beyond the coastal boundary. Those without FTE lack a formal connection to water, electricity and sanitation facilities, and participants raised water supply and quality, as well as poor sanitation and lack of toilet facilities, as key issues. However, much of the discussion in the workshop was on the need to build a seawall and where it should be constructed (again, influenced by land title).

A third 'hotspot' settlement is Ontong Java settlement, visited in 2019 as part of the new Adaptation Fund 'Climate Resilient Honiara' project (see later section; see also the chapter in this book written by Bruce and Marshall). It is low-lying with parts of the settlement below sea level. A major flood in 2014 demolished several houses along the river and caused the bank to be eroded and recede approximately six metres into the site. Participants advised that a priority action was for a flood-prevention wall to be built along the river to restrict further flood impacts from the river. If the communal title boundary is near the position of the bank before the flood, then there is an opportunity to reclaim some of the lost land in the construction of the flood-prevention wall. The Ontong Java settlement has a single 'Communal Title' (communal FTE) over the land, instead of a series of individual TOL or FTE parcels that exist in other settlements. This provides legal protection against others over all the settlement, while the community is left to itself to organise where buildings are located and constructed.

However, household size continues to increase, and the houses are densely sited, reducing air flow and increasing fire risk. As the settlement is located on one communal title, one possible response is to implement a process of participatory land readjustment where WASH services are improved, and site buildings and facilities are redesigned to be more in strata (individual ownership of part of a property, with shared ownership of the remainder), reducing the density of buildings on the site and improving the air flow between buildings. However, given the extent of overcrowding, this will also need to involve a new (second) settlement elsewhere and resettlement of some of the community to another place that allows access for fishing.

These three examples of 'hotspot' settlements provide a clear illustration of different land tenure arrangements and the many complex resilience issues that arise. Addressing these will require care and effective discussions with the communities and other key stakeholders, including the government, if: (i) land issues are to be addressed effectively, (ii) land tools are designed to fit local purpose, and (iii) agreed interventions improve both tenure security and community resilience.

Climate Resilient Honiara

Based on the HURCAP, a funding application for the Climate Resilient Honiara project was submitted to the UNFCCC Adaptation Fund by UN-Habitat on behalf of the Solomon Islands government. This was successful in being awarded funds in 2018, with RMIT University providing continuing scientific support in year one of the four-year project (from January 2019). Reflective of HURCAP, the programme of project activity is designed to deliver actions and capacity building at community, ward and city levels. There are four inter-related work packages at the community level. The first is developing climate action plans for all five case study hotspot settlements. The second is producing comprehensive community profiles for each using a mix of household and settlement surveys and various geospatial methods (including geospatial LiDAR maps). Outputs from this work package will also include a transferable methodology for others to carry out community profiling. Thirdly, the design of engineering solutions based on locally identified needs. The fourth work package is awareness raising and capacity building. At the ward level, activities include climate risk communication with women and youth groups (exploring non-written formats), urban organic agriculture, developing climate-resilient open spaces (including hard measures such as evacuation centres but also soft measures such as nature-based solutions), 'Planning for Climate Change' training with ward councillors, and good land administration in peri-urban areas. The city-level actions focus primarily on capacity building and will involve short training courses (based on a local needs assessment) that will be held in Honiara and Melbourne, as well as policy and actor mapping to improve integration with existing policies and initiatives.

Given the wide scope of different actions, a large multidisciplinary team from RMIT University (and other organisations where additional specialist expertise was needed) was assembled to work collaboratively on the different tasks. Skillsets range from the hard sciences (e.g., civil and environmental engineering), geospatial sciences (GIS), through to natural sciences (horticulture and nature-based solutions) and social sciences (land administration, media and communications, etc.). Some activities, such as climate action planning, require multidisciplinary inputs. While significant scientific support is provided in year one of the Climate Resilient Honiara project, some of this effort is being targeted towards capacity building with a range of local stakeholders to maximise the opportunities for the design and implementation of resilience actions to be locally managed and supported in subsequent years. It is hoped that this can be achieved at multiple scales, including engaging with communities (involving people in the design and implementation of projects and activities to develop new skills), capacity building activities with the city and national government (e.g., GIS training), working with groups such as the Honiara City Youth Council (e.g., youth members are involved with the household surveys and urban agriculture training), and engaging with other important local organisations (e.g.,

RMIT University and Solomon Islands National University have signed an MoU that will potentially support a partnership and collaborative activities that will hopefully endure beyond the life of the project).

It is also the intention of this new project to build synergies with other local projects and initiatives to ensure a more collective approach to moving towards a more climate-resilient Honiara. Examples include hosting joint training workshops for ward councillors on climate change adaptation and disaster risk reduction with ICLEI Local Governments for Sustainability (who are currently engaged with Honiara City Council on updating DRR plans and building links with Australian Councils), to design climate-resilient open spaces in close consultation with SPREP and their ecosystem-based adaptation case studies (PEBACC), and to look for implementation partnerships with international NGOs (Live and Learn, the Red Cross/Red Crescent Movement), local civil society organisations (Gurafesu Urban Agriculture Group) and relevant public organisations (Solomon Water).

Conclusions

The journey from vulnerability assessment to the implementation of climate-resilience actions has been enabled through a positive and long-term partnership between UN-Habitat, an Australian university and committed local organisations (both government and non-government). This has provided an alternative approach to the type of project that is typically consultancy-led, bringing benefits of long-term engagement, commitment and trust-building with local stakeholders. This has required a mutual understanding of how each project partner operates (both funder and university) and some degree of flexibility by all parties to 'align' applied university research with the demands of an important urban resilience agenda.

Underpinning the journey has been a highly participatory approach, which has enabled all citizens of Honiara, including people living in informal settlements, to have a voice in identifying priority issues and ultimately the development of a more equitable urban resilience and climate action plan. Moving forward, it is also intended that local people will have the opportunity to be involved with the implementation of actions through their own skillsets and resources (such as labour, carpentry skills and social networks), as well as various capacity building initiatives (enumerator training, training in urban agriculture techniques, etc). One engagement mechanism that had positive results was the creation of multi-stakeholder platforms that enabled open discussion and debate of issues and potential actions. Such platforms made clear that everyone has a role to play in enhancing urban resilience to climate impacts and urbanisation pressures, and that is not just the government's role to provide solutions or always act as the lead implementing partner. Furthermore, it was recognised that a focus on actions without the necessary capacity building will also prove ineffective in the longer-term.

One of the key lessons arising from this journey is that actions to adapt to climate change (as is being promoted by the international Green Climate Fund) need to be embedded in a broader resilience framework with actions targeting the drivers of current-day vulnerabilities as a foundation for longer-term climate adaptation. It makes little sense to target resilience to future changes in climate while many in Honiara are faced with poverty, development deficits, as well as being exposed to existing natural hazards that impact vulnerable communities in the current day.

Given the context of rapid urbanisation and population growth in peri-urban areas, there needs to be more effective engagement processes between the Honiara City Council and neighbouring Guadalcanal Province to scope issues and co-design solutions. Furthermore, principles of responsible land governance are needed to improve land tenure security, support the roll-out of Fixed Term Estates, and by extension increase the resilience of all urban residents. Fit-for-purpose and lower-cost land administration approaches are needed in this regard.

As noted in the discussion concerning endogenous, informal resilience, it is important to recognise the strengths of local institutions (structures and processes) and align with them wherever possible when designing resilience actions and capacity strengthening activities, i.e., avoiding imposing Western-style constructs that are unfit for local purpose, and hence unsustainable (e.g., one important challenge is to integrate climate science with local knowledge and traditional practice). In the Honiara context, it was found that local socio-cultural networks such as the Wantok system play a vital role in community well-being and being able to recover after the impact of extreme events. However, it is also clear that there are downsides to these 'extended family' relationships, as evidenced by situations of overcrowding and the sprawl of unplanned development. As such, neither 'endogenous' nor 'exogenous' approaches to urban climate resilience are able to operate without effective engagement across, and negotiation between, these two domains.

Ultimately, while the implementation of actions as part of the Climate Resilient Honiara project will have real-world impact in the case study settlements, the city's future resilience can only be achieved by an effective urban development masterplan. To this end, finalizing the National Urban Policy (currently in draft format) could provide a high-level framework at the national level, as well as giving guidance and support to the Framework for Resilient Development in the Pacific (SPC, 2016).

Notes

1. ICLEI Local Governments for Sustainability http://archive.iclei.org/index.php?id=9639, accessed 27 Feb 2019
2. ICLEI Local Government for Sustainability http://old.iclei.org/index.php?id=1201, accessed 27 Feb 2019
3. UN-Habitat https://unhabitat.org/urban-themes/climate-change/

4. Country Case Study: Solomon Islands On mainstreaming climate change into the National Urban Policy Framework (www.fukuoka.unhabitat.org/projects/asian_subregion/pdf/solomon%20islands_final.pdf)
5. UN-Habitat www.fukuoka.unhabitat.org/projects/solomon_islands/detail01_en.html

References

Betzold, C. (2015). Adapting to climate change in small island developing states. *Climatic Change*, 133, 481–489.

Biesbroek, G.R., Klostermann, J.E.M., Termeer, C.J.A.M. and Kabat, P. (2013). On the nature of barriers to climate change adaptation. *Regional Environmental Change*, 13, 1119–1129.

Eisenack, K., Moser, S.C., Hofmann, E., Klein, R.J.T., Oberlack, C., Pechan, A., Rotter, M. and Termeer, C.J.A.M. (2014). Explaining and overcoming barriers to climate change adaptation. *Nature Climate Change*, 4, 867–862.

Foukona, J. (2015). Urban land in Honiara: Strategies and rights to the city. *The Journal of Pacific History*, 50(4), 504–518.

Foukona, J. (2017). *Solomon Islands' Urban Land Tenure: Growing Complexity*. In Brief, 2017/05, State, Society and Governance in Melanesia. Canberra: Australian National University.

Friend, R. and Moench, M. (2013). What is the purpose of urban climate resilience? Implications for addressing poverty and vulnerability. *Urban Climate*, 6, 98–113.

Gero, A., Meheux, K. and Dominey-Howes, D. (2011). Integrating disaster risk reduction and climate change adaptation in the Pacific. *Climate and Development*, 3, 310–327.

Jones, P. (2012). Searching for a little bit of utopia: Understanding the growth of squatter and informal settlements in Pacific towns and cities. *Australian Planner*, 49, 327–338.

Keen, M. and Barbara, J. (2015). *Pacific Urbanisation: Changing Times*. In Brief, 2015/64, State, Society and Governance in Melanesia. Canberra: Australian National University.

Keen, M., Barbara, J., Carpenter, J., Evans, D. and Foukona, J. (2017). *Urban Development in Honiara—Harnessing Opportunities, Embracing Change*. State, Society and Governance in Melanesia. Canberra: Australian National University. Available at: http://ssgm.bellschool.anu.edu.au/sites/default/files/uploads/2017-05/urban_development_in_honiara_low_res.pdf.

Kiddle, G.L., McEvoy, D., Mitchell, D., Jones, P. and Mecartney, S. (2017). Unpacking the Pacific urban agenda: Resilience challenges and opportunities. *Sustainability*, 9(10).

Leichenko, R. (2011). Climate change and urban resilience. *Current Opinion in Environmental Sustainability*, 3(3), 164–168.

McEvoy, D., de Ville, N., Komugabe-Dixson, A. and Trundle, A. (2017). *Greater Port Vila Social Mapping and Analysis of Ecosystem Use*. Apia, Samoa: Secretariat of the Pacific Regional Environment Programme (SPREP). Available at: www.sprep.org/attachments/Publications/IOE/pebacc/port-vila-social-mapping-analysis-ecosystem-use.pdf.

McEvoy, D. and Mitchell, D. (2019). Climate resilient land governance in the global south. In S. Davoudi, R. Cowell, I. White and H. Blanco (eds.), *Routledge Companion to Environmental Planning*. Oxon: Routledge.

McEvoy, D., Mitchell, D. and Trundle, A. (2019). Land tenure and urban climate resilience in the South Pacific. *Climate and Development* [online]. https://doi.org/10.1080/17565529.2019.1594666.

Pacific Community (SPC), Secretariat of the Pacific Regional Environment Programme (SPREP), Pacific Islands Forum Secretariat (PIFS), United Nations Development Programme (UNDP), United Nations Office for Disaster Risk Reduction (UNISDR) and University of the South Pacific (USP) (2016) *Framework for Resilient Development in the Pacific: An Integrated Approach to Address Climate Change and Disaster Risk Management [FRDP] 2017–2030.*

Rey, T., Le De, L., Leone, F., Gilbert, D., Paton, D. and Johnston, D. (2017). An integrative approach to understand vulnerability and resilience post-disaster: The 2015 cyclone Pam in urban Vanuatu as case study. *Disaster Prevention and Management*, 26(3), 270–277.

Ride, A. and Bretherton, D. (2011). Solomon Islands. In A. Ride and D. Bretherton (eds.), *Community Resilience in Natural Disasters*. New York: Palgrave Macmillan.

Satterthwaite, D. (2013). The political underpinnings of cities' accumulated resilience to climate change. *Environment & Urbanization*, 25(2), 381–391.

Solomon Islands Government. (2016). *Honiara Urban Resilience & Climate Action Plan*. Authors: Trundle, A. and McEvoy, D. with UN-Habitat, Fukuoka, Japan. Available at: www.fukuoka.unhabitat.org/programmes/ccci/pdf/HURCAP_final_Endorsed.pdf.

Trundle, A. (2017). Governance and agency beyond boundaries climate resilience in Port Vila's peri-urban settlements. In M. Moloney, S. Funfgeld and H. Granberg (eds.), *Local Action on Climate Change: Opportunities & Constraints*. London: Routledge, 35–52.

Trundle, A., Barth, B. and McEvoy, D. (2018). Leveraging endogenous climate resilience: Urban adaptation in Pacific Small Island Developing States. *Environment and Development*, 31(1), 53–74.

Tyler, S. and Moench, M. (2012). A framework for urban climate resilience. *Climate and Development*, 4(4), 311–326.

UN ESCAP and UN-Habitat. (2015). *The State of Asian and Pacific Cities: 2015 Urban Transformations: Shifting from Quantity to Quality*. Available at: www.unescap.org/sites/default/files/The%20State%20of%20Asian%20and%20Pacific%20Cities%202015.pdf.

UN-Habitat. (2010). *Participatory Climate Change Assessments: A Toolkit Based on the Experience of Sorsogon City, Philippines*. Cities and Climate Change Discussion Paper 1. Authors: Mias-Mamonong, A.A., Flores, Y., Bernhard, B. and Radford, C.

UN-Habitat. (2014). *Climate Change Vulnerability Assessment. Honiara: Solomon Islands*. Abridged version. Available at: www.pacificclimatechange.net/sites/default/files/documents/Honiara_SI_Climate_Vulnerability_Assessment.pdf.

UN-Habitat and EcoPlan International. (2014). *Planning for Climate Change: A Strategic, Values-based Approach for Urban Planners*. Nairobi, Kenya: UN-Habitat.

Ziervogel, G., Pelling, M., Cartwright, A., Chu, E., Deshpande, T., Harris, L., Hyams, K., Kaunda, J., Klaus, B., Michael, K., Pasquini, L., Pharoah, R., Rodina, L., Scott, D. and Zweig, P. (2017). Inserting rights and justice into urban resilience: A focus on everyday risk. *Environment and Urbanization*, 29(1), 123–138.

Chapter 5

What Does Neighbourhood-Level Urban Resilience Look Like in Honiara?

Laura Bruce and Leeanne Marshall

Introduction

While urbanisation offers positive opportunities, in the Pacific, rapid and largely unmanaged urban expansion has resulted in development challenges such as lack of access to land and affordable housing which affect the 'liveability, productivity and sustainability' of Pacific island towns and cities (ADB, 2012: 95). These development challenges are nowhere more evident than in the informal settlements that are a common feature of many Pacific island towns and cities. It is estimated that up to 50 percent of the urban population in Melanesia is living in informal settlements (Jones and Sanderson, 2017), and informal settlement expansion is undoubtedly a feature of Honiara, the capital of the Solomon Islands, which is the focus of this chapter.

This chapter aims to identify and understand what people-led neighbourhood-level resilience looks like. Two neighbouring informal settlements in Honiara are discussed: Ontong Java (also known as Lord Howe settlement) and Renlau. Ontong Java and Renlau sit on either side of the mouth of the Matanikau river, which separates the two settlements on a section of the Honiara shoreline, collectively known as Mamanawata (see Figure 5.1). Translated, this means 'the water front'. As a result, both settlements are exposed to the threat of natural hazards and climate change impacts such as cyclones, sea surge and sea level rise. These shocks and stresses make this location highly vulnerable—Ontong Java is referenced widely as being a vulnerability hot spot due to its high-risk location (Solomon Islands Government, 2016; UN-Habitat, 2014).

This chapter is based on research and a field visit to Honiara undertaken by the authors that was supported by the Research for Development Impact Network (RDI Network) .[1] Honiara was chosen as a case study location because it is a Pacific island city that faces the combined challenges of rapid unplanned urbanisation, vulnerability to natural hazards and the impact of climate change. In addition, the city experiences underlying development challenges which are clearly manifested in its informal settlements, where an estimated 35 percent of its urban population resides (SINSO, 2011).

Multiple factors that both 'push' people away from rural areas and 'pull' them towards the city exist as drivers for Honiara's urbanisation. Push

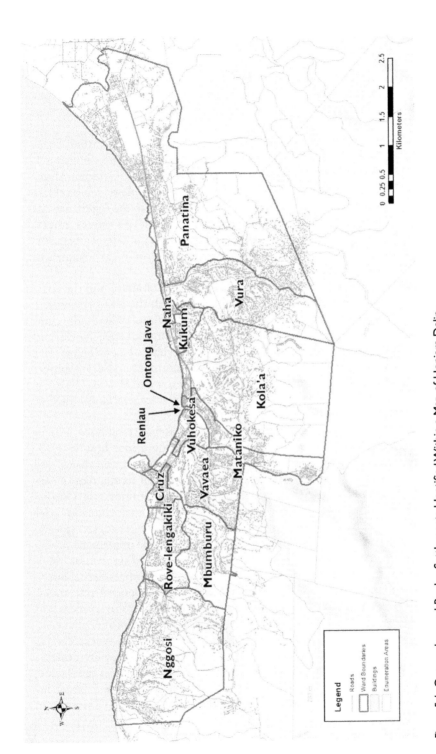

Figure 5.1 Ontong Java and Renlau Settlements Identified Within a Map of Honiara Delineated by Ward and Associated Peri-Urban Surrounds.

Source: Alexei Trundle (2016)

factors include a subsistence-based rural economy, population growth, limited economic opportunities, available services and the impacts of climate change. The city's pull factors of jobs, education and access to technology are drawing more people to Honiara, particularly younger people. These push and pull factors are set to continue, making the need to manage and respond to urbanisation issues all the more important.

Many global risks of climate change are concentrated in urban areas (IPCC, 2014). Pacific island vulnerability to climate change is highly relevant to the urban context, as most Pacific towns and cities, including Honiara, are based on coasts and are therefore more vulnerable to sea level rise and coastal flooding. To ensure that development gains in the region are not reversed, it is critical to support Pacific towns and cities to reduce vulnerability to natural hazards and adapt to the impacts of climate change. This is highly relevant to the case study locations focused on in this chapter, as both are situated on the coastal fringe of Honiara.

Given the threats noted previously, understanding Honiara and the communities that are the focus of this case study through the lens of resilience is extremely relevant. The concept of resilience concerns individuals, communities and urban systems being better able to withstand such shocks and stresses. Resilience is also an approach for 'doing development better' and has been widely used as a means of linking both disasters and development into one unified, people-centred approach (Sanderson and Sharma, 2016). It also figures prominently in the UN Sustainable Development Goals (SDGs), such as SDG 13, the 'urban' SDG.

This research applies a neighbourhood-level urban resilience lens in Ontong Java and Renlau settlements to gain an insight into how its communities address the combined challenges of urbanisation, the threat and impact of natural hazards and climate change, as well as ongoing development challenges. The research looked at how communities in Ontong Java and Renlau settlements are coping, adapting and transforming in order to address these multiple challenges and build their resilience, recognising that informal settlements are already places where people implement coping strategies on a daily basis in order to derive an income and survive. Its intention was not to provide a quantifiable measure or metric of resilience, but to identify fundamental aspects of neighbourhood-level resilience. Understanding 'what resilience looks like' is an important first step for government and policy interventions which aim to support the building of local resilience.

The research is comprised of a literature review and field work. The literature review included a desktop review of academic and grey literature to identify urbanisation trends and resilience-building activities in the Pacific, including Honiara in particular. The literature review built on a larger literature review addressing climate change, vulnerability and urbanisation in the Pacific being undertaken by researchers at the University of New South Wales (UNSW).[2]

The fieldwork in Honiara comprised three focus group discussions and 14 semi-structured key informant interviews with participants from

Figure 5.2 View From Renlau to Ontong Java Settlement.
Source: Leeanne Marshall (2018)

non-government organisations (NGOs), government, local councils and the two local informal settlement neighbourhoods. A participatory action research approach was applied with the two communities. Transect walks with community members were used to triangulate information about the built environment, social structures and economic activities. Data collection took place in the Ontong Java and neighbouring Renlau settlement.

The remainder of this chapter is in four sections. This first section discusses urbanisation and informal settlements in the Solomon Islands. The second section discusses the concept of resilience. The third section reviews the significance of social capital to building resilience. The final discussion reasserts the value of a neighbourhood resilience approach and how its application in this setting identified different levels of resilience within the two neighbouring locations, and the need for further research on the impact of social capital on resilience.

Urbanisation, Urban Growth and Informal Settlements in Honiara

The Pacific is a region of increasing urban growth, something that is reflected strongly in the Solomon Islands where the urban growth rate is almost twice the rate of national population growth (Keen and Barbara, 2015). With a land area of 22 km² and 12 wards, Honiara is also the most densely populated area of the country. It has a population registered in the 2009 census of 64,609, which is equivalent to 12.5 percent of the country's total population (SINSO, 2011). The city grew to an estimated 87,000 residents in 2015 despite civil unrest disrupting rural-urban migration in the early 2000s (SINSO, 2011). These growth rates do not include the rapid population expansion in peri-urban areas since these are not included in census enumerations.

Honiara City Council (HCC) is mandated to provide effective urban management and planning in Honiara by the Town and Country Planning Act. However, the planning departments in both the HCC and the Ministry of Lands, Housing and Survey (MLHS) at the national level are under-resourced and lack technical capacity. This weak governance and lack of budgetary support, both at the local and the national level, has resulted in poor urban management (UN-Habitat, 2012). For instance, neither the HCC or the MLHS have a formal policy or approach to managing informal settlements (UN-Habitat, 2012), despite the fact that informal settlements in greater Honiara are growing quickly and exceeding the pace of urban growth (UN-Habitat, 2012).

The negative impacts of urbanisation and urban growth are evident in the expansion of poor-quality informal settlements (UN-Habitat, 2012). Over a third of Honiara's population live in Informal Settlement Zones (ISZs), although informal settlement extends beyond these government-defined areas (UN-Habitat, 2012). Both Ontong Java and Renlau are not actually government classified ISZs. Since these official ISZ areas only cover a portion of all informal dwellings in the city, the scale of informal settlements in Honiara is even greater than the official numbers suggest. Since their current numbers are underestimated and their continued expansion looks inevitable, efforts to identify and build the resilience of those living in informal settlements is of significant importance.

Informal settlements are characterised as illegal, according to the prevailing formal state system, or unplanned housing developments that lack universal access to services. Due to these factors, they are often places that experience concentrated levels of poverty and increased vulnerability to the impact of natural hazards and climate change. Informal settlements, however, can also be thought of as resilient—they continue to exist despite neglect from formal government interventions and as a result are comprised with a high degree of locally driven adaptive capacity and social capital. In this instance, their survival in the face of their longevity—both Ontong Java and Renlau have been in existence between 60 and nearly 70 years—is evidence of the strength of their own resilience.

Despite being in existence for many years, people interviewed in both Ontong Java and Renlau for this research stated that they rarely engaged with government representatives and, when it was required, they had little trust in the government. A Renlau resident interviewed for this research stated, 'We have councillors, members for this ward here. But where are their footsteps? What have they done?'[3] Government response or support in Ontong Java and Renlau has largely been absent, which suggests local coping mechanisms and social capital inevitably have and will continue to play a key role in supporting neighbourhood resilience.

It is important to acknowledge that land tenure complexities in the Pacific mean that informal land tenure arrangements have emerged in informal settlements which may support what is known as 'perceived security of tenure' (Payne, 2001). Informal tenure does not necessarily mean insecure tenure. Broader approaches which lie outside the traditional Western concept of legal land tenure recognise tenure security, and can be generated through other means such as increasing the rights of residents to settle on land, extending existing customary arrangements and even linking longevity to claims of legitimacy to the land on which they have settled (Payne, 2001). This is certainly the case in Renlau, which has a customary land arrangement where there is great trust in their long-held customary agreement despite an absence of paperwork or formal arrangements.

The British colonial legacy means that the municipal area of Honiara and its Western-influenced land tenure arrangements are separate to the customary land arrangements that largely occur outside its borders on the island of Guadalcanal, the island on which Honiara sits (see Figure 5.1 for a map of Honiara delineated by ward; land outside these borders is Guadalcanal customary land). While customary land ownership within the Honiara city boundary is unusual, pockets remain. It is in one of these pockets that the Renlau settlement sits.[4] However, the encroachment of informal settlements located on municipal boundaries on the outskirts of the city onto Guadalcanal customary lands is causing, and has historically caused, land-related disputes. It is also demonstrative of the tension that exists between Western-influenced formal land tenure within Honiara and customary arrangements outside (and in the case of this case study inside) its municipal boundaries. Subsequently, there is a highly complex land tenure context within the Solomon Islands. In this case study, even though Ontong Java and Renlau sit directly next to each other, they have significantly different land tenure arrangements.

Informal settlements, particularly those in the Melanesian context, present an interesting layer of social dynamics due to ethnic, clan and kinship connections such as *wantok* (Jones, 2012). The wontok system (literally 'one talk' or 'one language') is a system unique to many countries in Melanesia which means there is an accepted and strong obligation to give preference to and share resources with those who are related, speak the same or a similar language, or are even from the same island. Solomon Islanders are well known for moving back and forth between Honiara and the Provinces. As a result, strong familial, kinship and cultural ties link the originating villages with communities in the city whereby new arrivals to the city seek support through social networks such as 'wantokism'. Moore notes that 'people seldom arrive without contacts; every provincial village has members living in Honiara' (2015: 422).

This fluid movement lends the city a unique make-up which has been termed 'rural villages in the city' (Jones, 2016). These informal settlements 'exhibit the physical, social and cultural characteristics of rural villages, including ethnic and kinship groups, but within an urban setting' (ADB, 2012: x). These 'rural villages in the city', also termed 'village cities', are observed in the context of Honiara's informal settlements (Jones, 2016). Therefore, how these 'rural village in the city' characteristics interplay with resilience in Honiara's informal settlements is of key interest.

Urban Resilience

This chapter defines urban resilience as 'the measurable ability of any urban system, with its inhabitants, to maintain continuity through all shocks and stresses, while positively adapting and transforming toward sustainability' (UN-Habitat, 2018).

The reference to 'shocks and stresses' in this definition includes natural, technological, socioeconomic and political-cultural crises. This underpins the view that resilience is as much a development concern as it is a disaster management approach, and that it is applicable before, during, and after 'shocks and stresses' (Jones and Sanderson, 2017). This definition also notes that resilience occurs at multiple levels; however, the reference to 'inhabitants' highlights the importance of social resilience within communities (which is a particular focus of this research).

Definitions of social resilience concern social entities, for instance individuals and communities, and their capacity to make their cities more resilient (UN-Habitat, 2018). The socio-ecological origins of resilience support the multi-component focus of resilience, i.e., how an urban system and its inhabitants tolerate shocks and stress through coping strategies as well as the positive change that can result from a disturbance through learning and adaptation (Cutter et al., 2008). While community coping and adaptation strategies support resilience as a process, this definition also recognises resilience as a transformative goal, and that it is possible to formulate actions for resilience 'towards sustainability'.

There is a growing commitment to urban resilience in recent years, both internationally and regionally, for example the New Urban Agenda, the SDGs (as noted earlier) and the New Pacific Urban Agenda.[5] While the existence of international and regional resilience frameworks and approaches is of course valuable, enacting resilience-building activities takes place both nationally and locally, and there is certainly room to identify what a local, people-centred approach through neighbourhood-level resilience looks like in a Pacific island urban context. Recent research identifies that 'endogenous resilience' in the form of community-derived capacities operates at a sub-city level in the Solomon Islands, but is largely 'untapped by international development institutions' (Trundle et al., 2018; also discussed elsewhere in

Neighbourhood-Level Urban Resilience   81

this book—see McEvoy et al.), despite playing a critical role in Pacific urban livelihoods (Jones, 2012).

The Significance of Social Capital to Building Resilience

Social capital is composed of the norms and networks that enable people to act collectively (Woolcock and Narayan, 2000). It can be regarded as a determinant of the propensity for collective action or community participation. Therefore 'investing in social capital fosters community resilience that transcends natural hazards and positively affects collective governance and community health' (Aldrich et al., 2018).

While a number of scholars have developed conceptual frameworks for resilience that incorporate social capital (see, for instance, Cutter et al., 2010), there is no consensus on consistent factors or standard metrics to measure the dimensions of community resilience (Cutter et al., 2010). In this research, social capital is mostly concerned with the local and informal community-based special interest groups that can inform resilience by building, maintaining and strengthening coping capacity, adaptive capacity and transformative capacity (examples are given in the section that follows).

While community-based special interest groups that support social capital can have positive outcomes for individual and community resilience, it can also foster negative outcomes as these groups may operate on unequal terms and may exclude vulnerable members of the community based, for instance, on sex, religion or caste (Chambers, 1983).

Therefore, understanding the context and the types of social capital most useful for increasing community resilience is important. The unique 'rural village in the city characteristics' of Honiara's informal settlements also offer a further dimension of social capital in relation to social networks. Within Honiara's informal settlements, these social networks offer what might be called a resilience paradox; while ethnic clan and kinship connections provide support to new arrivals in the city context, they also risk draining incumbent urban dwellers of resources. This is particularly evident in the context of informal settlements, as most 'new arrivals' to the city seek support through kinship ties from communities who may already be overwhelmed (Moore, 2015).

Social Capital in Ontong Java and Renlau

This section discusses how this social capital manifests in Ontong Java and Renlau. While the research identified multiple fundamental aspects of resilience—income diversification, preparedness, response to natural hazards and the impact of climate change, and land tenure arrangements—it was observed that social capital had a key influence on these fundamental aspects of resilience, namely disaster preparedness and response and land tenure arrangements due to the presence of active and functioning community-based special interest groups.

Community-Based Special Interest Groups

The research observed the positive relationship between the existence of social capital and community action due to the existence of active and functioning special interest groups. The presence of a community disaster committee in the Ontong Java settlement has increased the community's capacity to cope and adapt to the impact of natural hazards and climate change. This is in part due to their participation in the 'Finnish Pacific Project' (FINPAC),[6] an initiative aimed at building resilience and reducing vulnerability of livelihoods to the effects of climate change undertaken by the National Disaster Management Office (NDMO) and the Solomon Islands Red Cross Society (SIRCS). The community has an existing early-warning system that has been tested, though not in the last year, with the community disaster committee. Residents reported that they also keep boats to assist with evacuation when needed. This preparedness and planning was absent from the neighbouring Renlau settlement, where there is no active community disaster committee.

In 2002, the community of Ontong Java was able to collectively secure a communal title Fixed-Term Estate (FTE), which is a lease of government-held land for a 50-year period. Despite the existence of a FTE, Ontong Java settlement is considered an informal settlement because its housing does not comply to the city's building codes and its inhabitants lack universal access to services. The funds for securing a communal title were raised by the community and the land is managed on an ongoing basis through an elected community Trust Board. The existence of an active and functioning special-interest group in the form of the Trust Board is an example of transformational capacity since it has secured long-term development advantages through tenure security. However, it is worth pointing out that while community action with formal government in regards to tenure worked to the advantage of the Ontong Java settlement, the land tenure situation in Honiara is complex, and this approach is not an affordable and available option to many. A resident of Ontong Java interviewed for this study noted that while it was inexpensive, it took a long time to secure the FTE, 'we've got patience, but we had to wait 10 years'.[7]

Despite being just across the river from the Ontong Java settlement, the community of Renlau has a different land tenure arrangement established with the customary land owners of Guadalcanal. This agreement was made in 1964 through a *chupu* (a barter exchange based on traditional goods such as pigs or betel nut) between the Guadalcanal people and the Renlau community leaders. Although these two land tenure arrangements are very different, both neighbourhoods report similar levels of perceived tenure security. While the Renlau community does not possess any formal documentation, there is great reverence for and trust placed in the long-held customary agreements, even though, technically, there are no customary land rights within the town boundary. There is a need therefore to look beyond formal governance land tenure and Western-influenced concepts of illegal and legal land tenure by understanding how informal land tenure arrangements have emerged. For instance, this may include finding mechanisms to legitimize customary arrangements to access to land to support resilience in informal settlements. For this reason, understanding the informal land tenure arrangements and their consequences within individual settlements is a key entry point to supporting resilience in Honiara.

Social Networks

In both study locations, it was observed that the presence of social networks or ties that bind individuals and communities supported the existence of these active and functioning community- based special interest groups. Since the Ontong Java settlement is composed of a single 'wantok' (discussed earlier), residents reported that it is easier to form active and effective specialinterest groups since they speak the same or a similar language. One resident of Ontong Java reported 'we are one people, one language'.[8] This is evidenced by the presence of active and well-functioning special interest groups such as the community disaster committee, youth and women's groups and the community Trust Board that all seek collective returns for the community. In Ontong Java settlement, these special interest groups that display effective community governance appear to be a consequence of strong social networks or ties based on wantok. The research identified that most of the community in the Ontong Java settlement are originally from two main villages on the Ontong Java atoll, to which they still have very strong connections and economic ties.

In contrast, a distinctive feature of the Renlau settlement is the diversity of the people who live there. Although the settlement is mostly made up of people from Malaita Province, they are from different places in the province. There is also a minority Polynesian community from Rennell and Bellona Province[9] who live on the far side of the settlement near the mouth of the Matanikau river. The researchers observed the absence of a single wantok, which in this instance weakened the social network in this settlement and may be one explanation for the absence of special interest groups. One explanation for this absence could be the number of diverse ethnic groups which live in the settlement. While this in itself should not inhibit resilience, the fact that the community has struggled to bring its members together means there is no identifiable mechanism for achieving consensus or a shared vision.

Wantok in this instance had a significant influence on social capital, though other factors such as motivated individuals and strong leadership are arguably just as important. Where settlements are composed of people with different origins, this does not automatically preclude social networks. However, in areas where language groupings are so large, closer kinship is often the basis for residential groupings (Moore, 2015). There are also many other forces that can support social networks across different ethnic and kinship groups; the unifying role

Figure 5.3 View From Ontong Java Settlement in Honiara, Which Sits on the Coast. In the distance, it is possible to see the shipping containers on Port Cruz, which serves as the city's port.

Source: Laura Bruce (2018)

of religion, for instance, has huge relevance in the Pacific context. The absence of a church in the Renlau settlement might further explain the challenge of supporting cohesion between the different island groups within Renlau. In contrast, Ontong Java does have a small community church, though the central location of both Ontong Java and Renlau mean that churches of various denominations are accessible locally outside the settlements.

Finally, does the existence of social capital in the form of strong social networks and active and functioning special interest groups in the Ontong Java settlement make the community more appealing to development and humanitarian projects and initiatives? According to Archer, 'Communities with high levels of trust and strong norms of reciprocity and collective action are generally regarded as being more suited to participatory projects' (Archer, 2009: 8). Such communities are more appealing to work with and the Ontong Java settlement features heavily in recent reports by UN-Habitat (2014) and UN-Habitat (2012) as a vulnerability hot spot. Recently, the Ontong Java settlement have been the recipient of aid interventions through FINPAC and the NGO World Vision. This raises questions about whether the existence of the community disaster committee hinged solely on social capital, as other factors such as donor intervention could also be considered.

Clan and Kinship Relations

This research found that socio-cultural links between the rural-urban context were strong in both settlements, which suggests the strong influence of clan and kinship connections on social capital. What does that mean for long-term investment in Honiara and the concept of neighbourhood urban identity within informal settlements? Residents reported that they identify more strongly with their island of origin or kinship group than with Honiara, and that some residents of Honiara go back to their province to vote instead of registering to vote in Honiara municipal elections. These findings are confirmed by the 2009 census which revealed short-term mobility in most Honiara wards, since most have more than ten percent of their population with a usual residence elsewhere (SINSO, 2011).

Currently, Honiara's ongoing rapid urbanisation and the subsequent proliferation of informal settlements suggests that ethnic, clan and kinship connections will continue to be of importance to new arrivals. Strong links between Ontong Java settlement and the island of origin were reported as a result of the return of the men to help with the annual harvesting of 'bêche-de-mer' (sea cucumber) in their villages of origin. The significant income derived from this activity appears to have encouraged further neighbourhood investment in the urban context. Therefore, in this instance, ties between the province and the urban context remain strong.

However, over time perhaps ongoing urbanisation may mean that linkages back to places of origin become less meaningful to the new urban generation (Keen and Carpenter, 2017). This research also observed that rapid urban growth has created competition for space and access to services in informal settlements. Residents of both case study locations identified overcrowding as a key challenge, and talked about the possibility of resettlement for those who had arrived more recently. The potential weakening of these kinship ties due to rapid urbanisation and the risk of burdening incumbent communities in the urban context has implications for the role of social capital on resilience.

Discussion

A neighbourhood-resilience lens was particularly helpful for understanding the differences between Ontong Java and Renlau. Despite being neighbouring settlements with almost identical exposure to natural hazards and the impacts of climate change, the level of resilience varied. This appeared to be due to the existence and strength of community-based special interest groups. This local manifestation of social capital had a strong influence on resilience outcomes related to preparedness and response to natural hazards and the impact of climate change, as well as land tenure arrangements.

The neighbourhood-resilience lens allowed for a deeper contextual analysis which identified the influence of 'rural village in the city characteristics' on informal settlements and their subsequent impact on social capital. This approach is important, as understanding the dynamics of the varying socio-cultural orders and the connectivity and interplay of Pacific norms, values, attitudes and aspirations in the urban setting is central to the process of Pacific urbanisation (ADB, 2012).

In Honiara's informal settlements, the existence of these unique social networks provides an opportunity to further deepen analysis on the role of social capital by addressing inter-community ties and state/business-community linkages. Therefore, a key finding from this work is the need to better understand the relationships between social capital and building resilience, through in particular an analysis of the three different types of social capital which include: bonding, bridging and linking (Szreter and Woolcock, 2004).

The way that these types of social capital interface in Pacific informal settlements would provide a fascinating insight into the types of social capital that support resilience, and the local community-driven capacity that already exists. For instance, 'bonding' demonstrates intra-community ties which are more likely between close family and friends and often based in race or ethnicity; this was clearly observed through 'wantok' in the Ontong Java settlement. At the next level, 'bridging' connects those who are quite different through 'inter-community ties' such as church, sports or schools. This is valuable in this context since the church provides a stable social network and leadership in all communities through Honiara's settlements (Moore, 2015).

Finally, 'linking' connects community with people in higher positions of authority. 'Urban wantokism can be viewed both horizontally and vertically' (Moore, 2015: 434–435) and can therefore link communities horizontally through 'bridging', as identified previously, but also vertically by 'linking' individuals with high status in business or in government at the local or national level. In the event of shocks or stresses, these connections have different implications. While 'bonding' social capital supports short-term resilience and may be sufficient for survival, 'bridging' and 'linking' social capital may have more long-term implications and are therefore more effective at building resilience economically and socially (Aldrich and Meyer, 2015).

While neighbourhood-level resilience supports a people-centred, community-level approach to urban development and disaster response, it cannot of course be examined in isolation. While the neighbourhood context and social capital matter, it is greatly affected by wider systemic issues such as weak governance resulting in poor urban management. Council, national and regional interlinkages are equally important to managing rapid urbanisation and urban resilience. While there are undoubtedly development challenges in the Ontong Java settlement, a greater need was observed in Renlau settlement, although it had less reported engagement with NGOs and development organisations.

In the Pacific, the interplay between formal and informal approaches to urban management must also be considered, particularly in relation to land tenure arrangements. In the case of land tenure, this case study recognises the value of local approaches that recognise perceived security of tenure and not just 'Western' constructs on legal tenure security. This observation is relevant to all resilience-building activities. For resilience as a concept to be relevant to the Pacific, it needs to reflect the uniqueness of the Pacific urban context. The neighbourhood-level resilience approach used in this research provides an opportunity to do this. Ultimately, urban resilience activities should be grounded in the realities of the Pacific context by using a neighbourhood-level resilience lens within informal settlements.

Notes

1. Further research by the same authors can be found in the 'Research in Development' series on the RDI Network website: https://rdinetwork.org.au/resources/the-research-in-development-series/
2. UNSW Built Environment Pacific and urbanisation literature review, forthcoming.
3. Individual interview (2018) conducted by the authors.
4. An explanation for this is that it is a remnant from earlier years when land was reserved for canoes (Moore, 2015).
5. https://unhabitat.org/welcoming-a-new-post-2015-pacific-urban-agenda/
6. The FINPAC Project (2012–2017) aimed to reduce vulnerability of PIC communities' livelihoods to the effects of climate change. It did this through increasing the capacity of the National Meteorological and Hydrological Services to deliver weather, climate and early-warning services in cooperation with and for the benefit of villagers in Pacific communities. More information on the project can be found at: https://unfccc.int/sites/default/files/mcfadzien.pdf.
7. Individual interview (2018) conducted by the authors.
8. Individual interview (2018) conducted by the authors.
9. The only Polynesian province in the predominantly Melanesian country.

References

Aldrich, D.P. and Meyer, M. (2015). Social capital and community resilience. *American Behavioral Scientist*, 59(2).
Aldrich, D.P., Meyer, M. and Page-Tan, C.M. (2018). Social capital and natural hazards governance. In *Oxford Research Encyclopedia of Natural Hazard Science*. Online publication. Available at: https://oxfordre.com/naturalhazardscience/view/10.1093/acrefore/9780199389407.001.0001/acrefore-9780199389407-e-254#.
Archer, D. (2009). *Social Capital and Participatory Slum Upgrading in Bangkok*. PhD dissertation. Thailand.
Asian Development Bank. (2012). *The State of Pacific Towns and Cities: Urbanization in ADB's Pacific Developing Member Countries*. Pacific Studies Series. Manila: Asian Development Bank.
Chambers, R. (1983). *Rural Development: Putting the Last First*. London: Longman.
Cutter, S.L., Barnes, L., Berry, M., Burton, C., Evans, E., Tate, E. and Webb, J. (2008). A place based model for understanding community resilience. *Global Environmental Change*, 18(4).
Cutter, S.L., Burton, C. and Emrich, C. T. (2010). Disaster resilience indicators for benchmarking baseline conditions. *Journal of Homeland Security and Emergency Management*, 7(1), 1–22.

IPCC. (2014). *Climate Change 2014, Impacts, Adaptation and Vulnerability, Summary for Policy Makers*. Available at: www.ipcc.ch/site/assets/uploads/2018/02/ar5_wgII_spm_en.pdf.

Jones, P. (2012). Searching for a little bit of utopia: Understanding the growth of squatter and informal settlements in Pacific towns and cities. *Australian Planner*, 49, 327–338.

Jones, P. (2016). *The Emergence of Pacific Urban Villages: Urbanization Trends in the Pacific Islands*. Pacific Studies Series. Manila: Asian Development Bank.

Jones, P. and Sanderson, D. (2017). Urban resilience: Informal and squatter settlements in the Pacific region. *Development Bulletin*, 78, 11–15.

Keen, M. and Barbara, J. (2015). *Pacific Urbanisation: Changing Times*. In Brief, 2015/64, State, Society and Governance in Melanesia. Canberra: Australian National University.

Keen, M. and Carpenter, J. (2017). Living on the fringes: Voices from those living in the settlements of Honiara. *Development Bulletin*, 78, 54–58.

Moore, C. (2015). Honiara: Arrival city and Pacific hybrid living space. *The Journal of Pacific History*, 50(4), 419–436.

Payne, G. (2001). Urban land tenure policy options: Titles or rights? *Habitat International*, 25(3), 415–429.

Sanderson, D. and Sharma, A. (2016). Making the case for resilience. In D. Sanderson and A. Sharma (eds.), *World Disasters Report: Resilience: Saving Lives Today, Investing for Tomorrow*. Geneva: IFRC, 11–26.

SINSO (Solomon Islands National Statistical Office). (2011). *2009 Population and Housing Census: Honiara*. Honiara: National Statistical Office.

Solomon Islands Government. (2016). *Honiara Urban Resilience & Climate Action Plan*. Authors: Trundle, A. and McEvoy, D. with UN-Habitat, Fukuoka: Japan. Available at: www.fukuoka.unhabitat.org/programmes/ccci/pdf/HURCAP_final_Endorsed.pdf.

Szreter, S. and Woolcock, M. (2004). Health by association? Social capital, social theory, and the political economy of public health. *International Journal of Epidemiology*, 33(4), 650–667.

Trundle, A., Barth, B. and McEvoy, D. (2018). Leveraging endogenous climate resilience: Urban adaptation in Pacific Small Island Developing States. *Environment and Urbanization*, 31(1), 53–74.

UN-Habitat. (2012). *Solomon Islands: Honiara Urban Profile*. Available at: https://unhabitat.org/solomon-islands-honiara-urban-profile/.

UN-Habitat. (2014). *Climate Change Vulnerability Assessment. Honiara: Solomon Islands*. Abridged version. Available at: www.pacificclimatechange.net/sites/default/files/documents/Honiara_SI_Climate_Vulnerability_Assessment.pdf.

UN-Habitat. (2018). *City Resilience Profiling Program, Social Resilience Guide*. Available at: http://urbanresiliencehub.org/wp-content/uploads/2018/11/Social-Resilience-Guide-SMALL-Pages.pdf.

University of New South Wales Built Environment (ongoing). *Matching Supply to Changing Demand: Gauging Future Urban Vulnerability in the Asia Pacific Region to Build Effective Resilience*. In-depth review.

Woolcock, M. and Narayan, D. (2000). Social capital: Implications for development theory, research, and policy. *The World Bank Research Observer*, 15(2), 225–249.

Chapter 6

Using a Systems Approach to Better Understand Urban Resilience in Port Vila, Vanuatu

Pamela Sitko, Walker Toma and Olivia Johnson

Introduction

Building urban resilience[1] relies upon understanding the individual parts of a city and how they connect and behave as one city. A systems approach is just that—viewing the city, its history, its context and its relationships as individual parts or 'systems' that together make up a whole. A systems approach recognises that much like a human body, when one part of a city is affected, there are implications for the city as a whole (Rossi, 1982).

A systems approach can be a useful lens for building urban resilience because it has the ability to analyse complexity at different scales while taking account of the connections between systems and the processes responsible for the connections. When towns and cities are not managed well, the systems within them generate poverty, inequity and risk, giving way to fragile economies, inadequate access to basic needs and disregard for human rights across the urban-rural spectrum. Interrogating the ways in which individual systems work together to create an overall sense of liveability, well-being, and ability to overcome shocks and stresses can provide an insight into how to build urban resilience.

The Asian Development Bank notes that managing rapid urbanisation in the Pacific has become one of the most pressing national and regional challenges in the new millennium (Jones, 2016). The need for better management encompasses meeting infrastructure backlogs for water, sanitation and drainage; addressing issues of land tenure and access to basis services in relation to the growth of informal settlements; the need for greater social inclusion and genuine participation; and the reduction of gender-based violence, all of which are present within Pacific contexts, especially in Melanesia (ADB, 2012). There is also a need to increase mitigation measures to address the impacts of climate change and disaster risk, as well as to support more-effective governance to undertake the management of rapid urbanisation through mechanisms such as urban planning.

To these ends, this chapter argues that a systems approach can help to unpack urban complexity, particularly a city's ability to withstand shocks and stresses arising from seemingly intractable problems related to rapid and unmanaged urbanisation, poverty and climate change. A systems approach—a method for identifying patterns of behaviour over time and the underlying factors that cause the behaviour—enables analysis of separate parts of the city while also seeking an understanding of the city as a whole.

A case study of Vanuatu's capital city, Port Vila, is used as an example of how a systems approach can assist with analysis of evolving parts or 'systems' of a city in a manageable and flexible way. By way of example, three different systems are selected for discussion in detail—the built environment, social inclusion and protection, and economic—to demonstrate application across diverse aspects of the city.

The discussion seeks to identify specific factors related to formal government policies, mechanisms and processes that contribute to the vulnerability and capacity of each system discussed. The chapter concludes with a reflection on the potential for using a systems approach in research and practice.

Methodology

Four methods were used to collect and analyse data for this chapter. Firstly, UN-Habitat's City Resilience Profiling Tool (CRPT)[2] was used as the framework for analysis. The tool understands cities as connected systems that influence and shape each other, resulting in a city that behaves as though it is one entity. Using this tool, data was collected on the demographics of Port Vila, as well as an analysis of key stakeholders (local government and others), shocks, stresses and cross-cutting issues such as gender and climate change. Importantly, the tool also provided a set of pre-determined questions to analyse eight urban systems: 1) The Built Environment, 2) Supply Chain and Logistics, 3) Basic Infrastructure, 4) Mobility, 5) Municipal Public Services, 6) Social Inclusion and Protection, 7) Economy and 8) Ecology. Figure 6.1 that follows is an interpretation of the city as eight connected systems based on UN-Habitat's CRPT.

In an effort to simply organise what can seem like chaos at first glance, 'components' are introduced for each system based on those found in the CRPT, demonstrating that the activities taking place in cities can be methodical, ordered and highly interdependent.

To illustrate a systems approach, this chapter will present and discuss three of the eight identified systems and their components. These are:

1. Built environment, which has four components: urban form, land tenure, housing and built assets.
2. Social protection, which has three components: social accountability, access to social protection floors for all and access to basic social services.
3. Economy, which includes three components: economic structure, fiscal stability and municipal finance, and market connectivity.

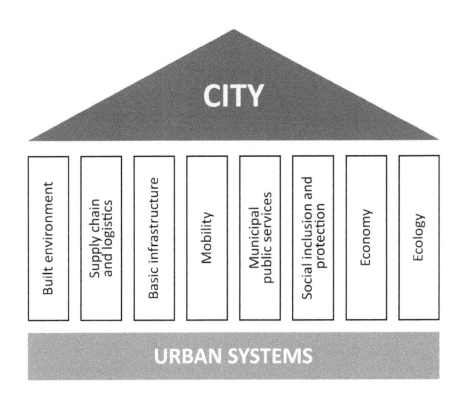

Figure 6.1 A Interpretation of the City as Eight Connected Systems Based on UN-Habitat's City Resilience Profiling Tool.

Source: Authors' own

Figure 6.2 summarises the three systems and their respective components. The components discussed here were developed as part of the CRPT for application to cities around the world, and therefore may not immediately reflect all aspects of urban life in Port Vila, or perhaps other urban centres in the Pacific. However, applying a global understanding of what cities require for inhabitants to thrive in the face of shocks and stresses may assist urban centres in the Pacific to identify gaps in policies and day-to-day operation. The tool, and others like it, seeks to generate evidence of such gaps so that different levels of government, communities and other such stakeholders have an evidence base to guide the resilience-building activities they design.

The second method involved a literature review. Searches about the build environment, social protection and economy were carried out in various combinations that included the words "Port Vila', 'resilience', 'vulnerability', 'capacity', 'systems', 'built environment', 'social inclusion', 'protection', 'health', 'accountability', 'governance', 'economy', 'markets', 'imports/

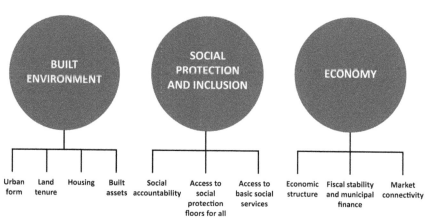

Figure 6.2 A Visual Representation of the Three Systems and the Components Discussed in This Chapter (Including: the built environment; social protection and inclusion; and economy based on UN-Habitat's CRPT).

Source: Authors' own

exports', 'land', 'kastom', 'tenure', informal settlements', 'urbanisation', 'climate change' and 'equity'. A total of 95 documents were reviewed, including gray literature (relating to geospatial information, institutional strategies, reports, assessments, budgets, evaluations, primary data collected about urban communities and neighbourhoods) and academic articles.

The third method involved interviews with 30 key informants who lived or worked in Port Vila based on their knowledge of the built environment, social protection or the economy. The fourth and final method presented and tested the initial findings at a two-day workshop held in Port Vila, attended by 17 urban specialists from municipal and national governments, non-government organisations (NGOs), the private sector and academia.

Inevitably, as with all research, there were limitations. As with any global tool, application relies on appropriate contextualisation. Where necessary, the questions in the tool were adjusted to reflect the context of Vanuatu, especially in relation to overlapping and sometimes conflicting responsibilities between the city and the national government. Extensive research on or with communities in Port Vila was not conducted, as the focus of the research was on formal government processes, mechanisms and policies. However, where possible, consideration of local attitudes, perceptions and behaviours were accounted for in the literature review.

The scope of this research is limited to the municipal boundaries of Port Vila. Boundaries can be problematic because of the people and factors they exclude. However, this study can be seen as a first step of many steps required to understand how a systems approach can be applied to Port Vila. Subsequent studies may be able to extend to Greater Port Vila and its surrounds.

Port Vila

Since gaining independence in 1980, Port Vila has served as Vanuatu's capital, administrative and economic centre, and location for its most prominent educational institutions. After gaining greater economic importance as a trade and transportation hub within the Vanuatu archipelago during the 18th and 19th centuries, Port Vila's recent history has largely been shaped by the country's establishment as a tax haven in the 1970s. The expansion and modernisation of the port and wharf in Vila Harbour over the past four decades has also been accompanied by increased tourism and a rapid growth in population.

The most recent national census estimates Port Vila's population to be approximately 51,000, or approximately 20 percent of Vanuatu's total population (Vanuatu National Statistics Office, 2016). However, a 2014 estimate by the Vanuatu National Statistics Office found the population inclusive of Greater Port Vila to be an estimated 85,000, indicating nearly 40 percent of the urban area's population resides outside of the administrative boundaries where the majority of recent growth has been concentrated (Vanuatu National Statistics Office, 2014).

Like most other Pacific nations, Vanuatu is highly dependent on foreign imports such as fossil fuels, on which the country relies not only for vehicular use, but also for electricity generation—over 80 percent of all electricity generation in Vanuatu relies on imported diesel fuel (Government of Vanuatu, 2014). While this trade-dependent economic composition is not uncommon with island nations, given the city's physical isolation and related dependencies, it remains vulnerable to economic shocks in global markets.

Port Vila faces extensive environmental threats, evident in its recent ranking as the 'world's most exposed city to natural disasters' (Verisk Maplecroft, 2015). Located within the South Pacific cyclone belt, and approximately 50 km east of the New Hebrides Trench, Port Vila is vulnerable to a number of natural hazards including earthquakes, wave action (including storm surge and tsunami), cyclones, heavy rainfall and flooding. Such threats, many of which are linked to climate change, are exacerbated by the existence of poverty, rapid urban growth, lack of institutional capacity and limited economic opportunity.

Having described the context of Port Vila, a discussion of three systems within the city will be presented.

System One: Built Environment

The built environment provides insight into the connections between historical and modern-day transformations of urban form—the shape, scale, quantity and quality of the built environment—(Oliveira, 2016) at different scales. An in-depth look at four key components can provide an understanding of the underlying factors that interact to shape the physical resilience of the city. Urban form, the first component of the built environment, provides an understanding of growth patterns within the city by tracing changes in its topography, buildings, plots and lots, open spaces and movement networks, such as streets and pedestrian lanes over time, be that years, decades or centuries (Moudon, 1997). The second component, land tenure, seeks to analyse the relationships people form with land by focusing on evolving social rules and legal systems that govern land use, ownership and, where applicable, property rights (Payne, 2004). Housing, the third component, seeks to identify the links between housing availability, affordability, quality of construction and the degree to which location impacts upon exposure to hazards. The fourth and final component is the physical adequacy of built assets such as hospitals, police stations and other emergency services designed to support city inhabitants when shocks and stresses occur.

A systems approach to understanding Port Vila's vulnerabilities within the built environment points to a number of concerns such as land grabbing, challenges related to working with rules from constitutional forms of tenure and *kastom*, hazard vulnerability, and a dearth of data related to land and property tenure. The discussion about the built environment focuses on two vulnerabilities. The first of which is hazard vulnerability, stemming from the location of Port Vila's city footprint (coastal and near fault lines) and subsequent high exposure to multiple hazards. According to a report, *Risk Mapping and Planning for Urban Preparedness* (Beca and NIWA, 2016), carried out for the Vanuatu Meteorological and Geo-hazards Department, 85 percent of the city is exposed to moderate levels of risk from earthquakes and wind while 15 percent is exposed to very high levels of risk, based on a 100-year mean return period. Vulnerability to hazards is increased when the quality of public and private buildings is low, building codes either do not exist or are not enforced, and the ability for the public to access information about risk is hindered, among other factors.

A second key vulnerability arises from a low level of available land and property administration data. The United Nations Economic Commission for Europe (UNECE) defines land administration as 'the process of determining, recording and disseminating information about ownership, value and use of land and its associated resources' (United Nations, 1996: 108). It is based on the belief that formal systems are necessary to register land and property, and that an effective land administration system fulfills the following criteria (United Nations, 1996: 7):

1. Guarantee ownership and security of tenure
2. Support land and property taxation
3. Provide security for credit
4. Develop and monitor land markets

5. Protect state lands
6. Reduce land disputes
7. Facilitate land reform
8. Improve urban planning and infrastructure development
9. Support environmental management
10. Produce statistical data

UN-Habitat argues that 'an effective administrative system for land is an essential part of resilience-building', highlighting the need for land surveys, records, awareness raising and increasing government capacity in relevant departments and bodies as a means of preventing and mitigating disasters (UN-Habitat, 2018: np).

When data is not reliable it cannot effectively mitigate and prevent the negative consequences of disasters. A 2015 climate change vulnerability report by RMIT University and UN-Habitat notes that existing data related to informal land ownership (and housing) may not convey a true depiction of the reality of the nation's capital. The report concluded that based on the way census data questions are formulated, '54 per cent of households were excluded from land tenure classification statistics across Greater Port Vila' (Trundle and McEvoy, 2015: 32).

Similarly, stresses around land tenure ownership occur if rules and regulations around land use are not strictly enforced. Lawyer and anthropologist Dr. Siobhan McDonnell contends that land administration issues, including those within Port Vila, stem from the exploitation of land for personal and political gain in addition to challenges related to implementing property law and a limited ability to hold officials accountable based on a '"culture of complicity" in land administration agencies' (McDonnell, 2017: np). One such example took place in 2012 when the former Minister for Lands approved 190 urban state land leases to family members, business and political associates, including 40 staff in the Department of Lands and Ministry of Lands (McDonnell, 2017). This example of the state exercising its power over commercially viable municipal land underscores the complicated web of political, social and cultural interactions that shape the ways in which the built environment is managed. Understanding corruption and institutional behavioural norms are as important as understanding the physical vulnerabilities that shape land-related transactions.

Capacities identified in relation to land use include the nation's 2013 Land Use Planning Policy (Government of Vanuatu, 2013), which guides land use planning in rural and urban areas (including provincial centres), foreshore and coastal development, risk management, land leases and legislation, among other things. Also of importance is Vanuatu's Land Sector Framework (2009–2018), which is described in Beca and NIWA's 2016 *Urban Risk Management Strategy: Risk Mapping and Planning for Urban Preparedness Report* as a critical step towards securing a 'sound foundation to integrate land use planning responses which promote resilience in Vanuatu's urban areas' while taking care to highlight that 'implementation of the existing legislation is weak' (Beca and NIWA, 2016: iii).

The report also notes that while land use planning is an appropriate tool for managing risks related to liquefaction and debris resulting from slope collapses, it does not address all issues to do with land, requiring other approaches such as development controls to address issues of seismic shaking in new and existing buildings. The resilience of the built environment also requires a strong community and individual approach that can be fuelled by providing public access to information about land, including the nature, frequency and location of risk. Drawing on community knowledge, kinship networks and local culture is an integral approach to reducing risk through disaster preparedness and mitigation, climate change adaptation and urban planning activities, especially when combined with top-down policy approaches (Rey et al., 2017).

Analysing the built environment as a system therefore highlights that institutional culture and behavioural norms shape the ways in which land tenure is understood and managed. Analysis of the land tenure component indicates the potential for reducing corruption by improving the accuracy of land and property data, and improving systems for gathering and storing it. The chapter will next provide a discussion of Port Vila's social inclusion and protection system.

System Two: Social Inclusion and Protection

The focus of a social inclusion and protection system is that of social resilience and the ways in which social safety nets are inclusively set up to meet the needs of the most vulnerable and marginalised population groups in the city. In Port Vila, the local authority has an extremely limited budget and capacity to carry out a number of the activities that commonly occur in cities in high-income countries. The social inclusion and protection mechanisms used in present-day Port Vila were developed at the national level, as is the case in many cities around the world, requiring strong collaboration between national and municipal governments to ensure relevance and appropriateness. To that end, recognising scale as particularly important in this system, two components have been selected for analysis, with a view to understanding the impact of national policies on people living in Vanuatu's urban centres.

The first component is social accountability, whereby citizen engagement in institutional performance is interrogated (Fox, 2015). The second is access to social protection for all, whereby access to a guaranteed basic income and a minimum level of essential social services is analysed (ILO and UNDG, 2014). For the purposes of this chapter, the linkages between social protection floors and basic services will be highlighted using an example of how national healthcare policies and activities may require adaptation to urban contexts.[3] This section endeavours to provide examples of vulnerabilities and capacities within social accountability, social protection floors and access to basic services, using healthcare as an example. Social inclusion is an integral concept running throughout the discussion with consideration of marginalised and vulnerable groups.

Social Accountability

Social accountability presupposes that institutions are clear about who is accountable and for what. It consists of institutions that are open to feedback and willing to adapt their actions based on advice from constituents. Effective enacting of social accountability mechanisms holds individuals, organisations and government bodies accountable for their actions by safely reporting concerns, complaints and abuses with the expectation of redress, where appropriate (Callamard, 2003). In essence, social accountability builds urban resilience through the exchange of information, good communication, awareness-raising, capacity building and knowledge generation with diverse stakeholders (Arroyo and Sirker, 2005).

An example of accountability capacity within Port Vila is that of a formal grievance redress mechanism (GRM). According to the World Bank, a grievance redress mechanism is a 'locally based, formalized way to accept, assess, and resolve community feedback or complaints' (Brown et al., 2014: 1). The Vanuatu Office of the Ombudsman, which is a national-level function, fulfils such a role at a municipal level through offices in Port Vila and Luganville. The Ombudsman is tasked with investigating complaints against public bodies such as government departments, agencies and ministries; public servants; leaders from provincial councils, municipalities, and statutory bodies and their board of directors; and companies partially or wholly owned by the government of Vanuatu. Issues of language rights are also investigated. The Ombudsman attempts to mediate complaints, and if they cannot be resolved, writes a preliminary report with recommendations, followed by a second report that is made public.

Vulnerabilities identified within this formal social-accountability mechanism relate to what the Ombudsman is tasked to do versus what happens in reality. The 2014 Vanuatu National Integrity System Assessment report notes that in addition to limited human resource capacity, the Ombudsman's office generally experiences a lack of follow-up by government bodies (the legislature, the executive, and other local or national agencies and departments that have had complaints lodged against them) on reports issued by the Ombudsman's office (Jowitt, 2014). Transparency International Vanuatu suggests that the ability to hold leadership to account is a barrier to improving social accountability, citing an example where leaders are required to 'file annual returns disclosing assets and liabilities' however, 'the law does not permit routine scrutiny of these returns' (Jowitt, 2014: 16). The Asian Development Bank points to culture, and in this instance, the significant role it can play in reducing the ways in which individuals and civil society organisations (CSOs) hold government to account noting that 'the culture of *wantok* and reciprocal obligation of clan and kin can impact on the ability of CSO staff to speak out against wrongdoing' (ADB, 2017: np). Further research that details the roles of *wantok* systems and NGOs in Port Vila is available and important to consider when looking at other forms of social accountability outside of official government redress mechanisms.

Access to Social Protection Floors for All and Access to Basic Social Services

Here a systems approach is used to analyse formal government mechanisms developed at a national level to address poverty, income inequality and social inclusion at various scales, with a specific focus on urban centres. A social protection floor can be defined as a national government policy to achieve developmental rights for the most vulnerable and marginalised, ensuring a minimum income and access to essential basic services through cash or in-kind assistance (ILO and WHO, 2009). Basic social services guarantee the protection of developmental rights through access to education, health care, social care and other protective services. such as those related to nutrition and food provision. Marginalised and vulnerable groups typically assisted through social protection include children, older people, persons with disabilities, informal workers and non-nationals, as outlined by the United National Office of the High Commissioner (OCHR, 2015). Historically and in the present day, most forms of social protection within Port Vila, and indeed across the country, come from social and cultural networks. However, this section focuses on formal basic services and mechanisms of protection delivered by the national government and its impact on municipal trends in terms of vulnerability and capacity.

Examples of vulnerability within health care in Port Vila, and Vanuatu more broadly, include a lack of equitable access to affordable health care facilities that are adequately resourced and equipped, limited health sector management capacity, and the need to reduce communicable and non-communicable diseases and improve overall health and well-being through the promotion of healthy lifestyle choices (WHO-Vanuatu, 2017). A more specific example is the need to refocus traditional approaches to HIV and AIDs awareness based on the demographics of the city. As of 2015, nine HIV-positive cases were reported nationally (the actual number is thought to be much higher) (WHO, 2018).

While there are a number of high-risk groups for transmission, one of the most difficult to communicate with in Port Vila is that of sex workers. Sex work is thought to have increased as a result of urbanisation, tourism, development, high unemployment rates, family violence and alcohol use (McMillan and Worth, 2011). Transactional sex work takes place informally in urban *nakamals* (kava bars), nightclubs, on the street, and among bus and taxi drivers who offer free transport to primarily young women and girls in exchange for sex (Vanuatu Ministry of Health, 2016). In 2016, a Pacific multi-country mapping and behavioural study on HIV and STI risk vulnerability recorded 2,000 female sex workers and 600 men who have sex with men/transgendered people (MSM/TG), most of whom were from Port Vila (UNDP et al., 2016). In the Pacific, where few sex workers formally identify as such, HIV and AIDS prevention programmes and services must operate differently to target informal and loose networks of sex workers who infrequently work together.

Key capacities identified in Vanuatu's HIV and AIDS prevention and treatment programme include having domestic HIV policies and guidelines, established partnerships between agencies, monitoring and evaluation systems, and data collection (McMillan and Worth, 2011). Health-care workers (doctors, nurses and pharmacists) are reported to have received training on Vanuatu's National Guideline on the Use of Antiretroviral Drugs for Treating and Preventing HIV Infection (WHO, 2018). Further opportunities identified by the International HIV Research group at the University of New South Wales suggests the Vanuatu Ministry of Health and the Vanuatu Family Health Association engage key population groups, especially MSM/TG, a group currently not engaged by either actor (McMillan and Worth, 2011).

This section drew upon examples of social accountability and the healthcare mechanisms for people with HIV and AIDs in an attempt to show that while Port Vila is host to a greater density of formalised social protection and inclusion infrastructure, it is also host to a greater diversity of norms, attitudes and behaviours which add dimensions of complexity to the ways in which social protection mechanisms serve the poorest and most vulnerable. Moreover, the impact of national policies and their ability to address urban vulnerability may require further nuancing to reflect trends within urban contexts.

System Three: Economy

Analysing information related to the economic composition of a city, such as its municipal finance and fiscal mechanisms, and the degree to which the local economy is connected to other markets, can provide an understanding of factors that influence economic resilience. While there are many ways to analyse urban economies, three key components have been selected to highlight economic vulnerabilities and capacities within Port Vila. These components include: local economic structure (a holistic assessment of how the economy is organised in terms of industries, business composition, labour and property markets); fiscal stability and municipal finance, which analyses the fiscal composition and financial capabilities of the local government; and market connectivity, wherein the intensity and efficacy of the local economy's connectivity to other markets is evaluated.

Economic Structure

Analysing the economic structure of an urban context is intended to evaluate the stability—and identify the potential vulnerabilities of—the local economy through a holistic assessment of market reliability. Common measures include diversity,[4] gross product and employment, as well as additional structural imbalances (inequality—that which is strictly based on income and that which is gender-related as well as the disconnect between income and real property value).

An evaluation of Port Vila's economic composition suggests key vulnerabilities may be related to median income (Vanuatu National Statistics Office and UNDP Pacific, 2013), limited manufacturing activity (Vanuatu National Statistics Office, 2011) and a nearly non-existent formal, circular economic activity (e.g., recycling, improved clustering and industrial integration).[5] While the existence of poverty exacerbates Port Vila's vulnerability to a range of hazards, its industrial composition, which requires greater dependency on international imports, restricts potential local capture of economic growth.

Housing affordability can serve as either a critical capacity or vulnerability for a city when facing complex, systemic impacts from different hazards. Although far from an ideal composition, the formal Port Vila housing market is relatively affordable given income trends. Although driven by a number of factors, housing affordability in Port Vila stems in large part from the ability for supply increase based on demand, through both formal and informal means. This flexibility within housing supply has allowed pricing levels to remain relatively in line with household income trends. In other words, while Port Vila must continue to cope with the stresses associated with informal housing, the low level of publicly subsidised housing and persistently high levels of poverty, the relatively low density and higher availability of land, in combination with communal living patterns and relatively inexpensive construction methods, help to control the increase in housing expenses. Although formal housing market prices have largely mirrored formal income patterns, the growth in informal housing, which is particularly focused on the urban periphery, remains a growing concern. While this chapter is focused on urban areas located within the municipal boundaries (where a relatively small proportion of households live in informal settlements), it is important to note that much of the recent housing expansion in the Greater Port Vila area has occurred in hazardous locations as well as on land with precarious tenure for many inhabitants, trends which should be closely monitored as the city continues to grow and market pressures build.

Fiscal Stability and Municipal Finance

An evaluation of the fiscal composition and financial capabilities of the local government allows for a holistic mapping of the revenue and expenditure composition of a local government, providing critical input for assessing its financial capacity and flexibility as it relates to service provision and capital investment. In particular, such an analysis is concerned with the composition of own-source revenues (i.e., generated through local taxes or fees), the distribution of expenditures to support municipal priorities and the extent to which a local government has access to, or is burdened from, public debt, among other relevant items.

Analysis of fiscal stability and municipal finance finds that the Port Vila Municipal Council (PVMC), like many local governments in the South Pacific, remains dependent on international funding sources for most capital investments and furthermore has a limited purview over service provision and a correspondingly minimal municipal budget. For instance, the PVMC has little responsibility for healthcare, education or the provision of basic utilities (water and electric), which are primarily overseen by the national government and a private utility company, respectively, resulting in a limited budgetary scope. Not only does such centralisation of service provision limit interaction between service delivery entities (duty bearers) and service recipients (rights holders), such a structure may exacerbate existing challenges related to social inclusion and protection stemming from national government and/or private enterprise provision of services. When duty-bearers (utility or other service providers in this case) are less connected to rights holders (service recipients) and limited redress mechanisms are available, the inclusion or coverage of all groups, especially those that are most vulnerable, is often more challenging. Furthermore, the PVMC budget remains largely incapable of supporting new initiatives or investing in medium- and long-term resilience-building efforts. Exacerbating this limitation is that property and land tax revenues, the primary source of fiscal revenues, are derived from aging parcel records and relies on ineffective collection processes.[6] The result is a gross shortfall in potential revenues. While revising collection methods would be both complex and challenging, requiring comprehensive mapping (and ongoing tracking and subsequent revision) of all existing structures and land records, investment could potentially be recouped through increased revenues stemming from a broadened tax base.

Despite these limitations, the PVMC possess two key interconnected fiscal capacities: a very high proportion of the municipal budget is derived from own-source revenues (as noted previously, primarily derived from land and property taxes) and a high level of expenditures are discretionary (i.e., resources are not earmarked or appropriated, but may be allocated at PVMC's discretion through budgetary processes) fiscal autonomy and flexibility. This combination provides the PVMC extensive flexibility and fiscal autonomy in prioritizing resources.

Market Connectivity

The third component, market connectively, evaluates the intensity and efficacy of the local economy's connectivity to other markets, be they regional, national or global. In this effort, connectivity (or access) is assessed at the local level (in terms of access to financial services such as banking) and at the regional and global scale through the mapping of linkages to other markets and analysis of goods movement (imports and exports).

Analysis of market connectivity suggests Port Vila is highly dependent on external markets for items such as diesel, gasoline, automobiles and textiles, among other things (MIT Atlas on Economic Complexity, 2018), which has led to inadequate market competition and workforce capacity (i.e., local workers lack the skills required to meet market demands). Like most South Pacific cities, Port Vila's economy primarily relies on low-value services such as tourism along with public-sector employment. Limited local manufacturing and other high-value-added industries correspond to the city's need to import the majority of high-value goods (cars, appliances, machine parts, agricultural equipment, pharmaceuticals, etc.) to meet demand. In relation to this import dependency, and given the relatively small market that Port Vila comprises, there is limited competition among local industries (e.g., there is a single utility provider), resulting in minimal innovation as well as workforce development and investment. Such import dependency, along with limited competition and minimal workforce capacity, increase the local economy's vulnerability to fluctuations in both the Port Vila and global economies. The local, provincial and national government could collaboration and prioritise investment in local economic and workforce development in order to build a more flexible, integrated, complex, and therefore resilient, local economy.

Numerous capacities fundamental to building a more resilient economy have also been identified through a systems analysis. One such capacity relates to the degree to which Port Vila has access to, and is integrated within, the formal banking system. While other, less recognised forms of banking are also present in the local economy (informal lending, investment, collective ownership, etc.), it is nonetheless an important attribute for a local economy to provide access to financial services for both individuals and businesses. Port Vila features a relatively high level of inclusion in formal banking (e.g., number of individuals who possess and regularly access a formal bank account), access (e.g., the number of ATMs present in the city) and access to mobile vending practices (Reserve Bank of Vanuatu, 2016). These capacities both provide the potential for investment in new industries and innovation of industry practices, and provide capacity for both industry and individuals to cope with the impacts of different shocks.

The financial infrastructure in place in Port Vila suggests that with greater market competition and a workforce possessing capacities better suited to local market demands, there exist local economic development opportunities that could be supported through focused and sustained governmental support.

Discussion

The systems analysis undertaken in this chapter aimed to demonstrate that a systems approach may be one of many approaches that can assist with unpacking urban resilience, specifically the underlying factors that create patterns of vulnerability and capacity. A systems approach underscores the importance of interrogating problems at different scales in order to identify links, overlaps and processes that influence parts of the city as well as the whole. This chapter focused on formal government activities, mechanisms, and policies and therefore primarily touched upon overlaps between municipal and national scales. However, further research could seek to explore complexity at an individual, household, neighbourhood and provincial level.

Overall, a systems approach recognises that cities are dynamic and unpredictable. Placing urban complexity into social, physical, political, economic and cultural categories may assist with understanding changes that have taken place over time, offering a better understanding of why a city operates as it does today. It also highlights that a problem such the lack of enforcement of rules and regulations in one system can be expected in other systems and their respective components. Understanding urban complexity from a systems approach may also provide space for development and disaster management practitioners to shift from single-sector analysis to a more integrated approach that can better support governments and communities to cope with multifaceted problems such as poverty, climate change and income inequality (Sitko and Goudswaard, 2019). Such attempts at operationalising systems approaches are already being made, as is demonstrated by the *City Resilience Framework (2014)* by Arup and the Rockefeller Foundation, the Global Alliance for Urban Crises (a network of 70 institutions from government, the private sector and non-for profits) as outlined in its document *Building Resilience in the Face of Urban Crises*, (Sitko and Massella, 2019) and organisations such as Mercy Corps' *Resilience Framework* (2018) and *Strategic Resilience Assessment Guidelines* (Levine et al., 2017), which are based on a systems approach.

Notes

1. Urban resilience can be defined as 'the capacity of cities to function, so that the people living and working in cities—particularly the poor and vulnerable—survive and thrive no matter what stresses or shocks they encounter' (Arup and Rockefeller, 2015: 3). Other useful definitions include UN-Habitat's understanding of urban resilience as 'the measurable ability of any urban system, with its inhabitants, to maintain continuity through all shocks and stresses, while positively adapting and transforming toward sustainability' (UN-Habitat, 2018).
2. UN-Habitat's City Resilience Profiling Tool (CRPT) maps the ways in which urban systems operate and influence one another. The CRPT sets out a framework for measuring how systems maintain continuity amidst shocks and stresses. Drawing on global frameworks such as the New Urban Agenda, Paris Agreement, Sustainable Development Goals and Sendai Framework, the tool aims to bridge development and disaster paradigms through the analysis of shocks and stresses together. It uses a multi-sectorial and multi-scalure approach, engaging stakeholders from the built environment, infrastructure, communications and those working on social, political, economic and environmental issues.
3. The CRPT analyses social protection and basic services separately.
4. The extent to which economic activity of a given defined geography is distributed among a number of categories such as industries, sectors, skill levels and employment levels.
5. Key informant interview (2018) conducted by the authors.
6. Key informant interview (2018) conducted by the authors.

References

Arroyo, D. and Sirker, K. (2005). *Stocktaking of Social Accountability Initiatives in the Asia and Pacific Region*. Washington, DC: The World Bank.

Arup and Rockefeller. (2015). *City Resilience Framework*. London: Arup and Rockefeller Foundation.

Asian Development Bank (ADB). (2012). *The State of Pacific Towns and Cities: Urbanization in ADB's Pacific Developing Member Countries*. Mandaluyong City: ADB.

Asian Development Bank (ADB). (2017). *Civil Society Briefs Vanuatu*. Sydney: ADB, np.

Asian Development Bank and Macintyre, M. (2012). Gender violence in Melanesia and the problem of millennium development goal no. 3. In M. Jolly, C. Stewart and C. Brewer (eds.), *Engendering Violence in Papua New Guinea*. Canberra: ANU E Press, 239–266.

Beca International Consultants (Beca) and GNS Science and the National Institute of Water and Atmospheric Research (NIWA). (2016). *Urban Risk Management Strategy: Risk Mapping and Planning for Urban Preparedness*. Online: Beca and NIWA.

Brown, M., Jenkins, B., Leon, P., Seyedian, A. and Inamdar, A. et al. (2014). *Global Review of Grievance Redress Mechanisms in World Bank Projects*. Washington, DC: World Bank Group.

Callamard, A. (2003). The HAP and humanitarian accountability. *The Humanitarian Exchange*, 23, 35–37. London: HPN.

Fox, J. (2015). Social accountability: What does the evidence really say? *World Development*, 72, 346–361.

Government of Vanuatu. (2013). *National Land Use Planning Policy*. Port Vila: Vanuatu Council of Ministers.

ILO and WHO. (2009). *The Social Protection Floor: A Joint Crisis Initiative of the UN Chief*. Executives Board for Co-ordination on the Social Protection Floor. Geneva: ILO and WHO.

International Labour Organisation (ILO) and United Nations Development Group (UNDG) Asia-Pacific. (2014). *UNDG Asia-Pacific Social Protection Issues Brief*. Bangkok: ILO.

Jones, P. (2016). *The Emergence of Pacific Urban Villages: Urbanization Trends in the Pacific Islands*. Pacific Studies Series. Manila: Asian Development Bank.

Jowitt, A. (2014). *National Integrity System Assessment Vanuatu 2014*. Port Vila: Transparency International Vanuatu.

Levine, E., et al. (2017). *Strategic Resilience Assessment Guidelines*. Portland: Mercy Corps.

McDonnell, S. (2017). Urban land grabbing by political elites: Exploring the political economy of land and the challenges of regulation. In S. McDonnell, M. Allen and C. Filer (eds.), *Kastom, Property and Ideology: Land Transformations in Melanesia*. Canberra: Australian National University Press, 283–304.

McMillan, K. and Worth, H. (2011). *Risky Business Vanuatu: Selling Sex in Port Vila*. Sydney: International HIV Research Group (UNSW).

Mercy Corps. (2018). *Mercy Corps' Resilience Framework*. Portland: Mercy Corps.

MIT Atlas on Economic Complexity. (2018). *Vanuatu*. Available at: https://atlas.media.mit.edu/en/profile/country/vut/.

Moudon, A.V. (1997). Urban morphology as an emerging interdisciplinary field. *Urban Morphology*, 1, 3–10.

Oliveira, V. (2016). *Urban Morphology: An Introduction to the Study of the Physical Form of Cities*. The Urban Book Series. Geneva: Springer.

Payne, G. (2004). Land tenure and property rights: An introduction. *Habitat International*, 28(2), 167–179.

Reserve Bank of Vanuatu. (2016). *Financial Services Demand Side Survey, Vanuatu*. Suva: Pacific Financial Inclusion Programme.

Rey, T., Le De, L. and Gilbert, D. (2017). An integrative approach to understand vulnerability and resilience post-disaster: The 2015 cyclone Pam in urban Vanuatu as case study. *Disaster Prevention and Management: An International Journal*, 26(3), 259–275.

Rossi, A. (1982). *The Architecture of the City*. Boston: MIT Press.

Sitko, P. and Goudswaard, S. (2019). *Development in the Urban Era: Six Strategies for Better Managing Urbanisation in Asia and the Pacific*. Sydney: RDI Network.

Sitko, P. and Massella, A. (2019). *Building Urban Resilience in the Face of Crisis: A Focus on People and Systems*. Geneva: Global Alliance for Urban Crises.

Trundle, A. and McEvoy, D. (2015). *Greater Port Vila Climate Vulnerability Assessment: Full Report (2015)*. Melbourne: RMIT and UN-Habitat.

UNDP, UNICEF and UNSW. (2016). *Pacific Multi-Country Mapping and Behavioural Study: HIV and STI Risk Vulnerability among Key Populations—Vanuatu*. Port Vila: UNDP, UNICEF and UNSW.

UN-Habitat. (2018). *City Resilience Profiling Tool*. Barcelona: UN-Habitat.

United Nations. (1996). *Land Administration Guidelines: With Special Reference to Countries in Transition*. New York: UNECE.

United Nations Office of the High Commissioner. (2015). *Social Protection Floors and Economic and Social Rights*. Geneva: OHCR.

Vanuatu Ministry of Health. (2016). *Global AIDS Monitoring Report for Vanuatu*. Port Vila: Vanuatu Ministry of Health.

Vanuatu National Statistics Office (VNSO). (2011). *2009 National Population and Housing Census (VNSO)*. Port Vila: VNSO.

Vanuatu National Statistics Office and UNDP Pacific. (2013). *2010 Household Income and Expenditure Survey*. Port Vila: Vanuatu National Statistics Office.

Vanuatu National Statistics Office (VNSO). (2014). *2009 Census Data Extracts—Greater Port Vila by Enumeration Area*. Unpublished—Spreadsheet Format (.xls) supplied to RMIT University, extracted July 25, 2014.

Vanuatu National Statistics Office (VNSO). (2016). *Vanuatu 2016 Post TC Pam Mini-Census Report*. Port Vila: VNSO.

Verisk Maplecroft. (2015). *Natural Hazards Risk Atlas*. Available at: https://www.maplecroft.com/insights/analysis/which-cities-are-most-exposed-to-natural-hazards/.

WHO. (2018). *Strengthening HIV Services in Vanuatu*. Online: WHO.

WHO-Vanuatu. (2017). *Country Cooperation Strategy 2018–2022*. Port Vila: WHO-Vanuatu.

Chapter 7

'This Is Our Garden Now'

Disasters and Belonging in an Urban Pacific

Jennifer Day and Tom Bamforth

The Problem: Unseen Urban Populations in Crisis

This chapter articulates a set of understandings about the structure of social life and governance in Pacific cities, and about in-built biases in the humanitarian system, that have created urban populations that are in part invisible and in part excluded from receiving emergency assistance during crises. The authors hope that this articulation will help make these populations more easily seen by humanitarians and governments so that they are targeted for assistance in the critical weeks after humanitarian emergencies occur.

We centre our narrative following a humanitarian emergency in Vanuatu, discussing similarities in other urban Pacific responses where relevant. We also focus specifically on the shelter component of humanitarian response. In April 2015, one month after the Category 5 Tropical Cyclone Pam (TCP) made landfall in Vanuatu, the Shelter Cluster became aware of a peri-urban population with significant post-disaster needs that was living within a ten-minute drive of the country's Parliament and National Disaster Management Office, and which had not received emergency shelter distributions. This was despite the presence in Vanuatu of more than 25 NGOs working in the shelter sector, and at least six countries' militaries (Australia, New Zealand, the USA, France, United Kingdom and Tonga) offering emergency assistance and aid.

Vanuatu is a South Pacific country comprised of 82 islands and 283,000 people (WorldOMeters, 2018). Roughly 16–25 percent of the population lives in the capital city, Port Vila (Jones and Sanderson, 2017; Vanuatu National Statistics Office, 2017). The 2016 Mini Census estimates the population of Port Vila to be 51,437 (Vanuatu National Statistics Office, 2017: 96). Jones and Sanderson (2017) estimate around 15,000 people live in the peri-urban communities that surround Port Vila. The Pacific region hosts some of the fastest urban growth in the world, with an overall average growth at around four percent annually and double-digit growth in peri-urban areas (Jones and Sanderson, 2017).

A critical part of the reflection about urban disasters, such as TC Pam that struck Port Vila, is how, in such an aid-rich environment, an urban neighbourhood could be overlooked by the humanitarian community and its own government for a month before receiving relief. These were not unknown places: Blacksands is the oldest permanent settlement of rural-urban migrants in Port Vila (Mecartney, 2000: 57). Directly adjacent, the settlement Manples is one of the fastest growing. These communities have housed migrants from Vanuatu's outer islands since at least the 1960s. As we argue in the remainder of this chapter, the neglect of Blacksands and Manples appears to be an unfortunate confluence of a rural bias within humanitarian aid, an intentional direction of resources by government away from these particular peri-urban settlements and a feeling by members of the community that they did not *belong* to the city. The chapter originated as a discussion between the two authors, both humanitarian practitioners, who in 2015 were trying to address a specific issue about urban response in Vanuatu. The chapter represents the course this discussion has taken— which we believe sheds light on wider cultural and contextual aspects of urban humanitarian action in the Pacific—and documents, through praxis, the evolution of an idea rather than an exposition of an argument.

Our Situatedness

This chapter is based on personal experiences of the authors during TC Pam—working directly with disaster-affected communities (Day) and in coordinating multiple humanitarian responses in the Pacific (Bamforth). What follows is intended as a reflection on the practice of international humanitarian aid in the Pacific, and the authors draw on TC Pam in Vanuatu as a basis for illustrating more generalisable trends in urban humanitarian response across the region. We contend that both the humanitarian community and government failed to 'see' (observe and acknowledge) thousands of people living close to the logistical centre of the humanitarian response. We further contend that the decision not to take urban needs seriously was possible because of the combination of governance gaps, the in-built rural bias in humanitarian programming, and the relative absence in Pacific countries that an urban identity can be articulated and extended. That the oversight was 'discovered' was an accident, and this chapter proposes some ways in which humanitarian action and advocacy will need to change in order to keep pace with rapid levels of urbanisation in the Pacific.

Jennifer Day is an academic who was in the process of designing a programme of academic work in Port Vila, the capital city of Vanuatu, prior to TC Pam, and who visited the city repeatedly during the emergency response. Tom Bamforth was, at the time, the Shelter Cluster Coordinator for the emergency response. One month after the cyclone, in collaboration with colleagues from Oxfam, in mid-May 2015, Day conducted a field survey in two peri-urban communities, Manples and Blacksands. The purpose of the survey was to substantiate her observation, made while visiting friends after the cyclone, that these communities had not received humanitarian shelter assistance. As an outcome of that survey, based on a rough estimate of sampled population densities, land area and the 2009 Census numbers, the estimate was that more than 6,000 people located in these communities—within a ten-minute drive of the National Disaster Management Office of Vanuatu in peri-urban Port Vila—had not received emergency shelter distributions.[1] No tarpaulins were on display in these communities, and survivors reported no visits from government or humanitarian actors. Survivors had largely rebuilt their *one-day houses* (a local term for houses built in a day) from scavenged building materials, much of which had been damaged in the cyclone. The repaired homes were incomplete and lacked walls, privacy and adequate roofing. Water intrusion through poorly repaired roofs threatened the health, belongings and assets of local residents. Figure 7.1 shows an image from Day's fieldwork in May 2015, of homes in Blacksands rebuilt without humanitarian assistance.

This initial observation—which can form the basis for humanitarian decision-making in the immediate aftermath of disasters where information is scarce—was subsequently verified by more-formal assessment processes. The government of Vanuatu/World Bank Post Disaster Needs Assessment (PDNA) drew attention to widespread damage around Port Vila and to the extensive informal and peri-urban settlements around the capital (Government of Vanuatu, 2015: 37). The Shelter Cluster Assessment in April 2015 found that 95 percent of housing had been damaged in urban Port Vila, of which 30 percent was destroyed, while 65 percent of households had not received emergency assistance (Shelter Cluster, 2015).

This paper consequently draws on the authors' personal reflections of their involvement in the response and subsequent discussions about the nature, biases and reasons for the omission of urban communities from response prioritisation more generally in the Pacific. Importantly, this was not an underfunded or under-resourced response, especially during the emergency phase. On the contrary, in her influential review of the humanitarian response, Barber (2015) criticized the excessive importation of aid structures, systems and financial resources into a small island state. This unusually resource-intensive context, where decisions were not made solely in order to make the most effective use of insufficient resources, provides a unique vantage point for practitioners themselves to reflect on how and why humanitarian decisions were made.

Rural Bias in Humanitarian Assistance

It turns out that the peri-urban communities of Blacksands and Manples had remained unallocated by aid agencies, whose attention was focused outside of the capital and its immediate surrounds. This direction of attention to outer islands is not unusual, and occurred in Cyclones Winston (Fiji, 2016)

Figure 7.1 Two Months After TCP, Many Homes in Blacksands Were Rebuilt Without Humanitarian Assistance. (Note the lack of tarpaulins.)

Source: Jennifer Day (2015)

and Gita (Tonga, 2016). On the part of aid agencies, this reflects a default position that vulnerability is, in large part, a product of distance from a capital city.

The Shelter Cluster is a coordination platform for humanitarian actors that supports government to manage emergency response in the shelter and settlements sector. In the early phases of the humanitarian response in Vanuatu, aid agencies in the Shelter Cluster largely provided tarpaulins to allow people to escape the elements and regain privacy. In later stages of an emergency, shelter assistance can also include building materials and tools, and technical or cash assistance for rebuilding. Generally, and in Vanuatu, the direct providers of this assistance are NGOs. Part of the role of a Shelter Cluster Coordinator is to ensure that geographic coverage of affected communities is as extensive as possible and is not duplicated. In Vanuatu, Bamforth and the Shelter Cluster achieved this by parsing the capital city and the outer islands and assigning various geographic segments to NGOs with the capacity to deliver shelter materials to those places. This initial geographical division of responsibilities between aid agencies initially excluded peri-urban Blacksands and Manples, which were never allocated to a responsible aid organisation.

Rural bias in humanitarian assistance does not tell us the whole story of Blacksands and Manples' non-allocation within the Shelter Cluster: other peri-urban communities in Port Vila were allocated to humanitarian organisations. For instance, humanitarian shelter distributions occurred in the peri-urban communities of Beverly Hills and in the peri-urban villages of Pango, Eratap and Erakor. In the next section, we describe the government's role in their non-allocation.

The Government's Rural Focus

The non-allocation of Blacksands and Manples to a responsible NGO for shelter response was not simply an oversight by the Shelter Cluster Coordinator and the cooperating NGOs. Rather, Bamforth—unfamiliar with these settlements and with limited information—acted under instruction by the government to focus relief on the outer islands. National government personnel working in the National Disaster Management Office (NDMO) at the time stated that, because of their proximity to town, people in Blacksands and Manples would not struggle to obtain building materials and other emergency aid. Working from the coordinator's office inside the NDMO headquarters, Bamforth was unable to verify the information he received from government workers until he received Day's field report. Acting under his organisation's[2] mandate to support the government, he had no reason to distrust this information. In the government-led response to Cyclones Winston and Gita, Bamforth received a similar prevailing sense from the government that urban communities, who often work in a monetised economy rather than a subsistence one, were wealthier and could cope on their own.

Governments in the Pacific, including in Vanuatu, have historically been reluctant to govern the cities. Port Vila, for instance, does not currently have a building code or town plan (Cullwick, 2017). At the time of the TC Pam response in 2015, the latest available census estimates of population were from 2009. They were outdated and inaccurate. The Shelter Cluster was working with population estimates for these peri-urban areas that enumerated the population at about one-third of the actual population.

Urban growth outpaces rural growth in all eight South Pacific countries except Samoa (Keen and Barbara, 2015). These dense settlements host a large portion of the urban population—within the Port Vila municipal boundary, the 2015 PDNA found that 49 percent of residents lived without formal tenure in more than 30 informal settlements, with an unknown number living beyond the formal urban limits (Government of Vanuatu, 2015: 35). Yet most countries in the South Pacific do not have government ministries that are dedicated to urban development (Keen and Barbara, 2015), and as the census estimates at the time of TC Pam illustrates, there is often little official awareness of the rate and extent of population growth on the urban periphery.

The government's rural focus around TC Pam must be explained in the context of the complexities of land at the edge of Port Vila. Pacific countries, including Vanuatu, often acknowledge both customary and introduced land ownership systems in their constitutions. Most land belongs by default to its customary owners, while land belonging to the state is often limited to the central business district of major cities. The boundaries of Port Vila were delineated through the Land Reform Order No. 26 of 1981, shortly after the country achieved independence in 1980. The Constitution of the Republic of Vanuatu (Comparative Constitutions Project, 2019) states that all land in Vanuatu belongs to its indigenous custom owners and their descendants (article 73). The land on which the capital sits is designated as municipal land that is effectively owned by the state. Peri-urban lands adjacent to the municipal boundary remain under customary ownership. The communities noted in this paper, Blacksands and Manples, sit on customary lands, though many of the residents are not customary owners. That is, they may have customary lands on other islands, but they live in these peri-urban settlements under various tenure arrangements, from formal leaseholds to informal agreements and squatting.

In contrast to Blacksands and Manples, peri-urban settlements that were provided with humanitarian shelter assistance after TC Pam—such as Beverly Hills—tend to have tenures that are formalised in the introduced system of land leases. As humanitarian response and development programmes focus on customary landowners or those with formal leaseholds, substantial numbers of people living in settlements on the urban periphery tend to be overlooked and are made even more marginal, as they may have little or no legal tenure.

It would be an oversimplification to say that Blacksands and Manples are 'informal settlements', if the term is used to denote squatting (Regenvanu, 2017). Tenure arrangements on these customary lands are also a product of both the introduced and the customary systems. Settlement occurs under a wide range of processes that include oral permission with no financial exchange, exchange of non-monetary products such as garden produce or monetary exchange. Under the introduced system, customary landowners may enter into formal long-term lease arrangements for periods of up to 75 years. In actuality, very few settlements in Vanuatu are occupied by squatters (Regenvanu, 2017). Still, there are currently rumours of pending evictions of 'squatters' in Blacksands.

Another issue, in addition to the perceived informality of Blacksands and Manples, is political representation. Despite the customary formality of these settlements and although many people reside permanently in the city, they often still vote on their home islands. Politicians directing incoming emergency aid from the capital have strong incentives to be seen to be doing something for their island constituencies. In 2015, no department of government—national, provincial or municipal—was responsible for managing the growth and planning of the peri-urban settlements around Port Vila (Personal discussion with the then-Director of Local Authorities, Ms. Cherol Ala, May 2015).

Belonging in the City

Belonging to the city as voters and formal leaseholders is part of a more-complicated story about belonging in Port Vila. In this section, we describe how people's feelings of belonging—and a *politics of belonging*—impacted Blacksands and Manples residents' willingness to ask for humanitarian assistance, and indeed, believe that they were entitled to it.

People in Vanuatu are attuned to having a place where they belong—known locally (in Bislama) as a *man ples* (Bonnemaison, 1985; Jones, 2016). These places of belonging are generally associated with their home islands—not the city. A product of this association with other places is that many people do not feel that they *belong* to the city. Here, we use Yuval-Davis' (2006) construction of belonging. Yuval-Davis disaggregates feelings of belonging into three analytical levels and advocates study at all of these. Belonging as a *social location* is a composition of multiple social constructions that may change over a person's lifetime. In Pacific cities, being a rural migrant is one such construction, as are gender, class and sexual preference. She points out that some aspects of social location are more prominent than others in certain discourses. In Blacksands and Manples, for instance, the belonging generated from status as a rural migrant was particularly salient in the context of a humanitarian emergency.

For instance, in the same trip where Day documented the people living without assistance after TC Pam, one Blacksands resident and customary owner told her how the original customary arrangement allowed three or four families to reside on a particular piece of land. Three decades later, there are 40 people and at least eight families now living in one-day houses on the same piece of land. When most of these homes were destroyed in TC Pam, both the customary owner and the migrants began to question the arrangement. The landowner wanted to limit the reconstruction of permanent structures—structures like the community's concrete-block church, which had safeguarded some members of the community during the cyclone—in order that future displacements of the additional population would be easier should he wish to initiate them at another time. Accustomed to thinking about their *man ples* outside the city and themselves as squatters in Blacksands, the residents in the overstressed communities did not seek assistance from the humanitarian community or the government. Instead, they rebuilt both their houses and their expectations similarly to how that had been before: in a precarious equilibrium that could change with the next cyclone or the whim of the landowner.

Emerging belonging among peri-urban residents can be aligned with another of Yuval-Davis' constructions of belonging, on identification and emotional attachment. The Pacific is witnessing the development of a greater urban consciousness as city-life becomes more common and more entrenched among the post-independence generations. As concepts of being and belonging evolve, *man ples* may also be coming to refer to urban communities as well. Despite feelings that their current settlements had outgrown the original customary arrangements, people in Port Vila are emotionally attached to their urban communities and the resources they have emplaced there in the form of housing and rents. Identity is more complex, but there is evidence that identity is expanding to encompass urban livelihoods and multiculturalism. For instance, a now-common T-shirt design among young people has the language, 'Straight Outta Blacksans'—representation of an urban neighbourhood as a form of identity. 'We are not from the islands anymore; this is our garden now', Bamforth was told by a gang member in an informal settlement in Port Moresby called Burns Peak. 'Gardening' in this encounter was useful euphemistically to refer to the gang's main source of income: petty theft, especially of mobile phones.

Yuval-Davis' third analytical level of belonging is related to how social location and emotional attachment/identify distinguish groups. Earlier, this chapter described how governance structures in Vanuatu create a vacuum of governance and political representation in the peri-urban settlements. That the Shelter Cluster was advised by the government to direct resources to the outer islands and not towards peri-urban settlements, suggests that a 'politics of belonging' (Yuval-Davis, 2006: 204) was at least partly responsible for creating a legitimate, urban 'us' that warranted humanitarian assistance and a migrant, peri-urban 'them' that did not. She ties this conception of belonging closely to notions of citizenship: full and legitimate belonging. Citizenship can be applied to many kinds of settings, including nations and cities (p. 206). Non-urban citizens excluded by political processes and humanitarian acquiescence to non-intervention appears to fit into these notions of belonging and citizenship.

Lessons for Humanitarians

As we have demonstrated, it is possible that responsibility for ensuring that urban people receive humanitarian assistance can be assumed by *nobody* in some places in the urban Pacific. How governance and belonging work in the Pacific gives some idea of how this could occur. This is, of course, a partial explanation—but one that may provide actionable ideas.

Here, we offer some suggestions on how humanitarian structures could leverage the these lessons about belonging in the context of Pacific governance and capacity so that humanitarian response is more responsive to an urbanizing Pacific. As we discuss in this section, there are already some good humanitarian tools and processes developed that can capture the needs of informal and semi-formal places like Blacksands and Manples, including those not enumerated in census data. Still, the experience in Vanuatu suggests that something else is needed to ensure that they receive attention in humanitarian emergencies. It is beyond our scope here to assert whether further efforts should be in the form of preparedness or government accountability, new tools or some other intervention. Instead, our assertions focus on what agencies working at any of these levels should consider as they work to ensure that all urban people receive assistance in humanitarian emergencies.

Recognising Urban Man Ples

As we have described previously, a feeling of belonging is missing in many urban communities in the Pacific—but there are suggestions that urban identity is emerging. Humanitarians should seek to understand, support and advocate for urban belonging as a part of humanitarian response. Humanitarians have an existing suite of tools to advocate for urban belonging. There is an increasing legal basis for the 'right to housing' that underpins the advocacy role shelter agencies and the Shelter Cluster can play in addressing land tenure and housing issues in disaster response. These include the 'right to adequate housing' in the International Covenant on Economic, Social and Cultural Rights (ICESCR; United Nations Office of the High Commissioner for Human Rights, 1966) and the Pinheiro Principles (United

Nations Economic and Social Council, 2005), which protect the right to property restitution for refugees and displaced people, and the *Guiding Principles on Internal Displacement* (United Nations, 1998). These rights-based approaches underpin the shelter component of the Sphere Standards that provides guidance for all humanitarian agencies on minimum standards and principles in humanitarian response (Sphere, 2018). The right to adequate housing is based on the right to live somewhere in security, peace and dignity (and the right to non-discrimination in this context).

Crucially, these criteria also define housing—rather than shelter—more comprehensively, linking it with other human rights such freedom of movement. This underpins a core element of shelter programming and advocacy in general, which is that shelter and housing are embedded progressively within community rehabilitation and is not a product or commodity for distribution. This provides shelter agencies with an entry point for programming, policy and advocacy, especially in urban settings (NRC/IFRC, 2016).

These rights-driven approaches do not yet address the lack of *feeling* among urban dwellers that they belong in the city. Recognition of urban *man ples* is an area where humanitarian guidance could contribute in the Pacific. There are starting points available—indications that exclusion of people from urban belonging is changing in the Pacific. The Elang Etas peri-urban community in Port Vila is a place where feelings of *man ples* seems to be forming among people. Families interviewed in subsequent research studies (Day and Wewerinke-Singh, 2019; Day et al., 2019) have described how they began paying for land under a customary arrangement in order to establish a *ples* for their children—because those children no longer have a place on their island. The community's founder—who had a dream in the 1990s about providing an affordable place for migrants to live near Port Vila—described how he made arrangements with a customary owner and under a lease arrangement to start clearing the jungle. So, when the peri-urban Elang Etas community faced an eviction threat in 2018, the Elang Etas Community Association (EECA) formed. This is a grass-roots community organisation which has initiated fundraising processes, opening a cava bar and has started to organise its constituents to advocate for water, transportation and economic development, in addition to land rights. EECA may be an example of how other urban communities in the region can claim their 'right to the city' (Harvey, 2003; Lefebvre, 1996) and start to generate urban identities that primarily tie people to the city rather than a home island. Civil society organisations should be engaged as a foundational part of the process of creating urban communities.

Building Local Capacity About Urban Belonging

Given the leadership of national governments in managing disaster response, both local and international aid agencies need to shape their responses around government policy, often incorporating its strengths, weaknesses, biases and blind spots. Following Cyclones Pam, Winston and Gita, humanitarian agencies followed official census statistics and political processes, which did not always reflect of the condition of urban people. Governments are the front line of any emergency response, and humanitarians are obliged honour their sovereignty, use their processes and support their aspirations. There are, however, important moments of advocacy during emergency responses, where humanitarians can inject a better understanding of belonging in cities.

Leveraging Institutional Change

While the training of aid workers is changing, the bulk of training and delivery models are still largely rural-focused—which means that aid workers do not often have an up-to-date working knowledge about how urban areas function in emergencies. The international humanitarian and development communities, however, have taken steps to begin addressing the particular problems of cities in crises. More could be done with these platforms to support urban belonging.

For instance, ALNAP, a global network of NGOs, intergovernmental organisations and donors seeking to improve humanitarian response, set up its Urban Response Community of Practice in acknowledgement that 'Urban areas and needs in crises differ in important ways from rural contexts, and force the humanitarian community to fundamentally rethink the way they can prepare for, and respond to, disasters and conflict in cities' (ALNAP, 2018). The Global Alliance for Urban Crises (GAUC) 'was established to bring together the different actors who can help to improve crisis preparedness and response in our increasingly urban world' (urbancrises. org). Humanitarian and development agencies have produced urban-specific toolkits, like the Urban Context Analysis Toolkit (Sage et al., 2017), which provides a guide for governments and humanitarians in providing assistance for people settled in cities either temporarily or permanently. The Regional Studies Association Research Network on Academic-Practitioner Collaboration for Urban Settlements, South Pacific (APCUS-SP; http://apcus.cdmps. org.au/), which emerged from the experience of responding to Cyclone Pam, is an academic-practitioner network founded by Day and Bamforth to create better connections between subject-area experts and humanitarians, government and aid counterparts.

The shelter sector has increasingly articulated the need to develop what are variously termed 'area-based', 'neighbourhood', 'integrated' or 'holistic' approaches to post-emergency programming and coordination. Importantly, aid agency response and recovery programmes remain focused on rural environments or camp settings; area-based approaches are an important step in adapting to the demands and complexities of urban response, often drawing on longer-term development approaches (Sanderson, 2017: 350–351).

With minor variations, these describe programming that is geographically targeted, participatory and multi-sectoral (Parker and Maynard, 2015: 4). The intent of area-based approaches is to enable agencies and coordinating platforms to meet the complexity of urban crises and to address meaningfully the common mantra of shelter-response agencies that it is 'more than just a roof'. The achievement of safe shelter, and ultimately housing, is predicated on the wider resources of the settlement including access to water, roads, markets, education, livelihoods, cultural and religious centres, and so forth. Additionally, area-based programming addresses a key criticism of the current cluster approach to coordination which is often sector-based and therefore approached through a silo (shelter agencies and WASH agencies reporting to their different cluster leads) and in which inter-cluster coordination is often weak. In providing a spatial framework for programming, coordination and analysis, agencies would be compelled to look at wider issues of settlement beyond a narrow sectoral focus and, in principle, accord better with patterns of human settlement (Setchell, 2018: 94).

These initiatives are much-needed and are positive first moves by the humanitarian sector. They require adjustment and expansion in the Pacific, however. Most of these approaches and platforms seem to take belonging as a given. That is, they appear to presume that people living in a city have an already-existing sense of belonging to the urban community, even if they lack formal tenure—that people require no recognition of their urban communities or support in asserting their presence as a community. Future iterations of area-based approaches could integrate concepts of belonging towards ensuring that people at the margins of Pacific cities never again go unseen by the humanitarian system.

Notes

1. The Vanuatu National Housing Corporation estimated 7,662 people and 1,568 households lived in the two communities in 2012 (Vanuatu National Housing Corporation, 2012).
2. Bamforth is employed by the International Federation of Red Cross and Red Crescent Societies (IFRC).

References

ALNAP. (2018). *Urban Response*. Available at: www.alnap.org/our-topics/urban-response.

Barber, R. (2015). *One Size Doesn't Fit All: Tailoring the International Response to the National Need Following Vanuatu's Cyclone Pam*. Available at: https://resourcecentre.savethechildren.net/node/9377/pdf/reflections-on-cyclone-pam_whs-v2.0-report.pdf.

Bonnemaison, J. (1985). The tree and the canoe: Roots and mobility in Vanuatu societies. *Pacific Viewpoint*, 26(1), 30–62.

Comparative Constitutions Project. (2019). *Vanuatu's Constitution of 1980 with Amendments through 2013.* Available at: www.constituteproject.org/constitution/Vanuatu_2013.pdf?lang=en.

Cullwick, J. (2017). Port Vila has no town plan: Town planner. *Vanuatu Daily Post,* 23 January.

Day, J. and Wewerinke-Singh, M. (2019). *Learning from the Urban Experience of Development-Induced Displacement: Toward More-Inclusive Displacement Policy in Vanuatu and the South Pacific.* Prepared as a background paper for the Global Report on Internal Migration 2018. Internal Displacement Monitoring Centre, Geneva.

Day, J., Wewerinke-Singh, M., and Price, S. (2019). Eviction is not a disaster. *Development Policy Review.* Published online on 30 July 2019. Print publication forthcoming.

Government of Vanuatu. (2015). *Vanuatu Post-Disaster Needs Assessment, Tropical Cyclone Pam, March 2015.* Port Vila: Prime Minister's Office.

Harvey, D. (2003). The right to the city. *International Journal of Urban and Regional Research,* 27(4), 939–941.

Jones, P. (2016). Informal urbanism as a product of socio-cultural expression: Insights from the Island Pacific. In S. Attia, S. Shabka, Z. Shafik and A. Ibrahim (eds.), *Dynamics and Resilience of Informal Areas: International Perspectives.* Switzerland: Springer, 165–181.

Jones, P. and Sanderson, D. (2017). Urban resilience: Informal and squatter settlements in the Pacific Region. *Development Bulletin,* 78, 11–15.

Keen, M. and Barbara, J. (2015). *Pacific Urbanisation: Changing Times.* In Brief, 2015/64, State, Society and Governance in Melanesia. Canberra: Australian National University.

Lefebvre, H. (1996). *Writings on Cities.* Oxford: Blackwell.

Mecartney, S.A.N. (2001). *Blacksands Settlement: A Case for Urban Permanence in Vanuatu.* Department of Geosciences, Division of Geography. Sydney: University of Sydney.

NRC/IFRC. (2016). *The Importance of Addressing Housing, Land, and Property Challenges in Humanitarian Response.* Available at: www.nrc.no/resources/reports/the-importance-of-addressing-housing-land-and-property-hlpchallenges-in-humanitarian-response/.

Parker, E. and Maynard, V. (2015). *Humanitarian Response to Urban Crises—A Review of Area Based Approaches.* IIED Working Paper.

Regenvanu, H.R. (2017). Foreward. In S. Mcdonnell, M. Allen and C. Filer (eds.), *Kastom, Property and Ideology: Land Transformations in Melanesia.* Canberra: Australian National University Press.

Sage, B., Meaux, A., Osofisan, W., Traynor, M., and Jove, T.R. (2017). *Urban Context Analysis Toolkit.* Available at: http://pubs.iied.org/10819IIED/.

Sanderson, D. (2017). Implementing area-based approaches in urban post disaster contexts. *Environment & Urbanization,* 29(2).

Setchell, C. (2018). The emerging importance of the settlements approach. In D. Sanderson and A. Sharma (eds.), *State of Humanitarian Shelter and Settlements.* Geneva: IFRC, 114–119.

Shelter Cluster. (2015). *Shelter and Settlements Vulnerability Assessment: Vanuatu, April 2015.* Prepared in collaboration with REACH.

Sphere Project. (2018). *Sphere Handbook: Humanitarian Charter and Minimum Standards in Humanitarian Response*. Available at: https://spherestandards.org/wp-content/uploads/Sphere-Handbook-2018-EN.pdf.

United Nations. (1998). *Guiding Principles on Internal Displacement*. Available at: https://www.unhcr.org/en-us/protection/idps/43ce1cff2/guiding-principles-internal-displacement.html.

United Nations Economic and Social Council. (2005). *Economic, Social, and Cultural Rights. Housing and Property Restitution in the Context of the Return of Refugees and Internally Displaced Persons*. Final Report of the Special Rapporteur, Paul Sergio Pinheiro.

United Nations Office of the High Commissioner for Human Rights. (1966). *International Covenant on Economic, Social and Cultural Rights*. Available at: https://www.ohchr.org/en/professionalinterest/pages/cescr.aspx.

Vanuatu National Housing Corporation. (2012). *Port Vila Informal Settlements Upgrading Projection – Basic Data on Port Vila Informal Settlements*. Government of Vanuatu, Port Vila.

WorldOMeters. (2018). *Vanuatu Population*. Available at: www.worldometers.info/world-population/vanuatu-population/ (accessed September 15, 2018).

Yuval-Davis, N. (2006). Belonging and the politics of belonging. *Patterns of Prejudice*, 40(3), 197–214.

Chapter 8

Resilience in Pacific Towns and Cities

The Social Dimensions of Change

Meg Keen and Paul Jones

Introduction

Rapid urbanisation and its management are undermining sustainable development in the Pacific islands with population growth rates and densities in cities now rivalling some of the highest internationally (Table 8.1). Pacific island cities are small by international standards, but their rapid growth rates, limited resources, inadequate infrastructure and low-lying coastal settlements collectively create formidable urban resilience challenges. Despite the mounting challenges, urban planning remains weak—institutional arrangements and the political will to act are largely lacking (Barbara and Keen, 2017). The subsequent policy neglect is exacerbated by planning approaches which are not addressing public interest issues and the growing number of informal settlements (Jones, 2016). Achieving a more resilient development of cities is pressing. Recently, new initiatives at the regional and local levels are beginning to get some traction, but still need much support and resourcing.

Pacific island cities have particular characteristics that affect their resilience and the opportunities for sustainable development. All primate cities are coastal (see Figure 8.1), hemmed in by ocean with many low-lying settlements prone to flooding (UN-Habitat, 2015; Trundle and McEvoy, 2015). Climate change and other external pressures magnify already existing urban challenges related to population growth, competition for land and service shortfalls (ADB, 2012; Jones, 2016; Thomas and Keen, 2017; Schrecongost and Wong, 2015). In these circumstances, the impacts of climatic events can be large and lasting. In 2015, Cyclone Pam hit Vanuatu hard with widespread flooding and damage to its capital Port Vila and economic costs equivalent to 64 percent of GDP; the recovery is still ongoing.

The vulnerability of densely populated Pacific island cities to severe climatic events are well known and graphically covered by news around the world, including flooded homes, damaged infrastructure, and displaced people and communities. Cyclones, tsunamis and coral bleaching affect the lives and livelihoods of the Pacific islands' people with pressures set to increase.

122 Meg Keen and Paul Jones

Table 8.1 Urban Population and Growth Rates Based on the Last Census.

Country	Last Census Enumerated Population	Last Census Urban Population (%)	Urban Growth Rate (%)
Melanesia			
Fiji	837,271	51	1.5
PNG	7,059,653	13	2.8
Solomon Islands	515,870	20	4.7
Vanuatu	234,023	24	3.5
Micronesia			
FSM	102,843	22	−2.2
Kiribati	109,693	57	2.1
Marshall Islands	53,158	74	1.4
Nauru	10,084	100	1.8
Palau	17,661	78	−1.0
Polynesia			
Samoa	187,820	20	−0.3
Tonga	103,252	23	2.4
Tuvalu	10,782	57	3.1

Source: Adapted from the SPC Pacific Islands Population Database based on the last census information.[1] Available at: https://sdd.spc.int/en/stats-by-topic/population-statistics. (accessed 4 November 2018)

Recent research indicates that climate change may be occurring more rapidly than previously assumed (Cheng et al., 2019), thus the intensity and severity of the impacts on Pacific islands' cities and societies will escalate given their unenviable status as some of the most vulnerable countries to climate change (World Risk Report, 2017).

To enhance environmental and human security, Pacific island countries (PICs) are working to strengthen resilience and adaptive capacity (SPC, 2016). Within this context, the aim of this chapter it twofold. Firstly, the chapter examines the concept of urban resilience as it has been applied in the Pacific islands' context, arguing that resilience is not articulated and practiced in a way that sufficiently reflects the Pacific urban experience. Secondly, the chapter introduces an analytical framework which encompasses the key components of urban resilience—Responsiveness, Adaptation, Facilitation and Transformation (RAFT)—which can be applied in PICs. Using examples, the RAFT principles show how current policies and practices do not fully incorporate the complex social and physical systems of PIC towns and cities. We conclude that in PICs, especially those with rapidly growing informal settlements, the RAFT framework helps to reveal and address pressing urban problems that will require more than 'tweaking the system'. To achieve urban resilience, policymakers will need to become more responsive to diverse urban populations and their needs and, most importantly, more willing to transform urban governance systems to better suit the social and ecological contexts.

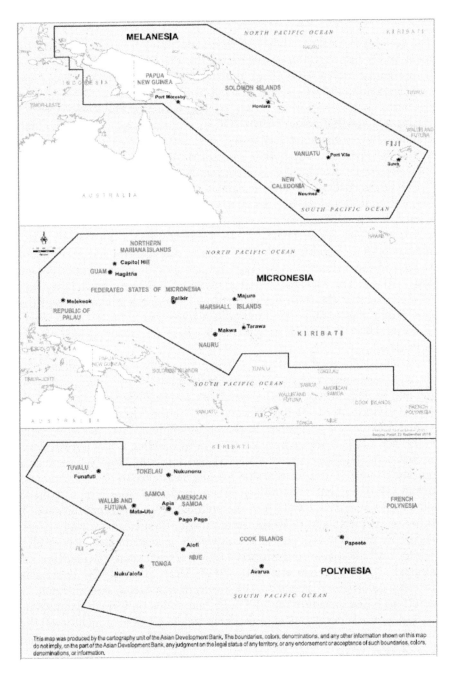

Figure 8.1 Pacific Island Countries and Cities.
Source: Paul Jones and ADB (2016)

Resilience: Putting Theory Into Practice

The concept of resilience helps to define the 'how' of sustainable development and is a powerful narrative to describe the ways in which individuals, communities and societies adapt, transform and co-evolve when faced with environmental, socioeconomic and political challenges. A useful working definition of resilience in the urban context is that of The Rockefeller 100 Resilient Cities initiative: 'Urban resilience is the capacity of individuals, communities, institutions, businesses, and systems within a city to survive, adapt, and grow no matter what kinds of chronic stresses and acute shocks they experience' (Rockefeller Foundation, 2015).

The urban resilience concept is applied across development, planning and humanitarian domains, but not always in a consistent manner and often with differing emphases on processes, goals, ecology and institutions (IFRC, 2016; UNIDSR, 2019; DFID, 2011). It is becoming a 'buzzword' that is used as both a catch-all and specific term by aid agencies and governments to refer to the diverse processes that manage shocks and stresses (Jones and Sanderson, 2017). The lack of policy, planning and conceptual clarity leads to concerns that the resilience concept will become a pliable concept that can be all things to all people (and policymakers), or 'captured' by powerful interests who can apply it as a means to shape the policy agenda to their advantage.

Gaining conceptual clarity is challenging because the term resilience has different meanings across its originating disciplines of psychology, engineering and ecology. It can describe the ability to resist change, to stabilise the existing system, or to adapt and bounce back to the original state of the individual, building or ecosystem. In the urban context, there are times when resistance and persistence have value, such as building urban infrastructure to maintain and support critical services and activities. However, these characteristics are not always desirable because resistance to change can create urban instability and vulnerability. When applied to cities, urban resilience often lacks adequate attention to the political economy of urbanisation. In other words, it fails to question the status quo that can be socially unjust, driven by elite interests and environmentally unsustainable, such as PICs' urban land allocation and property rights arrangements (Mecartney and Connell, 2017; Foukona and Allen, 2017; McDonnell, 2017). Approaches to enhance urban resilience are often system-reinforcing and anchored on solutions based in institutions and policies founded on formal planning and path-dependent development approaches (derived from colonial times) that may have contributed to urban malaise, such as informal settlements without services.

For the concept of resilience to get traction and become a driver of sustainability in the Pacific islands, it will need to be tailored and adapted to urban contexts and take into account complex social and ecological system dynamics. Key elements of processes that can achieve resilience in human settlements will need to be defined. The literature on social resilience provides useful guidance of how urban planning and management can be more responsive in urban contexts, highlighting the importance of social dimensions to change:

- *Social Learning*—facilitating and harnessing the capacity of humans to adapt and learn;
- *Integration*—responding across socio-ecological systems and scales (not just focusing on areas within the physical or administrative limits of the city or within one sector);
- *Transformation*—accepting that systems may need to transform in response to new needs, or pressures, including governance, planning and regulatory processes.

(Maclean et al., 2017; IFRC, 2016: 14–15)

Given the dynamic and densely populated nature of Pacific cities, the implication is that urban resilience will be iterative and people-centred process, not a final state, or constrained to any one sector, theme or level of governance. It is a 'mobilising metaphor' more than a 'performance indicator' (Béné et al., 2018). This view of resilience as a mobilising metaphor fits with an adaptive management or systemic approach that is responsive to diverse stakeholders and new challenges. The pursuit of urban resilience is political and needs to be inclusive of the full range of people living in the city to address pressing issues such as inequitable access to services, economic opportunities and political decision-making (Bahadur, 2016). Asking the key questions of 'resilience for who?' as well as 'resilience of what?' can reveal the hidden human and political dimensions of policies aimed at achieving resilience, and how different types of institutional arrangements, such as planning processes and service provision, affect inclusion in (or exclusion from) urban development processes (Jones, 2017).

In Pacific islands cities, achieving urban resilience necessarily requires looking beyond formal governance arrangements to assess adaptive capacity in all areas of the city. Currently, over 40–50 percent of the residents of cities are living in 'informal' settlements without urban services and neglected by formal institutions, with improvements to housing and drainage often done by communities (see Figure 8.2). Regulations concerning urban land development are rarely relevant (or even legally applicable) to the rapidly expanding urban and peri-urban areas under customary land management that fall outside of formal urban planning processes. Even planning and regulatory processes governing public and privatised land are often honoured more in the breach than observance.

Across Pacific cities the rise of informal (or squatter) settlements or 'urban villages' is pervasive. Given the lack of government services, many of these

Figure 8.2 In Many PICs, the Formal Planning System Fails to Provide Adequate Access to Sanitation, Water and Other Basic Services for Residents. In Kiribati, community groups work together to meet their shelter requirements by using and reusing traditional and modern materials and leveraging social networks to meet basic needs.

Source: Paul Jones

communities are centred around the adaptation of traditional socio-cultural orders based on kin and place-based relationships, ethnic associations and customary norms to enhance urban resilience. In these urban settings, the social dimensions of urban resilience, including the adaptive capacity of communities, is rarely acknowledged in urban policy and planning, notwithstanding the work of some Pacific scholars writing about human security and urban inclusivity (e.g., Connell and Lea, 1993; Cocklin and Keen, 2000; Jones, 2016; Storey, 2003; UNDP, 1996). Cities such as Honiara (Solomon Islands), Port Moresby (Papua New Guinea) and Suva (Fiji) are now taking steps to upgrade these settlements to enable their residents to gain land tenure and maintain social networks within these urban villages, but progress has been slow.

Given these circumstances, urban partnerships—public, private, civil society and especially 'bottom-up' arrangements—are essential components for facilitating the resilient and sustainable development of cities. If applied well, resilience policies can help ensure that those currently falling outside of formal planning systems, which in many Pacific cities is the bulk of the population, have an effective voice and access to resources to shape urban decision-making and their urban living environments. Recent research in informal settlements reflects the current feelings of exclusion from urban planning, economic opportunities and technical assistance, raising concerns about how residents' interests are being represented and the lack of power to affect urban planning and decision-making (Keen and Carpenter, 2017). Steps to better convene diverse stakeholder groups and governments have the potential to achieve more inclusive and integrated urban management across artificial boundaries such as initial efforts under the greater Honiara planning efforts that straddle the Honiara City Council, the Guadalcanal province, land holders and state-owned enterprises (Barbara et al., 2016).

In some cases, adapting or tweaking the system may not be enough to achieve sustainable long-term development that is equitable and ecologically sustainable. Rather, social and physical transformation to alter the nature of the system, that is its form, function and governance, may be required (Walker et al., 2004). For example, formerly illegal vending activities in the informal economic sector are being increasingly recognised and valued as an important part of the social fabric. In PNG, there is now a National Policy for the Informal Economy 2011–2015 that aims to support (rather than discourage or prohibit) the important role that informal activities play in livelihoods and the national economy (see Figure 8.3). Fiji's government has recently changed regulations to better recognise and invest in informal roadside markets, realising that recognition and support of community food markets can help to enhance urban livelihoods and food security in contrast to the ongoing efforts to deny work rights and shut markets down (Keen and Ride, 2019; Maebuta and Maebuta, 2009). Organisations such as UN Women are also supporting women in Fiji, Solomon Islands and Vanuatu, and creating new institutional arrangements to increase access to livelihoods, market land and financial services, as well as strengthen the political voice of women. Their programmes, along with other civil society groups, seek to transform cultural values detrimental to women's safety and advancement.

To summarise, the resilience literature and experience within Pacific islands' cities reveals deficits in the articulation and implementation of resilience strategies. Four key dimensions of urban resilience appear particularly important to enhance success and are encapsulated in the RAFT acronym:

Responsiveness to social norms, values and relationships often tied to local socio-cultural orders;

Adaptation of urban forms, functions and institutional arrangements to address pressures, challenges, and opportunities across sectors and jurisdictions;

Figure 8.3 Some PIC Governments, Such as Papua New Guinea, are Making Legislative Changes to Acknowledge the Critical Role the Informal Sector Plays in Supporting Urban Food Security and Livelihoods.

Source: Paul Jones

Facilitation and convening of diverse interest and residential groups to inform decision-making and co-produce resilience solutions;

Transformation to alter the nature or functions of the urban system to better achieve urban resilience.

Resilience: The Policies and the Practice in the Pacific Islands

The following section assesses in more detail how PIC policies and practices aimed at enhancing urban resilience are playing out on the ground with respect to urban responsiveness, adaptation, facilitation and transformation (RAFT). Our analyses of Pacific experiences focus on the social dimensions of resilience which include culture, community networks, inclusive planning, and self-organised governance and institutional arrangements (Ross and Berkes, 2014; Maclean et al., 2017). The aim is to engage with thinking about what urban resilience policies and practices are currently and what they 'should be', accepting that urban resilience will include processes of social and physical adaptation and transformation to meet the needs of urban residents.

Responsiveness

At the regional level, the Framework for the Resilient Development of the Pacific 2017–30, provides a template on which national and local-level policy can build, but it also reflects the rural policy bias in PICs (Barbara and Keen, 2017). The Framework does not explicitly mention cities/towns and their unique challenges despite their highly vulnerable status and rapid growth. It focuses predominantly on climate change and disaster risks, with much less attention on how these magnify already-existing social, ecological and demographic pressures, such as those emanating from urban areas. The regional focus of the Framework means it does not deal with many specifics, but there is acknowledgement that achieving more resilience in the region depends on political will, greater transparency of whose interests and values are being served, and the socio-political, cultural and institutional roots of vulnerability. Overall, however, the document deals weakly with how governments can become more responsive to social values, behaviours and actions that affect urban resilience, despite the growing population that live in cities.

The Pacific Urban Agenda (PUA) is more comprehensive with respect to urban resilience issues, but has achieved little policy traction or behaviour change as neither governments nor donors have committed to its implementation. Where lead regional agencies such as the Pacific Islands Forum have endorsed the PUA, very little implementation has occurred at the national or local levels (Kiddle et al., 2017). This does not bode well for the top-down Sustainable Development Goals, or SDGs (such as SDG 11, commonly known as the urban SDG), that also deal with the key issues of social equity and spatial inequalities, environmental and social resilience, urban livelihoods and governance. In general, the SDGs are not well-adapted to Pacific islands place and culture, nor relevant to the lived (and often subsistent) urban experience of people in Pacific cities. Indicators will need adaptation to context. Rationalisation, tailoring, and adaptation of the PUA and SDGs can occur if the resources, will and leadership are present. However, all are currently lacking, suggesting national and urban managers are not yet convinced that the regional resilience frameworks are well-suited to their local needs. A recent report on Pacific urban development identified multiple approaches needed to improve urban responsiveness including: transformation of land planning and allocation systems to better address customary land and informal settlements, working with communities to define solutions for informal work and settlement vulnerabilities, development of hybrid systems more responsive to law and order and gender-based

Meg Keen and Paul Jones

violence issues, and enhancing community-based social protection systems (Thomas and Keen, 2017).

Adaptation

Despite the rapid expansion of cities across the Pacific islands, there is remarkably little planning for their growth. The limited planning that is done is through the formal systems of governments and development partners, thus, efforts to strengthen informal settlements where residents show generally high levels of adaptation, resilience and self-organisation remain inadequate. The inability by governments, development and regional agencies to consider the RAFT principles and put people at the centre of development is not surprising given the neglect of informal settlements and the negativity surrounding them and their residents. Informal settlements and livelihoods such as market and street vending are judged within the framework of the formal planning system and simple formal/informal binary. In most cases, this is based on Western concepts of urban management which are poorly suited to the Pacific where a preconceived idea of conformity and order sets the boundaries for what is acceptable.

Mechanisms to bridge the formal and informal systems remain weak, yet essential, to resilience and strengthening adaptive capacity. With limited resources and reach of government institutions, informal systems underpin much of urban functionality and responsiveness to pressures such as those related to service or housing shortfalls, financial exclusions, limited jobs or climate disasters (Moore, 2015). Local governments are slowly admitting implicitly or explicitly that they do not have the capacity to deliver on many basic services and that supporting existing systems of governance, often informal, is a more practical and efficient option (Suhartini and Jones, 2019). This need to adapt urban planning to urban realities and accept that some adaptation of governance processes will inevitably underpin urban resilience has long been acknowledged in the Pacific, but not often acted upon.

In their critical analyses of urban land systems in Melanesian cities, Chand and Yala (2008) conclude that informal land arrangements are not sophisticated and are unlikely to evolve naturally to the point whereby they can mitigate the negative consequences such as overcrowding, poverty, crime and underservicing. Thus, evolving hybrid systems of governance (Silva, 2016) must be a major objective of contemporary Pacific planning. As noted by Pacific islands land authority Joseph Foukona, adaptation and evolution of the land management system could be of great benefit:

> There is no single solution. . . . In addition to [new] legal frameworks and clarity over rules and responsibilities, non-legal dispute resolution processes and support services for customary landowners could help

ensure equity and fairness in urban land development. Efficient and uncomplicated ways to enforce agreements between landowners and developers would also create more certainty for all.

(quoted in Keen et al., 2017: 71)

Current government institutions are largely ineffective at managing urban land and resilience issues, measures that are adaptive and transformative are required that build on existing social arrangements for land management and strengthen them by embedding them in supportive urban and national planning frameworks.

Facilitation

The continued implementation of top-down urban policies with mixed implementation success is partially a consequence of the difficulties of integrating policymaking and implementation across scales of governance from international to national and local. Where there has been success, international and regional initiatives have facilitated participatory and place-based processes. For example, the UN-Habitat city vulnerability assessments combine scientific studies, citizen participation and policy/plan-maker engagement (see for example Trundle and McEvoy, 2016; Trundle and McEvoy, 2015).

As a result, urban resilience 'action plans', including those addressing housing, water, sanitation and waste, health, ecosystem services, community governance, and disaster risk reduction and management are currently being developed. This policy work elevates the notion of urban resilience beyond the secular focus of climate change adaptation and risk of natural disasters and hazards to the wider development setting including that of disadvantaged (informal/squatter settlement) residents in the most need. The Honiara Urban Resilience and Climate Action Plan (HURCAP) 2016 builds on vulnerability assessments and is a joint strategy of the Honiara City Council and Solomon Island government, funded by UN-Habitat, with the key objective of strengthening the resilience of Honiara. The planning process engages vulnerable communities in informal settlements to reduce the impact of natural hazards and facilitate the creation of a community-based platform to implement climate change adaptation measures and enhance community resilience.

The challenge is in implementing and coordinating action across sectors and scales, and sustaining the engagement of communities even after project funding dries up. In the few communities where actions to improve resilience have been independently initiated and sustained, such as Panatina Valley in Honiara, communities have strengthened their internal governance and capacity to leverage wider urban networks and resources. These projects demonstrate the value of responsive, adaptive and facilitated approaches to urban planning that help expand supportive networks.

Despite these successes, across the Pacific, partnerships for urban development remain largely project-based and sectoral with erratic and inconsistent involvement of communities (see Figure 8.4). Urban planning and management have been dominated by technical planning processes that rarely facilitate the engagement of the many marginalised communities and workers (see Jones, 2017; Kiddle and Hay, 2017; Keen and Carpenter, 2017; Keen et al., 2017). Many regional initiatives that have the potential to boost urban resilience are weakened by the failure to include informal settlements and sectors, and to coordinate action across agencies, jurisdictions and time. There are still too few effective platforms to facilitate better urban management, planning and social inclusion across political boundaries and over the long-term.

Transformation

Incremental change or adaptive management can deal with some pressures. However, growing urban inequality, urban exclusions and uneven resource distribution often require social and institutional transformations that

Figure 8.4 There is Little Point Building Sea Walls to Combat Climate Change, as Seen Here in Betio, South Tarawa, if Local Communities and Systems are Not Engaged and Involved in Long-Term Maintenance.

Source: Paul Jones

challenge current political and technical systems that create, rather than mitigate, vulnerability. Change and transformation have long been part of humanity's evolutionary history (Gunderson and Holling, 2002), and cities are no exception. Cities need spaces and platforms that support critical reflection and self-organisation, rather than constrain them (Silva, 2016). A weakness of current resilience thinking is that it focuses mostly on incremental change, with less attention to the transformative processes that may be needed to alter entrenched systems and power dynamics that undermine sustainability, urban land management and equity (Bahadur, 2016; Jones, 2017). As noted previously, integrating informal and marginalised sectors of the city into central governance and planning systems requires institutional changes underpinned by changes to values and behaviours. The 5th Pacific Urban Forum was held in Nadi in July 2019 and stimulated critical reflections on entrenched and unsustainable urban management processes, with acknowledgment that securing change would require reforms to urban land tenure, better integration of informal economies and settlements into policy and planning frameworks, and a more systemic approach to governance that did not treat urban and rural development as unrelated processes (Keen and Kiddle, 2019). A recurring theme throughout the forum was the need to integrate cultural norms, traditional knowledge and governance into the urban fabric. Delegates summarised in one word their view of sustainable urban development—top among these one-word summaries was 'belonging', 'diversity' and 'localisation', aspirations for cities that will require power shifts and urban management transformations.

Transformative urban management requires more inclusive planning, but also a reconceptualisation of urban issues as one part of a larger interacting system. Increasingly, pressures on urban systems are from external sources, such as rural-urban migration or climate pressures, with local systems ill-equipped to convene relevant stakeholders to effect action or coordinate the integration of policy responses to meet current needs, let alone future ones. In this environment, urban planning and development challenges are escalating, but PIC capacity and political commitment for sustained action continues to be 'missing in action' and often only focused on a part of the system (ADB, 2012). Achieving more sustainable Pacific cities will require a shift from a largely technical and singular thematic approach, such as one limited to climate change or land use planning, to a more human-centred approach with a stronger understanding of the political economy of cities, the power dynamics of decision-making, and the drivers of change that transcend social and ecological systems.

Resilience for Sustainable Development: Towards the Inclusive City

> Sustainability and resilience depend on a society's innovative capacity . . . solutions must be found by innovating in urban systems at different scales

and across sectors. This firmly frames the urban system as an opportunity for sustainability and drives us to recognize that the answer to increased resilience might not lie in its ecological dimension, but rather in the social.

(Ernstson et al., 2010: 538)

Local populations are the first and last responders in any crisis, climatic or otherwise (IFRC, 2013). Whether those populations live in informal settlements or gated communities, their inclusion in building urban resilience matters. To achieve urban resilience, much more attention to social inclusion, political agency and partnerships is needed to achieve RAFT principles that underpin urban resilience. Urban resilience is not, and cannot be, apolitical because urban planning and decision-making are political acts embedded in social and power structures. In many cases, building urban resilience can require transformation rather than restoration or reinforcement; it must be part of a political process of change and evolution within the city, and between the city and its wider regional support and supply networks.

Building resilience requires partnerships that span sectors, social groupings and levels of government. In many cities, we still need to create the platforms and mechanisms to facilitate these dialogues, and to establish the rights of urban dwellers to be politically engaged, to access basic services and to work productively. Creating resilience is not just about disaster preparedness, though that is an important component. It must create or enhance the institutional and, importantly, multi-layered governance arrangements that support diverse livelihoods and settlement patterns, and create rules and regulations that are fit for place and culture. In cities where customary land tenure and subsistence activities persist, resilience building cannot be merely about strengthening formal or colonial-based urban systems that exclude these social arrangements. It must be about considering and understanding people-place relationships and their associated values and decision-making processes. Hybrid arrangements that bridge formal and informal urban governance systems can help to give urban resilience social and policy traction.

With so many growing urban needs, demands and expectations in Pacific island cities and so few resources, regional capacity sharing and convening power are key elements of resilience building. Globally, networks such as the 100 Resilient Cities help to facilitate learning and knowledge brokering, but unfortunately, they exclude PICs with their much smaller cities, but no smaller needs. Localised or regionalised solutions are needed which are adapted to cultural contexts. The Pacific Urban Forum 2019 could be the basis for a regional convening platform, but only if this time around it establishes supportive mechanisms for action that reach down to local and community levels. New initiatives need to critically consider power dynamics, governance and incentives that drive decisions from urban land allocations to community-based service delivery and support. Ultimately, urban processes need to be anchored on policies and actions which are responsive, adaptive, facilitative and transformative, that is, providing a RAFT for resilience.

Note

1. In some cases, census date can be up to ten years old, so numbers and percentages are only indicative. In PNG and Solomon Islands, government estimates put urban populations as a proportion of the total population rather higher because of continuing in-migration and urban growth after the census period. Designations of urban boundaries vary, with 'urban' growth happening in nominally rural areas in several PICs, and commuting becoming increasingly significant. In all cases, therefore, percentages are likely to be underestimates of urbanisation.

References

Asian Development Bank (ADB). (2012). *The State of Pacific Towns and Cities, Urbanization in ADB's Developing Member Countries*. Pacific Studies Series. Manila: ADB.

Bahadur, A. (2016). *Reimagining Resilience: Bringing Resilience, Transformation and Vulnerability Closer for Tackling Climate Change*. Asian Cities Climate Change Resilience Network (ACCCRN), Monitoring the Field, February 2013. Working Paper. Reissued January 2016.

Barbara, J., Carpenter, J. and Keen, M. (2016). *Visions for Henderson: A workshop on managing peri-urban growth in Solomon Islands*. In Brief 2016/32, Department of Pacific Affairs. Canberra: Australian National University.

Barbara, J. and Keen, M. (2017). Urbanisation in Melanesia: The politics of change. *Development Bulletin*, 78, 16–20.

Béné, C.M.L., McGranahan, G., Cannon, T., Grupte, J. and Tanner, T. (2018). Resilience as a policy narrative: Potentials and limits in the context of urban planning. *Climate and Development*, 10(2), 116–133.

Chand, S. and Yala, C. (2008). Informal land systems within urban settlements in Honiara and Port Moresby. In *Making Land Work, Volume 2*. Canberra: AusAID.

Cheng, L., Abraham, J., Huasfather, A. and Trenberth, K. (2019). How fast are the oceans warming? *Science*, 363(6423), 128–129.

Cocklin, C. and Keen, M. (2000). Urbanization in the Pacific: Environmental change, vulnerability and human security. *Environment Conservation*, 27(4), 392–403.

Connell, J. and Lea, J. (1993). *Planning the Future: Melanesian Cities in 2010*. Pacific 2010: Pacific Policy Paper 11. Canberra, NCDS: Australian National University.

Department for International Development (DFID). (2011). *Defining Disaster Resilience: A DFID Approach Paper*. London. Available at: www.dfid.gov.uk/Documents/publications1/Defining-Disaster-Resilience-DFID-Approach-Paper.pdf (accessed January 12, 2019).

Ernstson, H., Van der Leeuw, S., Redman, C., Meffert, D., Davis, G., Alfsen, C. and Elmqvist, T. (2010). Urban transition: On urban resilience and human-dominated ecosystems. *Ambio*, 39(8), 531–545.

Foukona, J. and Allen, M. (2017). Urban land in Solomon Islands: Powers of exclusion and counter-exclusion. In S. McDonnell, M. Allen and C. Filer (eds.), *Kastom, Property and Ideology: Land Transformation in Melanesia*. Canberra: Australian National University Press, 85–110.

Gunderson, L. and Holling, C. (2002). Resilience and adaptive cycles. In L. Gunderson and C. Holling (eds.), *Panarchy: Understanding Transformations in Human and Natural Systems*. Washington, DC: Island Press, 25–62.

International Federation of Red Cross and Red Crescent Societies (IFRC). (2013). *Annual Report 2013*. Geneva. Available at: https://www.ifrc.org/Global/Docu ments/Secretariat/201411/IFRC%20Annual%20Report%202013_FINAL.pdf.

International Federation of Red Cross and Red Crescent Societies (IFRC). (2016). *World Disaster Report—Resilience: Saving Lives Today, Investing for Tomorrow*. Geneva: IFRC.

Jones, P. (2016). *The Emergence of Pacific Urban Villages: Urbanization Trends in the Pacific Islands*. Pacific Studies Series. Manila: Asian Development Bank.

Jones, P. (2017). Informal and squatter settlements: The self-made urban order shaping Pacific towns and cities. *Development Bulletin*, 78, 30–35.

Jones, P. and Sanderson, D. (2017). Urban resilience and informal and squatter settlements in the Pacific region. *Development Bulletin*, 78, 11–15.

Keen, M., Barbara, J., Carpenter, J., Evans, D. and Foukona, J. (2017). *Urban Development in Honiara: Harnessing Opportunities, Embracing Change*. Canberra: Australian National University.

Keen, M. and Carpenter, J. (2017). Living on the fringes: Voices from those living in the settlements of Honiara. *Development Bulletin*, 78, 54–58.

Keen, M. and Kiddle, L. (2019). *A PUF of Fresh Air? Pacific Urban Forum 2019*. In Brief 2019/15, Department of Pacific Affairs. Canberra: Australian National University. Available at: http://dpa.bellschool.anu.edu.au/sites/default/files/publica tions/attachments/2019-07/dpa_ib_2019_15_in_brief_keen_kiddle_final_0.pdf.

Keen, M. and Ride, A. (2019). Trading places: Inclusive cities and market vending in the Pacific Islands. *Asia Pacific Viewpoint*, 60(3), 239–251.

Kiddle, L. and Hay, I. (2017). Informal settlements upgrading: Lessons from Suva and Honiara. *Development Bulletin*, 78, 25–29.

Kiddle, L., McEvoy, D., Mitchell, D., Jones, P. and Mecartney, S. (2017). Unpacking the Pacific urban agenda: Resilience challenges and opportunities. *Journal of Sustainability*, 9(1878), 1–15.

Maclean, K., Ross, H. Cuthill, M. and Witt, B. (2017). Converging disciplinary understandings of social aspects of resilience. *Journal of Environmental Planning and Management*, 60(3), 519–537.

Maebuta, H. and Maebuta, J. (2009). Generating livelihoods: A study of urban squatter settlements in Solomon Islands. *Pacific Economic Bulletin*, 24(3), 118–131.

McDonnell, S. (2017). Urban land grabbing by political elites: Exploring the political economy of land and the challenges of regulation. In S. McDonnell, M. Allen and C. Filer (eds.), *Kastom, Property and Ideology: Land Transformation in Melanesia*. Canberra: Australian National University Press, 283–304.

Mecartney, S. and Connell, J. (2017). Urban Melanesia: The challenges of managing land, modernity and tradition. In S. McDonnell, M. Allen and C. Filer (eds.), *Kastom, Property and Ideology: Land Transformation in Melanesia*. Canberra: Australian National University Press, 57–84.

Moore, C. (2015). Honiara: Arrival city and Pacific hybrid living space. *The Journal of Pacific History*, 50(4), 419–436.

Pacific Community (SPC). (2016). *Framework for the Resilient Development in the Pacific: Framework for Resilient Development in the Pacific: An Integrated Approach to Address Climate Change and Disaster Risk Management 2017–2030.* Suva: SPC.

Rockefeller Foundation. (2015). *100 Resilient Cities.* Available at: www.rockefeller foundation.org/ourwork/topics/resilience (accessed January 10, 2019).

Ross, H. and Berkes, F. (2014). Research approaches for understanding, enhancing, and monitoring community resilience. *Society & Natural Resources*, 27(4), 787–804.

Schrecongost, A. and Wong, K. (2015). *Unsettled: Water and Sanitation in Urban Settlement Communities of the Pacific.* Sydney: World Bank.

Silva, P. (2016). Tactical urbanism: Towards an evolutionary cities' approach? *Environmental Planning B: Urban Analytics and City Science*, 43, 1040–1051.

Storey, D. (2003). The peri-urban Pacific: From exclusive to inclusive cities. *Asia Pacific Viewpoint*, 44(3), 259–279.

Suhartini, N. and Jones, P. (2019). *Urban Governance and Informal Settlements: Lessons from the City of Jayapura, Indonesia.* Switzerland: Springer.

Thomas, P. and Keen, M. (eds.). (2017). Special Issue: Urban Development in the Pacific. Development. *Development Bulletin*, 78.

Trundle, A. and McEvoy, D. (2015). *Climate Change Vulnerability Assessment: Greater Port Vila.* Fukuoka: UN Habitat.

Trundle, A. and McEvoy, D. (2016). *Honiara Urban Resilience and Climate Action Plan.* Fukuoka: UN Habitat.

UN-Habitat. (2015). *Cities and Climate Change Initiative: Honiara, Solomon Islands Climate Change Vulnerability Assessment.* Kenya.

United Nations Development Programme (UNDP). (1996). *The State of Human Settlements and Urbanisation in the Pacific Islands.* Regional Report for the United Nations Conference on Human Settlements (Habitat II), Istanbul.

United Nations Office for Disaster Risk Reduction (UNIDSR). (2019). *United Nations Office for Disaster Risk Reduction - 2018 Annual Report.* Switzerland.

Walker, B., Holling, C., Carpenter, S. and Kinzig, A. (2004). Resilience, adaptability and transformability in social-ecological systems. *Ecology and Society*, 9(2), Article 5 [online].

World Risk Report. (2017). Available at: www.welthungerhilfe.org/fileadmin/pic tures/publications/en/studies_analysis/2017-publication-wolrd-risk-report-en.pdf (accessed February 6, 2019).

Part 2

Asia (and Beyond)

Chapter 9

Planning for Climate Change
Adapting to a More Sustainable Urban Future

Barbara Norman

Introduction

The rapid scale and pace of urbanisation throughout the Asia Pacific region continues, fuelled both by rural to urban migration and by natural increase (that is, people being born in the city). UN-Habitat (2018b) estimates that by 2050 up to three billion people will be added to the urban population. Furthermore, it is estimated that cities will consume about 70 percent of global energy consumption and generate 70 percent of global carbon emissions (UN-Habitat, 2018b). The scale of projected urbanisation to 2050 is massive, with 'ten cities exceeding 20 million people by 2030, leading with Tokyo, Japan, at 37 million followed by Delhi, India at 36 million and Shanghai, China, at nearly 31 million people' (Norman, 2018a: 126).

At the same time, urban communities are already experiencing the impacts of climate change, including a lack of fresh water, increasing temperatures (Lancet, 2015), coastal storms and floods. A key challenge in planning for climate change is implementing actions that will increase urban resilience in a highly dynamic urban environment.

Significant recent global agreements have recognised the nexus between the two global challenges of urbanisation and climate change. These include the United *Nations Sustainable Development Goals* (SDGs), the *Sendai Framework for Risk Reduction* (UNISDR, 2015) and the *New Urban Agenda* developed by UN-Habitat (UN-Habitat, 2016). This is in relation to both climate mitigation, i.e., the challenge of reducing global emissions, and adaptation, i.e., the challenge of living with the impacts of climate change.

The great extent of urbanisation is happening within China, Africa and India (UN-Habitat and UNESCAP, 2015). Underlying the trend of urbanisation across the Asia Pacific region is persistent poverty, environmental degradation and continuing inequality. It is estimated that a third of the urban residents in Asia and the Pacific are without access to adequate shelter, safe drinking water and sanitation, and clean energy. (UNESCAP, 2015).

The recent *New Urban Agenda* developed by UN-Habitat and adopted by the UN Assembly in November 2016 highlights the challenges facing an urbanising Global South. It extends SDG goal 11 on cities and urban communities by adding a process of implementation. The *New Urban Agenda* has a strong emphasis on climate change action for both reducing mitigation and adaptation. Investing in 'good urban planning' is highlighted throughout the actions. As the Executive Director of UN-Habitat, Maimunah Sharif stated, in her opening address to the ninth Word Urban Forum, Kuala Lum pur, 'The needs of [an] integrated and holistic development plan at national/central level, at regional/state level and at local level is very important to consciously implement the New Urban Agenda and 17 Sustainable Development Goals' (Sharif, 2018).

During 2018, UN-Habitat, the Human Settlements arm of the UN, prepared a synthesis report on the state of SDG 11 for their 'High- Level Forum' in New York (UN-Habitat, 2018b). The report highlighted the continuing need to manage urban growth, particularly increasing urban sprawl and urban slums, the need to reduce urban pollution and municipal waste, and the demand for smart, safe and efficient transport. Future challenges identified included developing sustainable buildings, healthy urban living infrastructure, and efficient cities for business and work. Underpinning all of the these, UN-Habitat identified the importance of having systems in place for urban monitoring and evaluation, including urban indicators and data such as urban observatories, strengthened by networks and partnerships (UN-Habitat, 2018b).

Climate Risks in the Asia Pacific Region

The climate risks for the Asia Pacific region involve more extreme weather, flooding, subsidence, storms, drought, fire, dust and sandstorms (IPCC, 2014b). At the same time, large urban centres, such as Shanghai, Tokyo, New Delhi and Jakarta, are spreading into possible future urban conglomerations, joining together to create, in effect, never-ending urban corridors.

The Asian Development Bank (ADB) has identified that coastal flooding is one of the major risks in the Asia Pacific region. This is particularly affecting the Pacific islanders. The expected number of people affected in low-lying coastal zones will substantially increase between now and 2060. It is expected that the population living in coastal zone in India will increase from 63.9 million to 216.4 million people, in the People's Republic of China an increase from 144 million to 244.8 million people, and in the Philippines from 13 million to 34.9 million people (ADB, 2017; Norman, 2018a: 52).

The fifth IPCC's (2014b) projections for Asia include increasing coastal flooding and glacial melting, decreasing crop yields, increasing climate-induced disease, heat-related deaths, and drought-related water and food scarcity. Collectively, these risks will have major impacts on communities throughout the Asia Pacific region, often exacerbating the conditions already affecting the most vulnerable members of the community. Coastal fishing villages are possibly at the greatest risk, particularly in the large deltas and low-lying Pacific islands.

Heat is increasingly being recognised as major killer in the future (The Lancet, 2015). The impact of heat on the health and well-being of urban communities is highlighted by the World Health Organisation (ibid). This is made worse by the increase in urban pollution from both external sources (brown cloud from forest fires) and urban congestion from rapidly expanding urban settlements (Norman, 2018a). The journal *The Lancet* concluded that, 'the effects of climate change are being felt today, and future projections represent an unacceptably high and potentially catastrophic risk to human health' (The Lancet, 2015).

The risk to existing coastal infrastructure is enormous, affecting ports, airports, communications and major transit for coastal settlements. Smart infrastructure, such as rapid transit, will need to adapt to the changing climate to ensure it will be viable over the longer term. For example, substantial capital investment into large infrastructure projects such as airports can require a 50-year time horizon. The immediate challenge is that much of the current and future urban growth in the Asia Pacific region is expected to be in coastal areas. This means that very careful scenario planning and analysis will need to be undertaken to mitigate climate risks, factoring in the latest climate science, in order to build safely and appropriately.

The biggest risk, however, concerns poorer communities (who are almost always also the most vulnerable) living in cities and regions that are affected by the negative impacts of climate change. These include communities in coastal zones and inland rural communities facing drought. This will almost certainly result in climate-induced forced migration of affected communities affecting the Asia Pacific region.

All of the climate risks explained previously highlight the range of impacts affecting communities between now and 2050, and beyond. A major feature of the Asia Pacific region is the scale and pace of change—the region of highest urban growth simultaneously facing climate change. This will have major consequences for urban governance and the future planning of settlements. A much more integrated approach to the built and natural environments is essential, which, among other things, includes a systems approach to urban settlements.

The IPCC's 2018 report (IPCC, 2018) provides a stark warning of the challenges of limiting global warming. A very clear message is that pathways to achieving no more than an increase in temperature of 1.5°C 'include a steep decline in coal, increased energy efficiency, the use of a wide range of technologies and behavioural changes'(IPCC, 2018). As the authors conclude, 'every action matters, every bit of warming matters, every year matters, every choice matters' (IPCC, 2018).

This provides a number of key messages relevant to managing urban growth in the Asia Pacific region in the context of climate change. This includes the following: that risks depend on the magnitude and rate of warming, geographic location, levels of development and vulnerability, and on the choices and implementation of adaptation and mitigation options; and that adaptation options specific to national contexts, if carefully selected together with enabling conditions, will have benefits for both sustainable development and poverty reduction (IPCC, 2018; Bazaz et al., 2018).

In summary, there is a great deal of work to be done on improving the sustainability of growing cities across the Asia Pacific region. However, in adopting strategies to reduce global warming to 1.5°C, there are multiple opportunities to leapfrog old technologies and urban management approaches by adopting renewable energy, smart infrastructure and transit, 'net zero carbon' built environments towards a greener and more resilient urban future.

The New Urban Agenda

Concurrent with a better understanding of climate change through the IPCC reports and the 2016 United Nations Framework Convention on Climate Change Paris Agreement, there has been an increasing global understanding of the need to manage urban growth in a much more sustainable way. The landmark urban settlements conference, Habitat III, convened by UN-Habitat and to date held once every 20 years, occurred in Ecuador's capital city Quito in October 2016. It brought together over 30,000 participants from 167 countries, including the Asia Pacific region.

The major outcome from Habitat III was the *New Urban Agenda (NUA)*. The NUA was framed by the earlier adoption of the UN SDGs and the 2016 Paris Agreement, and as such placed a strong emphasis not only the environment but also the health and well-being of urban communities. The NUA outlines some of the challenges of implementing positive change:

> We recognize that the implementation of the New Urban Agenda requires an enabling environment and a wide range of means of implementation, including access to science, technology and innovation and enhanced knowledge-sharing on mutually agreed terms, as well as capacity development and mobilization of financial resources, taking into account the commitment of developed and developing countries and tapping into all available traditional and innovative sources at the global, regional, national, subnational and local levels, as well as enhanced international cooperation and partnerships among Governments at all levels, the private sector, civil society, the United Nations system and other actors, based on the principles of equality, non-discrimination, accountability, respect for human rights and solidarity, especially for those who are the poorest and most vulnerable.
>
> (UN-Habitat, 2016, Article 126)

The NUA is wide-ranging, covering the complexities of managing more sustainable urban growth. The NUA 'identifies the need for more integrated urban planning and management to respond to these complex challenges' (Norman, 2018a, 69). It highlights the critical need to include the considerations of climate change into everyday decision-making in urban areas—urban strategies, plans, policies and implementation of urban design, building and construction.

The World Urban Forum

The World Urban Forum, established in 2001, is held every two years, convened by UN-Habitat. It specifically focuses on urban development particularly in low- and middle-income countries. The official declaration from the ninth World Urban Forum (WUF), held in Kuala Lumpur in 2018, states the following concerning global challenges:

> We recognize that today we face emerging challenges that require urgent actions, including:
>
> - Recognizing that crises are increasingly urban, which calls for inclusive urbanisation tools adapted to local contexts and to the nature of natural and human made disasters and conflicts, as well as to guide humanitarian assistance, fast track recovery, and contribute to building and sustaining peace.
> - Managing the complexities of increased migration into cities, at all levels, leveraging positive contributions of all and using more inclusive planning approaches that facilitate social cohesion and create economic opportunities;
> - Understanding the impact of new technologies and potential of open and accessible data, which require governance and design models that help to ensure no one is left behind;
> - Addressing growing social and cultural inequalities, lack of access to economic opportunities, that are increasingly manifested in cities;
> - Responding to environmental degradation and climate change concerns.
>
> (UN-Habitat, 2018a)

Key outcomes from WUF 9 included:

- Strengthening the role of subnational and local governments, urban governance systems that ensure continuous dialogue among different levels of government and participation of all actors, and increasing multilevel and cross-sectoral coordination, transparency and accountability;

- Encouraging sharing of creative solutions and innovative practices which enable a shift in mindset necessary to drive change;
- Building inclusive partnerships and strengthening age and gender responsive environments to ensure meaningful participation and engagement at all levels.
- Adopting integrated territorial development, including through appropriate urban planning and design instruments, to ensure sustainable management and use of natural resources and land, appropriate compactness and density, diversity of uses, and revitalization of cultural heritage;
- Deploying monitoring and reporting mechanisms, including assessment of impacts, that encourage best practices for effective policy making.

(UN-Habitat, 2018a)

Planning for Climate Change in the Asia Pacific Region

The impacts of climate change will clearly vary across the Asia and the Pacific. Current projections by the IPCC indicate that the key impacts will be coastal flooding through sea level rise and coastal storms, glacial melting, decrease in crop yields, climate-induced disease, heat-related deaths, and drought-related water and food scarcity. One of largest risks is lack of water security exacerbated by rising temperatures, population increase and growing demands by agriculture. Coastal inundation for the small island states in the Pacific is a high risk (IPCC, 2014b).

Megacities in Asia are already a prominent feature of the landscape with more than ten urban areas approaching 20 million or more people, including the greater areas of Tokyo (37 million), Jakarta (30 million), Seoul (24 million), Karachi (22 million), Shanghai (23 million), Manila (24 million), Delhi (25 million), Beijing (21 million), Guangzhou (20 million), Kyoto (20 million) and Mumbai' (18 million) (Norman, 2018a: 45). Planning for climate change will be critical to minimise the risk to these areas.

Therefore planning for climate change in the Asia Pacific region presents enormous challenges in terms of the both the pace and scale of change. Put simply, there are millions of people at risk from the impacts of climate change. However, where there are challenges, there are also opportunities.

The SDGs, the NUA and the IPCC reports all provide a strong foundation for action. In my recent book on *Sustainable Pathways for our Cities and Regions* (Norman, 2018a), I outlined seven sustainable pathways as solutions to better manage urban growth in the context of environmental constraints, particularly climate change.

Table 9.1 that follows summarises the seven pathways based on a series on interviews of international leaders, in-country fieldwork (including

Table 9.1 Seven Sustainable Pathways for Cities and Regions.

	Sustainable pathways	Contribution	Application examples
1	Planning within planetary boundaries	An Earth systems contribution to more sustainable urban futures over time	A future "environmental checklist" for every city to improve its environment and minimise global impact
2	Long-term vision with targets	Strategic and timely investment in staged development that meets community and regional needs	New York Regional Plan Great Kuala Lumpur Master Plan Copenhagen Region Finger Plan
3	Adaptive integrated planning	Short- and long-term spatial planning involving the communities that facilitates timely and coordinated sustainable development	One NYC Copenhagen's cloudburst plan ACT climate change adaptation strategy (Canberra)
4	National sustainable development strategies	A global framework to inform national sustainable development strategies	Denmark Wales Malaysia
5	Net-zero carbon and liveable precincts	Implementing leading-edge precinct planning and design that is zero-carbon, resilient and liveable	Copenhagen's urban design solutions New York City resilient neighbourhood plans
6	Innovative platforms for collaboration, investment and evaluation	Providing innovative platforms that can better connect cutting-edge research with policy decisions with communities to support informed innovative decisions, e.g., sustainable development commissions	R20 World Green Buildings Council UN Sustainable Development Solutions Network (SDSN) International Council for Local Environmental Initiatives (ICLEI) Canberra Urban and Regional Futures (CURF)
7	Green growth	Renewable energy, rapid transit, water-sensitive urban design, air quality, green infrastructure	Singapore (smart infrastructure) Canberra (renewable energy) Copenhagen (green infrastructure) Kuala Lumpur (rapid transit) New York City (urban resilience)

Source: Barbara Norman (2018)

Singapore and Kuala Lumpur) and literature reviews. The seven sustainable pathways are recommendations that have a much greater focus on planning, achieved through the following: (i) planning within planetary boundaries, (ii) long-term vision with targets, (iii) adaptive integrated planning, (iv) national sustainable development strategies, (v) net-zero carbon precincts, (vi) innovative platforms for collaboration and evaluation, and (vii) green growth.

One of the key messages is that investment in good strategic planning that incorporates adapting to the impacts of climate change is essential. This should include ensuring that major urban and regional planning strategies embed climate change adaptation policies across the spectrum from major new developments to urban renewal to day-to-day decision-making processes. We build and rebuild cities every day and that provides a unique opportunity to make a very significant change in the near-term: water-sensitive urban design, renewable energy, climate-sensitive urban design and smart infrastructure through public investment. This will require a more integrated approach to managing urban development, better connecting the built and natural environments. There has been massive recent investment in rapid public transit across the Asia Pacific region. However, much more needs to be done in greening and cooling our cities in the region. Singapore is an example of increasing urban density and 'greenery' at the same time by including 'living-infrastructure' considerations in every step along the decision-making process of urban development (Norman, 2018a: 133).

A second key message is that clear targets within a long-term vision can be very effective. A clear example is the increasing number of cities and regions committing to a 100 percent renewable energy target. These include Canberra, Australia, which is on track to achieve 100 percent renewable electricity by 2020. Set as a target by the government in 2012, it provided a very clear direction and pathway to achieve this goal, and importantly provided a signal to private-sector investment. This also provides an excellent example of how a medium-sized city can transition to a 100 percent renewable future (ACT Government, 2019).

A third important message is that new technologies will play a vital role in making cities and towns more sustainable. An advantage in the Asia Pacific region is that in many places it will enable a leapfrogging from no energy source, or very little, to more independent local renewable energy—solar, wind and hydro. Solar cells in relatively inaccessible places (for example villages in northern India) are providing enough energy for cooking, charging a mobile phone and light in the evening for school children to do their homework. This is bringing economic, social and environmental benefits to isolated communities.

The adoption of new technologies in 'smart cities' must also be implemented with a deeper understanding that a city cannot be divorced from its regional ecosystem. Cities are not autonomous, but an 'urban system within wider systems including Earth systems (water, energy, carbon, biodiversity and so on), social migration, global capital and more' (Norman, 2018b).

Finally, more and more networks are developing that can better support planning professionals in low- and middle-income countries and assist with local capacity building on both mitigation and adaptation. *Planners for climate action* (P4CA) is one such example. Initiated by UN-Habitat, P4CA seeks to bring a key professional group connected across the world, sharing their knowledge and practice on climate change. Launched in February 2019 in Nairobi, the mission of P4CA is to catalyse and accelerate climate action through responsible and transformative urban and territorial planning practice, education and research, with the following objectives:

- Practice: Integrate climate change in the professional practices of all planners and their institutions through integrated approaches that reduce emissions, and prepare human settlements to adapt to climate change;
- Capacity-building: Build the capacity of all planners by ensuring that all graduate-level urban/regional planning curricula prepare planners to be effective climate change professionals;
- Research: Support and commission research that can strengthen knowledge at the intersection of planning practices and climate change.

(UN-Habitat, 2019)

This new global planning network provides the opportunity for built-environment professionals to work together in better mainstreaming climate change action into land use planning, encouraging more integrated planning, designing with nature, climate-sensitive urban design and green infrastructure.

Conclusions

While planning for climate change is a challenge for all countries, it is especially so in the Asia Pacific region. This is because the region is at the centre of global urban growth and is also facing some of the greatest impacts of climate change. While much of the discussion planning for climate change has global application, there are important distinctive conclusions for this region. In summary these are:

1. The Asia Pacific region brings enormous diversity and expertise as well some of the most extremes of poverty, environmental degradation and economic disparity.

2. The scale and pace of change vastly exceeds the rest of the world, bringing both enormous risks and opportunities.
3. The immediate ability to adopt technology and leapfrog into the 21st century including renewable energy, rapid urban transit, net-zero carbon developments and water-sensitive urban design.
4. The opportunity to implement a sustainable urban agenda that better embeds the natural environment into the built environment (i.e., the need to design with nature) to improve the health and well-being of communities at the same time as improving environment and economic outcomes.
5. The opportunity to introduce better forms of urban governance to manage large urban conglomerations.

Planning for climate change in the Asia Pacific region therefore will require collaboration between the sectors, across nations and environments, taking solutions beyond the 'normal'. This will involve investing in better-integrated urban planning, investing in living infrastructure, maintaining healthy ecosystems, innovation across the board, and developing clear targets and pathways for all to adapt to new climate futures where 'no one is left behind'.

Even if we collectively achieve minimising the increase in global temperature to 1.5°C, there will be many challenges for urban and rural communities. However, as the IPPC concludes, 'mainstreaming sustainable development policies and the inclusion of climate proofing concepts in national development initiatives are likely to reduce pressure on national resources and improve the management of risk' (IPCC, 2014a). And on that note, there remains hope and a more resilient pathway forward.

References

ACT Government. (2019). *100% Renewable Energy Target*. Available at: www.environment.act.gov.au/energy/cleaner-energy/renewable-energy-target-legislation-reporting.

Asian Development Bank (ADB). (2017). *A Region at Risk: The Human Dimension of Climate Change in Asia and the Pacific*. Manila: ADB.

Bazaz, A., et al. (2018). *Summary for Urban Policy Makers: What the IPCC Special Report on Global Warming of 1.5°C Means for Cities?* Prepared for the Global Covenant of Mayors for Climate and Energy and C40 Cities Climate Leadership Group.

Intergovernmental Panel on Climate Change (IPCC). (2014a). *Climate Change 2014, Synthesis Report*. Contribution of Working Groups 1, 2 and 3 to the Fifth Assessment Report. Geneva: IPCC.

Intergovernmental Panel on Climate Change (IPCC). (2014b). Climate Change 2014, Impacts, Adaptation and Vulnerability, Part B, Regional Aspects, Asia. Available at: www.ipcc.ch/report/ar5/wg2/asia/.

Intergovernmental Panel on Climate Change (IPCC). (2018). *IPCC Special Report on Global Warming of 1.5°C*. Available at: www.ipcc.ch/sr15/about/multimedia/.

The Lancet Commission on Health and Climate Change. (2015). Health and climate change: Policy responses to protect public health. *The Lancet*. Available at: www.thelancet.com/pdfs/journals/lancet/PIIS0140-6736(15)60854-6.pdf.

Norman, B. (2018a). *Sustainable Pathways for Our Cities and Regions: Planning Within Planetary Boundaries*. London and New York: Routledge.

Norman, B. (2018b). 'Are autonomous cities our urban future?' *Nature Communication*, 9, Article Number 2111. Available at: www.nature.com/articles/s41467-018-04505-0.

Sharif, M. (2018). *Opening Speech by Madam Mohd Sharif to World Urban Forum 2018*. Available at: http://wuf9.org/media-centre/news/wuf9-opening-speech-by-madam-maimunah-mohd-sharif-under-secretary-general-and-executive-director-un-habitat/.

UN Human Settlements Program (UN-Habitat). (2016). *The New Urban Agenda, adopted by the United Nations on 26 October 2016, Quito, Ecuador*. Available at: http://habitat3.org/the-new-urban-agenda/.

UN Human Settlements Program (UN-Habitat). (2018a). *Kuala Lumpur Declaration on Cities 2030, 9th World Urban Forum Declaration*. Available at: https://wuf9.org/kuala-lumpur-declaration/.

UN Human Settlements Program (UN-Habitat). (2018b). *Tracking Progress Towards Inclusive, Safe, Resilient and Sustainable Cities and Human Settlements*. SDG 11 Synthesis Report. High Level Political Forum, 2018.

UN Human Settlements Program (UN-Habitat). (2019). *Planners for Climate Action*. Available at: www.planners4climate.org/.

UN Human Settlements Program (UN-Habitat) and UN Economic and Social Commission for Asia and the Pacific (UNESCAP). (2015). *The State of Asian and Pacific Cities 2015—Urban Transformations, Shifting from Quantity to Quality*. Available at: www.unescap.org/sites/default/files/The%20State%20of%20Asian%20and%20Pacific%20Cities%202015.pdf.

United Nations (UN). (2015). *Sustainable Development Goals (SDGs)*. New York.

United Nations International Strategy for Disaster Reduction (UNISDR). (2015). *Sendai Framework for Disaster Risk Reduction 2015–2030*. Geneva, Switzerland: UNISDR.

Chapter 10

Community Resilience Through Self-Help Housing Adaptations

Examples From Nepal and the Philippines

Sandra Carrasco and Neeraj Dangol

Introduction

This chapter explores informal dwellers' motivation for spontaneous construction of housing adaptations to produce safer housing environments with necessary living space. Globally, government leadership has been recognised as at the core of effective urban disaster risk reduction, aiming to create resilient communities as it is referred to in the Sendai Framework for Disaster Risk Reduction 2015–2030 (UNISDR, 2015). Disaster risk-reduction planning, however, rarely includes spontaneous people's initiatives. Lewis (2013a) claims that the emergence of spontaneous resilience is difficult without 'authoritative direction and administration', i.e., government involvement. Conversely, participative and inclusive approaches are needed 'to make cities and human settlements safe, resilient and sustainable', as stated in the Goal 11 of the Sustainable Development Goals (United Nations, 2015).

Although urban development planning is in the hands of policymakers and authorities, the *New Urban Agenda* (UN-Habitat, 2016) calls for the recognition of local communities' capacities and their active involvement through incremental and self-built schemes (UN-Habitat, 2016). In addition, the Rockefeller Foundation (2014) defines city resilience as 'the capacity of cities to function, so that the people living and working in cities survive and thrive no matter what stresses or shocks they encounter' (Rockefeller Foundation, 2014). This has a particular emphasis on the poor and vulnerable and also highlights their capacities to 'survive, adapt and grow'.

Government agencies work mostly within the parameters of what is regulated, formalised or allowed. In the case of informal settlements or unrecognised construction within formally built settlements, government officials find themselves out of alternatives, even when there is the political will to support informal dwellers (as evidenced, for example, in a study about the Indonesian city of Surabaya's informal riverside settlements [Taylor, 2015]).

Moreover, government frameworks find difficulties in recognising housing co-production through residents' self-help construction. Studies on large housing projects, such as social and post-disaster housing projects, reveal mismatches between government-backed housing programmes and the urgency for resident-built housing extensions and in-house modifications. For instance, researchers observed the need for housing modification in post-disaster housing in the city of Cagayan de Oro in the Philippines (Carrasco et al., 2016), post-disaster reconstructed houses in Cankiri Province in Turkey (Dikmen et al., 2016), post-tsunami reconstructed settlements in Aceh, Indonesia (O'Brien and Ahmed, 2012), and in government-built housing in metropolitan Bangkok (Natakun and O'Brien, 2009).

Despite the urgency of people themselves to adapt their houses, government officials often believe that recognising people's spontaneous and unsupervised construction of housing adaptations in any way would allow people to build slums (Tipple and Ameen, 1999). Studies on self-help housing adaptations find that governments claim that recognising informal housing constructions would mean the legitimisation of the production of squatters (Porio, 2013) or, in case of resettled communities, re-create the squatter conditions in which they used to live before (Carrasco et al., 2016). Regardless of governments' position about allowing, limiting or prohibiting the self-production of the built environment, people consciously or not make decisions and take actions defying the status quo of centralised power to address their own problems (Holston, 2008). This redefines the meaning of inclusion of the excluded and citizenship, challenging the conventionally understood roles of marginalised communities through insurgent practices emerging from 'under the skin of the city' (Miraftab, 2009; Perlman, 2005). These grassroots practices are the result of the urgency to survive and are spontaneous and imaginative solutions to withstand disruptive challenges such as hazard exposure (Chatterjee, 2010; Dangol and Day, 2017; Jabeen and Johnson, 2013) and displacement (Taylor, 2015).

This chapter focuses on the adaptive capacities of informal urban dwellers to transform their housing in two locations: flood-prone informal riverside communities in Kathmandu in Nepal and disaster-induced resettled communities in the city of Cagayan de Oro in the Philippines. The study aims to explore the residents' perceptions of risk and how the housing adaptations were built. The households' responses are compared with observations of the quality and effectiveness of the housing adaptations in order to find coherences or inconsistencies in the self-production of safer housing environments with necessary living spaces.

The information for this chapter was collected during fieldwork in the city of Cagayan de Oro, Philippines in 2014, and Kathmandu, Nepal in 2016 by the authors. In Cagayan de Oro, four communities within the largest resettlement site were selected. The original study is part of doctoral research that included data collected between July and August 2014, 28 months after Typhoon Washi hit the city. The data collection included a questionnaire survey to 240 resettled households and semi-structured interviews with 20 households and observations. In Kathmandu, the data was collected as part of doctoral research observing residents' flood-adaptation initiatives in informal riverside areas. The external support to the informal residents' communities was absent. The original study included the collection of primary data through in-depth semi-structured interviews and inspection of houses conducted between June and September 2016 to 40 households of three informal settlements in Kathmandu.

The analysis of the case studies aims to understand informal settlers' motivations to construct spontaneous adaptations of housing. Although the collected data presents a realistic local situation based on people's empirical practices, the limited number of case studies would differ from statistical quantitative studies that might consider larger sample sizes. Moreover, the changing nature of housing would require multiple studies to have an accurate image of the incremental process, trends and consequences of the self-help construction of housing adaptations.

Housing Adaptations Towards Resilience

Adaptations are considered to be manifestations of adaptive capacity to make changes required to better deal with extreme events (Smit and Wandel, 2006). People's adaptive capacities to accommodate the unexpected changes in their socio-spatial conditions—such as disasters—require the development of flexible community approaches to incorporate the series of changes in residential dwellings in line with changing in household requirements (Bouzarovski, 2015). The capacities that enable changes to influence resilience, either intentionally or unintentionally (Walker et al., 2004), and the multiple nature and levels of adaptations refer to anticipatory or reactive, autonomous or planned changes (Smit and Wandel, 2006). Although adaptability influences resilience, fundamental changes in the system are produced through the deployment of adaptive capacities, which are referred to as transformability (Walker et al., 2004). Although a comprehensive study would require the analysis of the multiple dimensions of transformation, this chapter focuses on the socio-spatial adaptation that enabled the transformation of the physical environment.

Self-help initiatives in the tangible built environment often fall within the perception of informality, which is usually assumed as prone to be degraded to a state of precarity through a process of 'slumization' (Davis, 2006). The tense coexistence between formality and informality lies on the definition of which is perceived as legitimate or not. However, understanding informality as the expression of de facto possession and its sovereignty in a state of exception requires challenging the planning system which produces the planning and the unplannable (Roy, 2005).

Generally, government positions about self-help initiatives have historically been accompanied by a deeply rooted stigma that justifies the eradication of informal settlements (Perlman, 2005), and the restriction of the improvements and adaptations of housing and neighbourhoods (Lizarralde, 2014; Carrasco et al., 2016). The concerns regarding the spontaneous development of the built environment are based on the limitations in terms of quality of construction, materials and the skills required of the residents to carry out these tasks by themselves (Greene and Rojas, 2008; Narafu et al., 2010; O'Brien and Ahmed, 2012). Seabrook (1996) stressed that the transition from government-supported programmes to entirely self-help programmes is infeasible.

The different warnings against the uncontrollable nature of self-help construction are frequently accompanied by recommendations for assisted self-help schemes by government agencies or NGOs (UN-Habitat, 2005; Lizarralde, 2014; Carrasco et al., 2016) which call for an 'enabling strategy' where slum-dwellers are co-developers of housing and redevelopment projects (Mukhija, 2003). The reality of the daily life of informal dwellers, regardless of whether they have been 'beneficiaries' of government-sponsored resettlement projects or if they are still living in precarious neighbourhoods, is attached to the stigma of poverty and the tendency to be marginalised as current or former 'slum dwellers'. Therefore, informal settlers and their adaptive capacities to cope with stresses are discouraged and dismissed by local authorities (Satterthwaite et al., 2007; Carmin et al., 2012) since they are considered invalid alternatives for development, as these capacities could only guarantee a sheer survival (Amin, 2013). However, this study found that in the absence of external support, people take action on their own due to the urgency to keep their family safe from natural hazards or to provide liveable spaces for the families, challenging the official validation.

The following sections present seven case studies of self-help housing adaptations observed at the household level in the locations described earlier. The case studies are discussed in terms of residents' risk awareness, motivations to implement adaptations, characteristics and effectiveness of adaptations.

Riverside Informal Dwellers in Kathmandu, Nepal

This section presents three case studies of informal dwellers in one of the Kathmandu's riverbank informal settlements, at Shantinagar area situated along the Bagmati River. Shantinagar emerged in the early 2000s. It is located near highly commercial areas of the city and the international airport. The settlement has easy access to urban amenities such as hospitals, schools, public transportation, markets, cinemas and commercial complexes. It has 693 houses according to a survey conducted in 2013 (NBBSS and NMES, 2013).

A large portion of this settlement is affected by the flood incidents every year (Rai, 2015). The houses which are situated next to the river are profoundly affected. The residents have built a series of housing adaptations which are mainly conceived as spontaneous initiatives to protect their houses from the rise of the river waters that cause floods during the annual monsoon seasons. Due to the limited technical studies regarding the effectiveness of resident-built flood adaptations in informal settlements, the researchers presented the different types of adaptations observed to local engineers who provided insights about the efficiency of these constructions to cope with floods. Additionally, the residents' empirical perceptions regarding the effectiveness of adaptations were considered.

Case Study One

The household make-up in this case (Figure 10.1) is a nuclear family with two children. The main occupation of the breadwinner of the family is working in construction, while both children are at school. The average monthly family income is Nepalese Rupee (Rs) 15,000 (Approx. USD 150).

1. *Risk awareness*: The family perceived a high flood risk because they experienced recurring flood impacts. Flood incidents have repeatedly partially damaged their house and their belongings. They were aware of the increase in flood intensity and frequency in recent years.
2. *Motivations for adaptation*: The main reason was to protect the family and their belongings from the water during floods, as they also perceive higher intensity and frequency of these events. Their main limitation is their weak financial condition that prevents them from upgrading adaptations.
3. *Characteristics of adaptations*: The family gradually raised the ground level and the entrance, as can be seen in Figure 10.1. As the brick walls are becoming lower, the family raises the roof and uses makeshift materials—such as bamboo poles and plastic sheets—for the walls. Although the family planned to raise the brick walls, they cannot afford it at the moment. Additionally, the fear of eviction also prevents them from higher investments in housing adaptations as they perceive an uncertain future of their home and tenure security.
4. *Effectiveness of the adaptation*: Based on observations and visual assessments from local experts, the level of adaptation implemented can be considered lower compared to other adaptations found in the settlement. The residents also stated that what they implemented was not enough to reduce the flood impacts. As they have the skill of building construction, they implemented the adaptation measures by themselves.

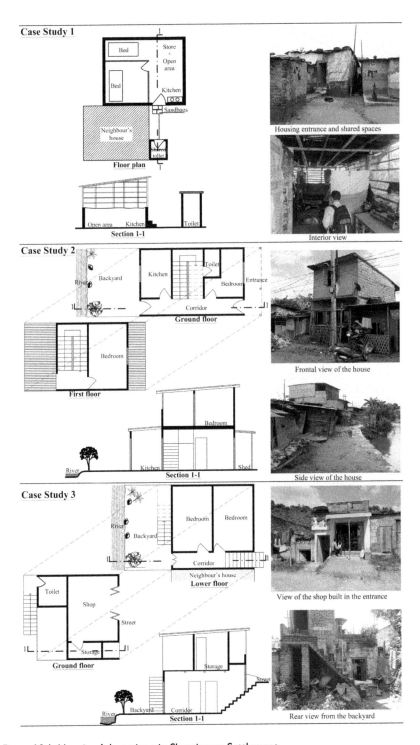

Figure 10.1 Housing Adaptations in Shantinagar Settlement.

Source: Author's own

Case Study Two

The family residing in the selected house (Figure 10.1) is composed of seven family members as an extended family covering three generations—parents, two sons, daughter, daughter-in-law and grandchild. The family income comes from the retirement pensions of both parents and remittances from one of the sons who is living abroad. The average monthly family income is Rs 40,000 (Approx. USD 400), which is considered higher in the community.

1. *Risk awareness*: The family believed that the floods they faced in the past were life-threatening experiences, especially the flood the previous year, as they barely managed to escape. In a hurry to protect their lives, the residents did not have time to protect their belongings, which were damaged.
2. *Motivations for adaptation*: To have safer spaces within their house to protect the family members as well as their belongings. Although the threats were recurrent, the family did not have enough financial capacity to invest in construction until the elder son started to earn money, and they then decided to build an upper level.
3. *Characteristics of adaptations*: The family firstly understood that they needed an upper level to protect their belongings and so that there would be safe spaces for the family during the monsoon seasons and the consequent floods. Although the formally established neighbours objected to this construction, the family kept improving their house. Moreover, they also felt that they were recognised by the government because they were provided with basic services, which the family perceived as security of tenure and a lower risk of eviction. It also supported their motivation to invest in the adaptation.
4. *Effectiveness of the adaptation*: The level of adaptation implemented can be considered high. The residents also experienced that the flood impacts reduced considerably in comparison to previous years. As seen in Figure 10.1, the upper floor provided them with a safer place to stay and keep valuable belongings. They hired local masons and workers to build the house. Mostly concrete blocks were used to build the walls and corrugated galvanised metal sheets were used as the roof and some portions of the wall. The improvement of the house seemed enough to reduce the flood impacts until severe flooding occurs.

Case Study Three

The household in this case study (Figure 10.1) is also an extended family with five family members—single mother, son, daughter, daughter-in-law and grandchild. Concerning the occupations of the breadwinners, the single mother runs kiosk from home and the son works as a security guard. The average monthly family income is Rs 15,000 (Approx. USD150).

1. *Risk awareness*: Flood incidents have repeatedly damaged the family belongings. Moreover, backflow from the toilet worsened past flood impacts. The impacts were not limited to damages to belongings, but also included impacts on the health of most of the family members. They were aware of the increase in flood intensity and frequency in recent years, which increased their risk perception.
2. *Motivations for adaptation*: To reduce the backflow from the toilet and reduce the health risks in the family. They were also aware of the damages to their belongings.
3. *Characteristics of adaptations*: The family moved the toilet to the upper level. Additionally, to reduce repeated damage to their belongings by flood water, they raised the ground level at the riverside and used sandbag walls to hold the raised ground. Objections from the formal neighbours and eviction notices discouraged them from spending fullheartedly on the adaptation measures. Moreover, the single mother had a hard time managing money for daily necessities. Only when her son started earning could she manage enough money to implement flood adaptations and to improve the housing condition. Conflicting relationships with the adjacent neighbour also affected the implementation of the adaptations because they could affect his property negatively.
4. *Effectiveness of the adaptation*: The level of adaptation implemented can be considered at a moderate level. It could withstand the less intense floods; however, in cases of high-intensity floods, the adaptation measures would prove ineffective. This was accepted by the residents as well. They hired local masons to build the toilet on the upper level. They worked themselves to raise the ground at the riverside and to build the sandbag walls at the river's edge.

Resettled Communities in Cagayan de Oro, Philippines

This section presents the situation of resettled families in the city of Cagayan de Oro, which was hit by an unexpectedly intense typhoon in December 2011. Typhoon Washi caused an unprecedented displacement of the urban population. The residents of informal settlements located on the riverbank were the target of government-driven resettlement. The four case studies presented were selected from two villages in the largest resettlement site in the city: Mahogany Village, whose houses were built with permanent materials such as concrete blocks and reinforced concrete structural elements; and the Filipino-Chinese Friendship Village, whose houses were built with non-permanent prefabricated materials. Both housing typologies followed the minimum requirements for social housing in the country—National Building Code of the Philippines and the Minimum Design Standards and Requirements for Economic and Socialized Housing Projects—that defines a housing unit as an indoor open space and a toilet with a combined minimum area of 21 square metres. These houses are occupied by families of up to 12 people, as found in the fieldwork, and in principle do not enable expansion of the liveable area, except for mezzanines or lofts in Mahogany's houses, to be carried out either by the government or by the residents themselves.

The families suffered multiple shocks from the traumatic and disastrous event, removal from their homes and adaptation to their new lives in a new environment with basic housing conditions. The residents performed a series of self-help adaptions to the government-supplied houses, in most of the cases adding living spaces or even renovating the entire house. These adaptations were driven by different motivations, and the performance and implications of their quality are explained in each case. The safety concerns were focused on two main threats that the families are exposed to, namely earthquakes and typhoons. The risk of floods was dismissed for the observation as it was assumed that appropriate technical assessments were conducted by the government prior to the construction of houses in resettlement sites. The references for the observations of seismic performance and wind resistance are based on studies from Imai et al. (2015), Nishijima and Espina (2015), Shelter Cluster and Department of Social Welfare and development (2014), and the Institute of Strategy for Disaster risk reduction (2008). This section presents the state of the housing adaptations two years after the families moved into their current houses.

Case Study Four

The household of house selected for this case study (see Figure 10.2) is a nuclear family composed of both parents and three children. Prior to resettlement, the family house was destroyed by the typhoon. The occupations of the breadwinners of the family are hawker and shopkeeper. The family has an average daily income of Philippines Peso (PhP) 100 to 200 (approximately USD1.90–3.81) considered as a medium in the community.

1. *Risk awareness and safety perception before the typhoon*: The family perceived two main threats, typhoons and floods, both with a regular frequency. Residents also expressed that both threats put them in equally regular difficulties to cope with the hazards and to overcome their impacts.
2. *Risk awareness and safety perception in relocation sites*: Residents only see floods as a possible threat, as there is a creek nearby the settlement. The residents feel confident about the quality of the houses provided by the government. However, the residents still observe that they might have to face medium difficulties to cope with possible floods and their impacts on the family.
3. *Current living conditions and housing adaptations*: The family observed an improvement in their housing and living conditions compared to

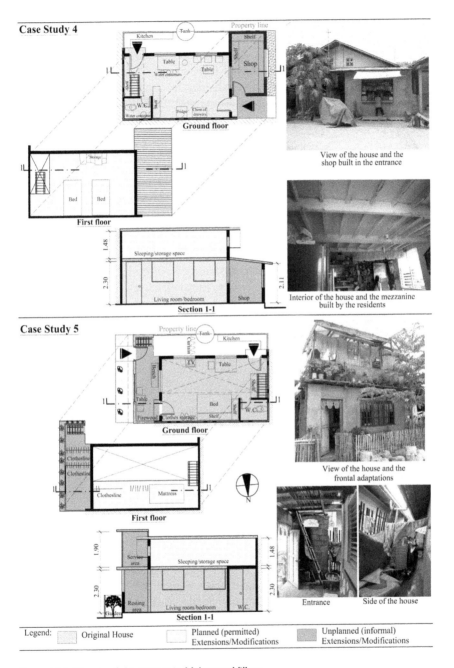

Figure 10.2 Housing Adaptations in Mahogany Village.

Source: Author's own

the former informal settlement. Housing adaptations were motivated by the need to have an income source. The family built frontal and side extensions to open a shop. Additionally, the family built a mezzanine inside the provided house. The housing adaptations were built two months after the family moved into the new house. The construction was performed by the members themselves using hollow concrete blocks for walls and galvanised iron sheets with timber structure for the roof. The areas of the extensions are: Loft = 17.23 m², shop = 5.73 m² and entrance = 2.32 m².

4. *Wind-resistance performance*: The absence of technical guidance produces uncertainty in the quality of the construction. There are no foundations, which makes the walls weak to resist strong winds and they might collapse. However, the roof structure is connected to the wall with rebar, the interval between wooden roof fasteners is between 30 to 60 cm, and the eave is also between 30 to 60 cm. This indicates a medium resistance of the roofing to strong winds.

Seismic performance: No foundations were built for the walls of the extensions. Also, there are no structural elements, such as columns and beams. Although hollow concrete blocks were used to build the walls, the absence of a foundation, structural elements, lack of attachment to the main building and the absence of steel bars makes the extensions poorly built to resist earthquakes.

Case Study Five

The makeup of the household in Case Study 5 (see Figure 10.2) is an extended family composed of nine family members. The family has both parents, two adult sons, a daughter-in-law and three infants. The father is the head of the family and the main breadwinner. He works in construction; the average family daily income is more than PhP 200 (approximately more than USD 3.81), which for the local community is considered within the higher income groups.

1. *Risk awareness and safety perception before the typhoon*: The family house in the former settlement was built with durable materials such as concrete blocks and the roofing was a mix of the concrete structure and, in some parts, corrugated galvanised sheets with a wooden structure. The house was partially damaged because of the typhoon in 2011. The family observed floods as the main threat that they were exposed to with a high frequency and it was extremely difficult to cope with the high impacts that flood caused in the family.

2. *Risk awareness and safety perception in relocation sites*: The family still observes floods as the threat for their house and family. However, their perception in terms of frequency and the difficulty to cope and the

possible impacts in the family have been reduced. They do not perceive earthquakes and typhoons as potential threats to their family or house.

3. *Current living conditions and housing adaptations*: The family perceives the quality of their living conditions in the new settlement equal. The main motivation to adapt the house was the need for space for family activities together with the need to have fresher spaces during the day due to the extreme heat in the provided house. Thus, they built a two-story extension in the entrance of the house and a mezzanine inside the original house. These spaces are used as resting areas and as storage of wood for cooking. The extensions were built four months after the family moved into the new house. The materials for the frontal ground floor extension are concrete blocks and wood for the first floor. The mezzanine was built with timber. The areas of the extensions are: Resting space=5.52 m^2 (ground floor) and 8.08 m^2 (in the first floor), and the mezzanine=8.78 m^2.

4. *Wind-resistance performance*: The builder had construction experience; however, there were no foundations for the walls, columns and beams. The roofing materials are non-permanent, including the wooden structure and corrugated plastic sheets. The walls on the first floor are made of timber poles and plywood; the connections of the roof structure and the walls are only nails. The interval between fasteners is more than 60 cm and the eaves are between 30 to 60 cm. These characteristics provide few chances to withstand strong winds.

   Seismic performance: The extensions lacked important structural elements such as proper foundations, columns and even steel bars in the walls to withstand a possible earthquake. Although the frequency of seismic events is unpredictable, the house could be heavily damaged or even collapse in an earthquake.

Case Study Six

The household (see Figure 10.3) is a nuclear family composed of five members: both parents and three children/young adults, aged 11 to 20 years old. The main income source for the family is the local shop and internet cafe that the family have established in their house. The average daily family income is more than PhP 200 (more than USD 3.81), which makes them one of the privileged in the community.

1. *Risk awareness and safety perception before the typhoon*: The family's former house was precariously built with local materials and was destroyed by the typhoon. The family perceived exposure to typhoons, floods, earthquakes and landslides. The family also expressed that coping with floods was the most challenging, followed by the typhoons and landslides. However, landslides were the hazards that caused a higher impact on the family.

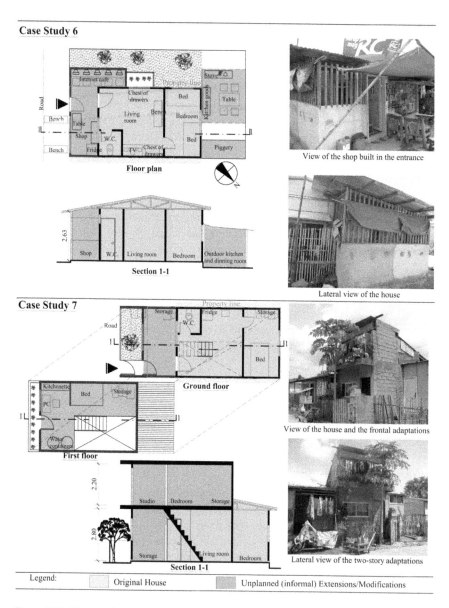

Figure 10.3 Housing Adaptations in Filipino-Chinese Friendship Village.
Source: Adapted from Carrasco et al. (2017)

2. *Risk awareness and safety perception in relocation sites*: The family feels that it would be very difficult to cope with flooding and that such an event would cause a high impact on the family. One of the reasons for this perception is the low quality of the house provided in the resettlement

site. The houses were considered permanent structures despite the use of prefabricated materials commonly used for temporary housing. Additionally, the location of the house in the settlement next a creek makes the family fear the rise of the waters in cases of heavy rains.

3. *Current living conditions and housing adaptations*: The family observes an improvement in their living conditions compared to their former houses. The motivations to build housing adaptations were the need to have an income source, to add spaces for family needs and relief from uncomfortable and hot interior spaces in the original house. The adaptations included the extension in the frontal area of the house that partly expands to the side of the original house. There are non-permanent/ makeshift additions in the rear of the house. The family took a long time to perform the permanent adaptations and they started two years after they moved into the new house. In the frontal extension, the walls were partly built with concrete blocks and the upper part was built with wood and roofed with corrugated galvanised metal sheets. The area extended is 9.18 m² (shop and internet café).

4. *Wind-resistance performance*: The extensions were built by the family without technical assistance. The walls have no foundations or structural elements such as columns. The walls were built with hollow concrete blocks up to one-meter high, and the upper part of the walls was precariously built with timber. The roof structure is only attached to the walls by nails and the spacing between fasteners in the roof structure are between 30 to 60 cm. Therefore, the extensions are in risk of collapse or significant damage if an intense typhoon hits the area again.

   Seismic performance: The lack of foundation and structural elements already makes the extensions weak to seismic forces. Additionally, the lack of proper roof attachments to the main building and the weak roofing structure makes the construction weak.

Case Study Seven

The family residing in the studied house (Figure 10.3) is a nuclear family composed of both parents and three kids. The occupation of the family head is a labourer and the average daily income is higher than PhP 200 (higher than USD 3.81). They are also considered as a higher income family in the community.

1. *Risk awareness and safety perception before the typhoon*: The house in the former settlement was precariously built and was destroyed by the typhoon. The household perceived exposure to typhoons, floods, earthquakes and risk of landslides. Similar to the previous case study, the family observes floods as the most difficult hazard to cope with.

2. *Risk awareness and safety perception in relocation sites*: The perception of hazards has not changed, as the fear of floods is considered their main

concern. Although storms, earthquakes and landslides are considered by the residents, these hazards do not challenge their coping capacities.

3. *Current living conditions and housing adaptations*: The family perceives an improvement of their overall economic conditions, health, housing, neighbourhood and community life. The motivations to adapt the house were the uncomfortable high temperatures inside the house, the perceived weakness of the house and the reduced space to accommodate the family needs. The adaptations were built 14 months after the family moved into the house. The adaptations included frontal extensions and replacement of parts of the original house, all built with permanent materials such as reinforced concrete and concrete blocks. The house is the only one that has two stories. The areas of the extensions are ground floor=7.13 m^2 and in the first floor=12.75 m^2.

4. *Wind-resistance performance*: The housing adaptations were built by a mason. The two-story extensions include construction with concrete blocks and reinforced concrete in the structural elements and a concrete slab. The foundations were built with concrete and steel bars similar to columns and beams. There is a proper connection of the roof to the main structure. The roof structure is made of timber with a spacing between fasteners of 45 cm, covered by corrugated galvanised metal sheets, and the eaves are 45 cm wide. The structure is resistant to strong winds.

Seismic performance: The proper construction of walls with reinforced concrete foundations and structural elements, and walls built with hollow concrete blocks confined by columns and beams create a solid structure. In general, from the observation and based on the indicators for evaluation, the housing extensions would resist a possible earthquake.

Discussion and Conclusions

In the cases presented, families invested in different types of housing extensions considering permanent and non-permanent materials, complexity in use and area added. Despite the different socioeconomic conditions of the families, they are willing to invest in building housing adaptations to reduce the risk of future disastrous events. In the case of the riverside settlements in Kathmandu, families were driven by the need to protect their members from floods. Many of them perceived discouragement from the neighbouring residents of formal settlements. However, informal settlers experienced higher confidence after building extensions as well as pride and a sense of secure tenure of their houses despite the lack of a legal title. In the cases presented, the residents made the adaptations based on their empirical knowledge and experiences of regularly dealing with floods and aimed to reduce the risks, although the effectiveness of the adaptations to withstand future flooding events is not clear.

In resettlement sites in Cagayan de Oro, the families mainly built extensions to the government-provided houses to adapt to family needs and priorities in a new physical environment. In most of the cases, the families built the extensions by themselves using local knowledge and some notions of construction. When the complexity of the extensions overpassed local knowledge, the residents chose to hire qualified workers to ensure the quality of their investment, although the construction quality might not necessarily be guaranteed (Carrasco et al., 2016). Although the residents' risk awareness might be present in their daily lives, the housing extensions did not reflect the need to protect the family but to satisfy their needs or alleviate the failures in the houses provided.

These findings do not align with Lewis's (2013a) claim that the emergence of spontaneous resilience in a community would take longer, or might not happen, without an 'authoritative direction and administration'. In three cases of informal settlers' housing in Kathmandu without external support, residents managed to build their resiliency according to their capacities. In four cases in Cagayan de Oro, the families managed to build the extensions by themselves. It was found that in both locations, residents incrementally and continuously put in effort to develop their resilience through housing adaptations. This finding strengthens the necessity of the recognition of local communities' capacities and their involvement as put forward by UN-Habitat (2016) and Rockefeller Foundation (2014).

The housing adaptations built by the residents in both locations show how they developed capacities to adapt their physical environment to cope with challenging conditions. In fact, the residents' capacities to 'survive, adapt and grow' are presented and might be seen as a level of resilience achieved. However, this might not necessarily mean the reduction of all risks. Actually, some of the vulnerabilities might still be present in the communities and make them highly exposed to disasters. However, Perlman (2005) claimed that this should not be used to blame the poor for their own vulnerabilities. The transformative process of aiming to achieve resilience is regarded as 'more a process than an outcome' (UNDP, quoted by Kindra, 2013). Lewis (2013b) also says that in reality, processes of resilience and vulnerability could run in parallel. The cases presented here show a process of social resilience, as the families were able to take actions by themselves in times of adversity, and these difficulties had a direct influence in the transformation of their physical environment through the adaptation of their houses.

This chapter observed peoples' perspectives beyond the victimisation of the poor and focused on their own adaptive capacities, limitations and their active contribution to the progressive improvement of their housing by themselves. These incremental self-help practices are common construction practices in the Global South. One study estimated that 50 to 80 percent of the population in most developing nations build their homes progressively (Ferguson and Smets, 2010). Moreover, these schemes of incremental production of housing environments are considered one of the most efficient, affordable and sustainable ways to have and to increase access to housing (Tipple, 2000; UN-Habitat, 2005; Goethert, 2010). The absence of government support did not stop these 'marginalised' families from taking the challenges of housing into their own hands, and these could potentially expand to their neighbourhoods and city development. This perhaps suggests a possible reconsideration of government leadership as the core of urban disaster risk reduction aiming to create resilient communities as referred by the Sendai framework (UNISDR, 2015). However, it cannot be ignored that housing development by marginalised communities can increase their risk to hazards and adversities if they are residing at hazardous locations.

Finally, this chapter echoes Roy's (2005) claims that confronting the limitations of the policies and models for urban development provides a more realistic sense of conflicts and politics. The policies and models for urban development often ignore or reject informal housing adaptations initiated by communities in their disaster management frameworks. These policies and models can be challenged by understanding the resident-led process of housing production which would provide opportunities for residents and governments to plan for adequate housing production. Specifically, understanding the relationship between residents and institutional actors and, in particular, established housing providers (governments, NGOs and private developers) is essential in the development of resilient communities.

References

Amin, A. (2013). Telescopic urbanism and the poor. *City*, 17(4), 476–492.

Bouzarovski, S. (2015). *Retrofitting the City: Residential Flexibility, Resilience and the Built Environment*. London: Bloomsbury Publishing.

Carmin, J., Nadkarni, N. and Rhie, C. (2012). *Progress and Challenges in Urban Climate Adaptation Planning: Results of a Global Survey*. Cambridge, MA: Massachusetts Institute of Technology (MIT).

Carrasco, S., Ochiai, C. and Okazaki, K. (2016). Impacts of resident-initiated housing modifications in resettlement sites in Cagayan de Oro, Philippines. *International Journal of Disaster Risk Reduction*, 17, 100–113.

Carrasco, S., Ochiai, C. and Okazaki, K. (2017). Residential satisfaction and housing modifications: A study in disaster-induced resettlement sites in Cagayan de Oro, Philippines. *International Journal of Disaster Resilience in the Built Environment*, 8(2), 175–189.

Chatterjee, M. (2010). Slum dwellers response to flooding events in the megacities of India. *Mitigation and Adaptation Strategies for Global Change*, 15(4), 337–353.

Dangol, N. and Day, J. (2017). Flood adaptation by informal settlers in Kathmandu and their fear of eviction. *International Journal of Safety and Security Engineering*, 7(2), 147–156.

Da Silva, J. (2014). *City Resilience Framework*. London: The Rockefeller Foundation and Arup. Available at: https://assets.rockefellerfoundation.org/app/uploads/20140410162455/City-Resilience-Framework-2015.pdf (accessed October 2018).

Davis, M. (2006). *Planet of Slums*. London: Verso.

Dikmen, N. and Elias-Ozkan, S.T. (2016). Housing after disaster: A post occupancy evaluation of a reconstruction project. *International Journal of Disaster Risk Reduction*, 19, 167–178.

Ferguson, B. and Smets, P. (2010). Finance for incremental housing; current status and prospects for expansion. *Habitat International*, 34(3), 288–298.

Goethert, R. (2010). *Incremental Housing: A Proactive Urban Strategy*. Monday Developments. Boston, MA: Brandeis University.

Greene, M. and Rojas, E. (2008). Incremental construction: A strategy to facilitate access to housing. *Environment and Urbanization*, 20(1), 89–108.

Holston, J. (2008). *Insurgent Citizenship: Disjunctions of Democracy and Modernity in Brazil*. Princeton: Princeton University Press.

Imai, H., Nishimura, A., Lanuza, A., Penarubia, C., Ison, R.S., Tamayo, M.L., Narag, I.C., Soridum, R.U., Inoue, H., Sakuma, J. and Okazaki, K. (2015). Development of practical tools for vulnerability and safety evaluation of houses in the Philippines. *Journal of Disaster Research*, 10(1), 121–128.

Jabeen, H. and Johnson, C. (2013). Perceptions of climate variability and coping strategies in informal settlements in Dhaka, Bangladesh. In H. Joffe, T. Rossetto and J. Adams (eds.), *Cities at Risk: Advances in Natural and Technological Hazards Research*, Vol. 33. Springer: Dordrecht, 149–170.

Kindra, J. (2013). *Understanding Resilience*. IRIN UN Office for the Coordination of Humanitarian Affairs, 6. Available at www.thenewhumanitarian.org/analysis/2013/03/04/understanding-resilience (accessed April 15, 2019).

Lewis, J. (2013a). Some realities of resilience: A case-study of Wittenberge. *Disaster Prevention and Management*, 22(1), 48–62.

Lewis, J. (2013b). Some realities of resilience: An updated case study of storms and flooding at Chiswell, Dorset. *Disaster Prevention and Management*, 22(4), 300–311.

Lizarralde, G. (2014). *The Invisible Houses: Rethinking and Designing Low-Cost Housing in Developing Countries*. New York: Routledge.

Miraftab, F. (2009). Insurgent planning: Situating radical planning in the global south. *Planning Theory*, 8(1), 32–50.

Mukhija, V. (2003). *Squatters as Developers?: Slum Demolition and Redevelopment in Mumbai, India*. Hampshire: Ashgate Publishing.

Narafu, T., Ishiyama, Y., Okazaki, K., Ando, S., Imai, H., Pribadi, K.S. and Turer, A. (2010). A proposal for a comprehensive approach to safer non-engineered houses. *Journal of Asian Architecture and Building Engineering*, 9(2), 315–322.

Natakun, B. and O'Brien, D. (2009). Extending the house/extending the dream: Modifications to government-built housing in Bangkok Metropolitan Region. *Journal of Architectural/Planning Research and Studies*, 6(3), 45–64.

Nishijima, K., Espina, M.A. (2015). *Investigation of Wind Damage Processes by Typhoon Yolanda, Identification of Effective Damage Reduction Measures, and Its Facilitation to Recovery Work*. Japan-Philippine Urgent Collaborative Projects regarding "Typhoon Yolanda" within the J-RAPID Program 2015.

NBBSS and NMES. (2013). *Community Record*. Kathmandu.

O'Brien, D. and Ahmed, I. (2012). Stage two and beyond: Improving residents' capacity to modify reconstruction agency housing. *Kumamoto University*, 309–317.

Perlman, J.E. (2005). The myth of marginality revisited: The case of favelas in Rio de Janeiro. In L.M. Hanley, B.A. Ruble and J.S. Tulchin (eds.), *Becoming Global and the New Poverty of Cities*. Washington, DC: Woodrow Wilson International Center for Scholars, Comparative Urban Studies report.

Porio, E. (2013). The community mortgage programme: An innovative social housing programme in the Philippines and its outcomes. In D. Mitlin and D. Satterthwaite (eds.), *Empowering Squatter Citizen: Local Government, Civil Society and Urban Poverty Reduction*. London: Earthscan.

Rai, R. (2015). Bagmati flood hits squatters at Tinkune. *Republica*, 17 August. Retrieved from http://myrepublica.com/society/story/26570/bagmati-flood-hits-squatters-at-tinkune.html.

Roy, A. (2005). Urban informality: Toward an epistemology of planning. *Journal of the American Planning Association*, 71(2), 147–158.

Satterthwaite, D., Huq, S., Pelling, M., Reid, H. and Lankao, R. (2007). *Adapting to Climate Change in Urban Areas: The Possibilities and Constraints in Low-and Middle-Income Nations*, Vol. 1. London: International Institute for Environment and Development (IIED).

Seabrook, J. (1996). *In the Cities of the South: Scenes from a Developing World*. London: Verso.

Shelter Cluster and Department of Social Welfare and Development (DSWD). (2014). *8 Build Back Safer Key Messages*. Manila: DSWD.

Smit, B. and Wandel, J. (2006). Adaptation, adaptive capacity and vulnerability. *Global Environmental Change*, 16(3), 282–292.

Taylor, J. (2015). A tale of two cities: Comparing alternative approaches to reducing the vulnerability of riverbank communities in two Indonesian cities. *Environment and Urbanization*, 27(2), 621–636.

Tipple, A.G. (2000). *Extending Themselves: User-initiated Transformations of Government-built Housing in Developing Countries*. Liverpool: Liverpool University Press.

Tipple, A.G. and Ameen, M.S. (1999). User initiated extension activity in Bangladesh: Building slums or area improvement? *Environment and Urbanization*, 11(1), 165–184. https://doi.org/10.1177/095624789901100125.

UN-Habitat. (2005). *Financing Urban Shelter: Global Report on Human Settlements*. London: Earthscan and UN-Habitat.

UN-Habitat. (2016). *New Urban Agenda: Quito Declaration on Sustainable Cities and Human Settlements for All*. Quito, Ecuador: UN-Habitat.

United Nations. (2015). *Transforming Our World: The 2030 Agenda for Sustainable Development*. UN General Assembly. Available at: www.un.org/ga/search/view_doc.asp?symbol=A/RES/70/1&Lang=E (accessed October 2018).

United Nations International Strategy for Disaster Reduction (UNISDR). (2008). *Handbook on Good Building Design and Construction in the Philippines*. Manila, Bangkok and Geneva: UNISDR.

United Nations International Strategy for Disaster Reduction (UNISDR). (2015). Sendai framework for disaster risk reduction 2015–2030. In *3rd United Nations World Conference on DRR*. Sendai, Japan: UNISDR.

Walker, B., Holling, C.S., Carpenter, S. and Kinzig, A. (2004). Resilience, adaptability and transformability in social–ecological systems. *Ecology and Society*, 9(2).

Chapter 11

The Discourse and Practice of Resilience Policy in Phnom Penh

Laura Beckwith and Piseth Keo

Introduction

The arrival of the rainy season is usually met with mixed feelings in Cambodia's capital city, Phnom Penh. While the rains take the edge off the oppressive heat of the hot season, the near daily deluge brings traffic chaos, fills the already putrid canals with trash off the street, and floods the homes of those living on river banks or in areas with inadequate drainage. This is the unfortunate reality for the majority of the city. Managing flooding is not a new challenge for Phnom Penh, given its geography, situated at the confluence of the Mekong, Bassac and Sap rivers and receiving an average of 1.4 m of precipitation annually (Climate-data.org, 2019).

In fact, Phnom Penh was at one point blessed with the natural infrastructure to not just manage but thrive thanks to the seasonal flooding. A system of lakes dotted throughout the city centre and encompassing huge expanses of the peri-urban zone effectively absorbed the annual floods, feeding the cultivation of aquatic vegetables grown by urban farmers and treating the city's wastewater. Climate change and urban expansion into these areas are, however, threatening the benefits of this natural infrastructure.

Boeung Tompun in the south of Phnom Penh is one such area in the peri-urban zone. The wetland covers an area of 2,600 hectares and is the primary receptacle for wastewater run-off from the city (STT, 2016a). It is also home to numerous communities whose residents use the lake to grow aquatic vegetables which are sold in the local markets. Farming on the lake has never been easy, but evidence collected through field work in the Boeung Tompun area indicates that conditions are getting riskier. Farmers report that weather patterns have become erratic with heat and rain appearing unexpectedly at any point in the year. Climate modelling confirms that Cambodia is already experiencing climatic changes. Since 1960, annual average temperature has increased approximately 0.8 °C while the number of 'hot' days (those defined as more than 10 percent hotter than average) has increased 12.6 percent overall and up to 25.7 percent in September–November (McSweeney et al., 2008). Predictable weather is essential for a reliable harvest and farmers can no longer rely on the seasons as they once could.

Although environmental changes are worrying to urban farmers, there is a more immediate threat. The lake is part of what is slated to become a 'satellite city', one of many currently planned in Phnom Penh. Phase I of the project, led by the Cambodian company ING Holdings, is already underway, featuring the construction of high-end gated residential areas and luxury commercial centres (ING Holdings, 2015). The construction of this vast new city depends on in-filling the majority of Boeung Tompun and its neighbouring lake, Cheung Ek. In the final plans, less than 500 hectares will remain (Royal Government of Cambodia, 2008). Some local residents have been told that their village will be ring-fenced within this project and those with appropriate documentation will be accorded land title for their homes. However, it appears as though much of the wetland area they are currently using for farming will be lost.

This chapter discusses the meaning of resilience and how it is employed in climate change policy and practice in Cambodia, and specifically in Phnom Penh. After briefly examining how resilience features in national and municipal policies, the discursive and institutional factors as well as the power dynamics that impact its usage will be explored. The findings presented in

Figure 11.1 Phnom Penh Visible Behind the Morning Glory Fields on Boeung Tompun.
Source: Laura Beckwith

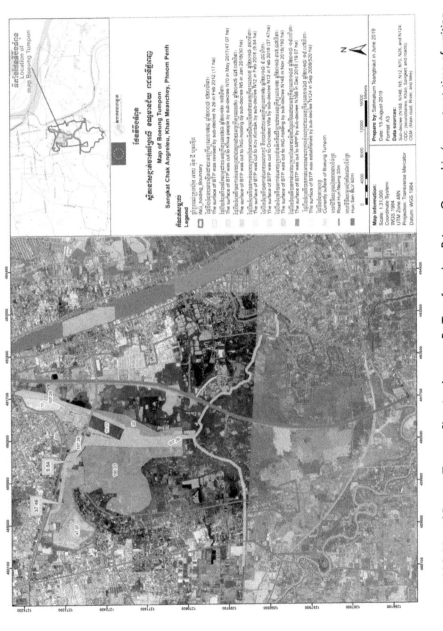

Figure 11.2 Map of Boeung Tompun Showing Areas to Be Transferred to Private Ownership (accurate at time of writing, July 2019).

Source: STT (2019)

this chapter are based on research conducted over eight months in Cambodia that sought to explore the political ecology of the policy and practice of climate change adaptation in the country's capital. Ethnographic field work with urban farmers was combined with policy and discourse analysis to offer insight into the institutional environment that frames governmental efforts to adapt to climate change in urban areas and to highlight the disconnect between policy rhetoric and the reality of urban planning in Phnom Penh. The chapter will conclude with a series of recommendations to overcome barriers to implementing resilience policies.

Resilience Policy in Cambodia

The case of Boeung Tompun exemplifies the multiple and interconnecting social, economic and climate risks to which Phnom Penh and particularly its most vulnerable inhabitants are exposed. These challenges require solutions that are multi-sectoral, multi-scalar and sufficiently flexible to adapt to an uncertain future.

As Cambodia's leaders seek to secure their country's future in the context of climate uncertainty, the government has adopted 'resilience' as a key objective of their climate change adaptation activities. This is particularly true at the national level, where resilience appears frequently in high-level policy documents in relation to climate change adaptation. In Cambodia's Climate Change Strategic Plan 2014–2023, the multi-sectoral document which guides the country's priorities for both mitigation and adaptation, two of eight strategic objectives are aimed at fostering 'climate resilience'. They are: Strategic Objective 1: Promote climate resilience through improving food, water and energy security; and Strategic Objective 3: Ensure climate resilience of critical ecosystems (Tonle Sap Lake, Mekong River, coastal ecosystems, highlands, etc.), biodiversity, protected areas and cultural heritage sites (Royal Government of Cambodia, 2014: xvii).

In other words, resilience is taken as the positive outcome of adaptation to climate change. Furthermore, Cambodia's Rectangular Strategy Phase 4 (2019–2023), which forms the basis of the National Strategic Development Plan, also includes building resilience as a priority both in relation to climate change as well as potential economic shocks (Royal Government of Cambodia, 2018). Within the national government, the term resilience has therefore been embraced at the highest levels.

Despite the risks that Phnom Penh will face from flooding and increased temperatures, resilience does not feature prominently as a policy objective at the municipal level. In the Phnom Penh Land Use Master Plan, which is the key planning document that guides the city's development through 2035, there is no mention of resilience as a planning priority (STT, 2016b). An official at Phnom Penh City Hall, when asked if the term resilience featured

The Discourse and Practice of Resilience 175

in his work, replied, 'Yes, we do use that word resilient also. We use it for infrastructure, upgrade infrastructure. For example, for the river bank. Right now we do the river bank to avoid the erosion' (Interview, official, 2018).[1] This use, however, does not appear to translate into a formal policy priority.

The presence or absence of resilience in written policy, however, does not necessarily indicate whether a resilience agenda is being implemented. As the use of the term increases, it is important to understand the discourse in which it is situated (Leach, 2008). The discourse of resilience includes the meanings and associations that govern when and how the word is used. This discourse is then enacted through the framework of institutions, the particularities of which have implications for the implementation of resilience policy. Institutions can be understood as 'regularized patterns of behaviours between individuals and groups in society' (Leach et al., 1999: 225). These can be either formal (such as laws and regulations) or informal (including unwritten practices that govern behaviour). Institutions are operated by human actions (Cleaver and De Koning, 2015; Leach et al., 1999) and as such can offer insight into actions that may not be written into policy. The operation of such institutions is shaped by relations of power, where power is defined as 'the ability of a given individual, corporate body, political organization, or political system (broadly defined) to further interests, shape behaviours (positively and negatively), and inform strategies for action' (Landau, 2007: 2). Overt forms of power such as force are most visible, but other forms of power such as regulation and corruption can shape how policies are implemented. An examination of the discourse of resilience in Cambodia, as well as the way it is interpreted through institutions and power relations, will improve understanding of how the concept is enacted at the policy level.

Cambodia's Resilience Discourse

Despite its prominence in national policy documents as the outcome of climate change adaptation, there has not been an attempt to define resilience specifically for the Cambodian context. A lexicon has been developed by the Cambodia Climate Change Alliance (a donor-funded initiative housed within the Ministry of Environment) which translates IPCC terminology into the Khmer language and was often cited in interviews with policy makers and development actors as the source for their definition of resilience. However, when asked to elaborate, many were hesitant to state the definition. In over 25 interviews with representatives from national and subnational levels of government as well as international donors, UN agencies and NGOs, all indicated that resilience featured as an objective in their climate change work. None, however, were able to confidently provide their institution's definition of resilience.

Interviewees were therefore invited to give their own personal description of resilience. All individuals interviewed had a sense of what resilience meant to them and their work and were able to give an informal definition but, for the most part, these were vague and highly normative. Respondents viewed resilience as a capacity and equated it with the ability to 'cope' with climate change. As one senior official at the Ministry of Environment said, 'Resilience is the capacity to survive, to cope with' (Interview, official, 2018). Furthermore, interviews with policy makers at the national level confirmed that resilience is often seen as the successful outcome of climate change adaptation or sometimes as a synonym for anticipatory adaptation, or actions that might be taken to prepare for the impacts of climate change before they occur. These differing but universally positive associations with the word resilience suggests that it is being used as a 'buzzword,' whereby its euphemistic and assumed positive qualities facilitate buy-in from all stakeholders (Cornwall, 2007).

The lack of an agreed definition however, means there is little opportunity to question the meaning of pursuing resilience as a policy objective. Instead, a shared objective is simply assumed, side-stepping any discussion of trade-offs or conflicting priorities. The lack of debate about the substance of a resilience agenda in Cambodia is due, at least in part, to the widespread belief among both civil society and government stakeholders that resilience is simply the current donor fad. This is evident in the prominence of the term resilience at the project level, appearing as an objective wherever there are resources from foreign donors. For example, much of the current work happening on climate change at the national level falls under the Strategic Program for Climate Resilience (SPCR), funded by the Climate Investment Fund through the Asian Development Bank and that seeks to 'mainstream climate resilience into national and sub-national development policies, plans and projects' (SPCR, 2018). Resilience is also a priority for the Cambodia Climate Change Alliance (CCCA), an initiative jointly funded by the EU, Sweden and UNDP that 'aims to strengthen national systems and capacities to support the coordination and implementation of Cambodia's climate change response, contributing to a greener, low carbon, climate-resilient, equitable, sustainable and knowledge-based society' (Ministry of Environment, 2014).

The ubiquity of the term however belies the lack of ownership felt by those responsible for its implementation. One government official within the Ministry of Environment offered: 'Some terminology is difficult for us to adapt. It's a new term for us and some people confuse resilience and adaptation' (Interview, official, 2018). Another official lamented that over his 30-year career he had seen a continuous cycle of new terminology introduced to replace the old with little substantial change in the meaning. However, he argued, 'If you want their budget you have to use their word' (Interview, official, 2018).

The Role of Institutions

The lack of vision for what resilience means is only part of the reason why the term is more rhetoric than reality in Cambodia's climate change policies. 'Lack of capacity' is often identified as the reason why many development initiatives fail or are only partially implemented. For example, a recent World Bank report on urban development in Phnom Penh lists its first recommendation as 'Improving Institutions and Governance' without which, it goes on to say, Phnom Penh will 'develop in an uncoordinated and fragmented manner, with infrastructure coming under increasing strain, increases in sprawl and congestion, worsening vulnerability to climate change, and a less liveable urban environment' (World Bank, 2018: 5). This perceived capacity gap can take multiple forms, from weaknesses in institutional capacity such as coordination and delineation of responsibilities through human capacity deficits. All of these problems were raised in interviews with different stakeholders as reasons why the policy agenda around climate change has not been fully implemented in Cambodia, particularly at the subnational level.

Coordination was identified by a senior official responsible for climate change within the Ministry of Environment as the biggest challenge for his office. He went on to explain that coordination problems arise not only from working with different line ministries as well as levels of government, but also Cambodia's international donors, some of whom he said have a 'different agenda' (Interview, official, 2018). A government-led Technical Working Group (TWG) on climate change has recently been established that is supposed to play a coordination role. However, a representative from an international agency admitted that the new TWG had been slow to get started. Their meetings had been infrequent and they were hampered by the fact that much of the climate change funding is coming as Official Development Assistance and is therefore going through the Council for the Development of Cambodia (CDC), adding another layer in the management of funds and information (Interview, UN, 2018). The necessity of multi-scalar and multi-sectoral responses to build resilience means effective coordination is critical.

The issues related to coordination are not unique to climate change policy and are found throughout government agencies, where unclear boundaries between ministries and levels of government create confusion and duplication of roles (Interview, donor, 2018). In addition to multiple line ministries at the national level involved to various degrees in both climate change programming and urban planning, the process of decentralisation in Cambodia over the past 17 years has created multiple layers of sub-national administration. Within Phnom Penh, the sub-national layers of government are: 1) the municipality or Phnom Penh Capital Hall; 2) twelve khan or districts; and 3) ninety-six sangkats[2] (Phnom Penh Capital Hall, 2019). The sangkat level in particular is expected to play a key role in planning for climate change in the city through the three-year Commune Investment Plan. With so many parties involved, a strong coordination and communication mechanism is needed, as well as a shared understanding of the objectives to be achieved. This will increase the ability of government to deliver coherent policy and to respond to changes as they emerge.

A related challenge is the need for technical capacity within the government to deliver appropriate programmes that will contribute to the stated objectives of achieving climate resilience. Tragically, the country's most educated were among those targeted by the Khmer Rouge whose brutal regime from 1975 to 1979 decimated the intellectual and bureaucratic capacity of the country (Fauveaud, 2016). This was followed by a decade of political instability and violence as multiple parties fought for control of the country. After relative peace was restored in 1993 under the UN Transitional Authority in Cambodia, institutions were rebuilt from scratch (United Nations, nd). The number of universities, particularly private institutions, is growing rapidly with four times the number of students enrolled in 2008 as in 2002 (UNESCO, 2010). But the percentage of the population with a post-secondary education is still only 6.1 percent (National Institute of Statistics, 2016) and universities are only beginning to provide programmes related to climate change (Interview_official, 2018). Therefore, technical capacity related to climate change and resilience building is scarce. While specialist agencies such as the CCCA provide some technical support, the long-term objective is for line ministries to be capable of analysing the impacts of climate change on their own programming. Currently, key informants to this research have indicated that this is not feasible (interview, donor, 2018; interview, official, 2018).

Furthermore, resilience has been theorised to include an element of reflective learning in order to continually respond to change (Folke et al., 2010). In the institutional setting governing climate change, the quality of the working environment in the Cambodian government fails to provide incentives for employees to even meet minimum standards let alone thrive in their jobs. This makes processes such as reflective learning incredibly difficult. Salaries for many government jobs are well below the cost of living in Phnom Penh, meaning government workers may seek out other work, attending to their governmental responsibilities for only a few hours a day, if at all (Jackson and Cheang, 2014). Furthermore, the strictly hierarchical nature of the Cambodian government means that senior employees are able to claim credit for the work of their subordinates, creating an environment where hard work achieves little recognition and motivation is low (Interview, donor, 2018). In this context, what is written into the policy matters little if none of it is being implemented. As one donor representative put it: 'We were successful . . . to form the establishment of climate resilience into the policies, the sectoral policies, the manual, but we failed to function it' (Interview, donor, 2018).

In the absence of an effective government response to emerging climate risks, individuals and groups are taking steps to adapt to the changes they are experiencing, both in terms of changing weather patterns as well as changes occurring as part of the process of urban expansion. Around Boeung Tompun in Phnom Penh, these two processes are transforming the urban wetland that supports the livelihoods of the farmers in the area. Cognizant of the changing conditions, farmers are employing multiple strategies to maintain the viability of urban farming. These include the increased use of chemical pesticides and fertilisers, negotiating access to areas of the lake with better water quality and taking on debt to replace income lost when crops are destroyed by unexpected weather. Although farmers have extensive knowledge of the ecological conditions in the area, their ability to enact strategies that foster resilience is limited by the political and economic environment that has placed constraints on collective action. The hostility directed towards civil society organizing, as evidenced by the scrutiny under which local human rights NGOs are forced to operate (see for example Kijewski and Chheng, 2018), has prevented the emergence of collective community-based responses to local climate risks. This limits the potential of local knowledge that might otherwise offer insight and innovative solutions to the city's challenges if properly supported.

Power at Play

Power imbalances among stakeholders involved in Phnom Penh's urban development mean the private interests of political and economic elites are winning out over the efforts that do exist to pursue resilience as a policy priority. Resilience receives little attention in urban areas in Cambodia partly because of the high risks faced by rural Cambodians to the expected impacts of climate change. However, the complex situation faced by the urban farmers of Boeung Tompun described earlier is just one example of the way Phnom Penh's vulnerable residents are threatened by both climate change and unequal urban development. As they struggle to make their livelihoods viable in the face of unpredictable weather, their land is being lost to urban expansion, forcing them out as property values rise.

Urban informal settlements are framed as dirty or polluted, justifying their removal to make way for seemingly cleaner, but resource-hogging, luxury developments in what have been termed 'green evictions' (Ghertner, 2011). The role of inadequate public services and discriminatory policies, particularly with respect to land ownership, in creating these conditions is not acknowledged (Interview, NGO, 2018). This narrative was employed to legitimate the removal of the residents of Boeung Kak in central Phnom Penh whose forcible eviction when the lake was filled in for development made international headlines (Fauveaud, 2016). It is also used to justify government inaction or failure to provide public services, especially in situations of uncertain land tenure (Interview, official, 2018).

This situation is related to a wider tendency in the urban planning process to adopt a technocratic or managerial approach to urban development with limited public involvement. According to a senior official within the Phnom Penh municipal government there was no open public consultation on the Master Plan (Interview, official, 2018). While sub-municipal levels of government such as district and sangkat leaders were consulted during the development of the plan (Interview, official, 2018), given the hierarchical and neo-patrimonial nature of Cambodian society and politics, it is questionable what weight community-level priorities are given, even by local officials, in the face of political interests at higher levels (Springer, 2011; Un and So, 2011; Eng, 2016).

Furthermore, while the Land Use Master Plan represents a significant forward step in regulating urban planning in Phnom Penh, historic patterns of corruption and cronyism in land speculation see patterns of 'institutionalized informality' continue to operate at the centre of urban development in Phnom Penh (Fauveaud, 2016). This lack of transparency and participation promotes a concentration of power and knowledge, preventing the recognition of localised risks and likewise overlooking community-led solutions to climate vulnerability.

The case of Boeung Tompun is emblematic of this type of deal making where private interests are pursued at the expense of legal requirements and public interest. Details of the deal made to sell the land to ING Holdings are scarce, even among officials of local and national governments interviewed for this research. While City Hall insisted that the lake itself would not be filled in, this assertion was immediately contradicted by the confirmation that less than 500 hectares of the lake (of the existing 2,600 hectares) is projected to remain (Interview, official, 2018). This is despite the fact that natural lakes are ostensibly protected under the 2001 Land Law (Sasin et al., 2015). Furthermore, the lake currently receives the majority of the city's wastewater. At present, the agricultural activity on the lake contributes to successfully treating many of the contaminants before the water is released into the local river system (Sovann et al., 2015), while the proposed plan to build a wastewater treatment plan in its place will be capable of treating only a small fraction of the current volume and will require not only an up-front cost for construction but ongoing running and maintenance costs (Nishikawa, 2018). The extraordinary power wielded by private developers to shape the vision of Phnom Penh's future has led to a fractured process of urban expansion which fails to take into account city-level priorities such as the preservation and development of essential systems such as wastewater management.

Making the Concept of Resilience Work in Phnom Penh

Having identified numerous challenges impeding effective translation of resilience policy into practice, this paper proposes four potential areas for improving the relevance of resilience to climate change policy in Cambodia. The list is not intended to be exhaustive but suggestive of some of the areas that could benefit from immediate attention in order to promote a more resilient and inclusive society.

First, the concept of 'resilience' should be carefully investigated, understood and locally defined by the array of institutional bodies, including international NGOs, corporations, state institutions, academic and research institutions, farmers and minority groups. These actors are linked together by concrete strategies and programmes (Adger et al., 2001; Arts, 2004) and together form a policy network which is responsible for 'the movement of objects, resources, knowledge, and materials' (Escobar, 1998: 56). The actors at the top of this policy network, specifically the National Council for Sustainable Development, which is the United Nations Framework Convention on Climate Change (UNFCCC) National Focal point, along with its key donors—United Nations Development Programme and the Asian Development Bank through CCCA and SPCR—are responsible for setting the strategic direction of policy and should therefore understand the key concepts involved with prioritizing resilience as part of the climate change policy discourse.

These concepts must be digested and translated into the Cambodian context before being introduced to other network members. Without clear understanding and guidance from policy leaders, other network members are left pursuing their own agendas, leading to potential conflicts in terms of scale, timeline or visions of resilience. Although resilience theory can be complex, a distillation of its fundamental concepts as applicable to the current challenges facing Cambodia would greatly benefit the multitude of actors involved in this policy sector to implement a shared vision. A booklet synthesizing the theory, training workshops and effective communication tools should be applied for awareness raising within the policy network members, and to encourage more participation in advocating and implementing resilience as a national policy. With active participation of all key actors involved in the formulation and implementation of resilience policy, a more grounded and relevant resilience agenda could be set.

The second policy area is the need to overcome coordination challenges between the diverse state and non-state actors, from national to subnational levels, who are members of the climate change policy network. Successes and failures of policy largely depend on connection and coordination among these actors. Evidence indicates that strong mediators are key catalysts for policy successes (Mahanty, 2002; Keo, 2018). To connect the actors in the climate change policy network in Cambodia, there is a need to identify players who can take on the role of mediators in the network. The Ministry of Planning, being the national authority responsible for setting the strategic direction for development, should provide leadership to effectively coordinate and provide institutional, political and financial support when necessary, where administrative units are ill-coordinated.

The Climate Change Department, through its donor-funded programmes—CCCA and SPCR—should provide guidance and coordination of technical capacity related to climate resilience. Creating interactive and responsive platforms, where members are able to interact, share policy ideas and provide comments, is essential for the improvement of policy formulation, implementation, monitoring, and evaluation, and to address challenges faced by members of the policy network. The existing Technical Working Group on Climate Change provides a foundation for this strategy. However, it should be more inclusive of local actors including local government and civil society as well as more responsive to its members. Better coordination and connection will give members a sense of belonging to the network that will motivate them to participate and provide support to network building.

The third policy priority is to improve the balance of power in terms of knowledge integration into policy formulation. The findings of this research echo much of the existing literature in political ecology, which recognises that indigenous and local knowledge, whose discourses are based on experiential learning or lived experiences, are ignored by bureaucrats who consider techno-scientific-based knowledge to be superior (Bryant and Wilson, 1998; Forsyth, 2003). In most cases, if not all, there are no questions raised about the fundamental ways in which scientific knowledge is interpreted, controlled and possibly manipulated to fit with specific goals (Escobar, 1998). Having failed to include local knowledge in the development of urban planning and climate change policy results in a situation where plans overlook the needs and challenges faced by those that the policy primarily intends to support.

To address this challenge, there is a need to apply an integrated approach for knowledge production for policy design. Studies adopting methodologies associated with modern science and technology should integrate an ethnographic approach, in which the local community is encouraged to fully participate in data collection and policy design. This will help policy makers have a broad knowledge of the challenges and needs of diverse localities, which can lay the foundation for appropriate solutions. This approach is challenging in that it requires time, sensitivity and diplomacy to integrate different types of knowledge, but the end result may be a vision of resilience which is inclusive of diverse constituencies. Within the SPCR, case studies related to best practices of local level adaptation to climate change have been collected, but this information must then be used to inform policy and importantly to reach beyond donor-funded projects. This practice is applicable across a wide range of policy areas.

The final recommendation focuses on the need to build effective formal institutions for the delivery of policy in Cambodia. It is essential to ensure that public servants drive state institutions to effectively provide public services for the benefit of the whole Cambodian population, not to suit the particular

The Discourse and Practice of Resilience 183

needs of a small group of elites. Capacity needs assessment and capacity building of the public servants is indeed significant, particularly as it relates to legal instrument formulation, policy development, implementation, and monitoring and evaluation. However, capacity building alone will not address the institutional challenges that undermine the work environment in Cambodian civil service. These must be addressed by reforming the politics of government institutions. Merit-based recruitment of the best talent and establishment of incentive schemes and a conducive environment for staff are key to securing the best performance from government staff. Capable and well-supported officials will be better positioned to take on the role of mediators, facilitating the participation of other stakeholders including the private sector and civil society to foster a vision of Cambodia's future that goes beyond coping with climate change and embraces the more ambitious elements of a resilience agenda, not least of which is attention to reducing inequality.

In conclusion, Cambodia has been recognised as facing serious threats from climate change (University of Notre Dame, 2017), yet the choice of resilience as a concept to lead the policy response appears to lack local ownership. While the concept of resilience has been enthusiastically adopted in national-level documents, it reflects the continued influence of donor funding in Cambodia, rather than an attempt to robustly engage with how the country will move forward into a future of climate uncertainty. The challenges identified with the implementation of resilience policy will not be solved simply by increasing the discourse of resilience. The barriers to delivering on commitments to resilience are fundamentally political and will only be resolved when development planning priorities expand beyond the pursuit of private enrichment for the country's elite. Until then, whether it is resilience or another buzzword that is used, the needs of Phnom Penh's most vulnerable are unlikely to be high on the agenda.

Notes

1. In order to preserve the anonymity of respondents, interviews have been referenced either as donors, government officials, UN or NGO.
2. Sangkats are the lowest level of elected government in urban areas (called communes in rural areas). The average population size of a commune/sangkat is 8,264 (JICA, 2009).

References

Adger, N.W., Benjaminsen, T.A., Brown, K. and Svarstad, H. (2001). Advancing a political ecology of global environmental discourses. *Development and Change*, 32(4), 681–715.
Arts, B. (2004). The global-local nexus: NGOs and the articulation of scale. *Tijdschrift voor economische en sociale geografie*, 95(5), 498–510.
Bryant, L.R. and Wilson, G.A. (1998). Rethinking environmental management. *Progress in Human Geography*, 22, 321–343.

Cleaver, F. and De Koning, J. (2015). Furthering critical institutionalism. *International Journal of the Commons*, 9(1).

Climate-data.org. (2019). *Climate Phnom Penh*. Climate-data.org. Available at: https://en.climate-data.org/asia/cambodia/phnom-penh/phnom-penh-4857/ (accessed March 7, 2019).

Cornwall, A. (2007). Buzzwords and fuzzwords: Deconstructing development discourse. *Development in Practice*, 17, 471–484.

Eng, N. (2016). Decentralization in Cambodia: New wine in old bottles. *Public Administration and Development*, 36, 250–262.

Escobar, A. (1998). Whose knowledge, whose nature? Biodiversity, conservation, and the political ecology of social movements. *Journal of Political Ecology*, 5(1), 53–82.

Fauveaud, G. (2016). Les pratiques urbanistiques de l'ombre des acteurs institutionnels et privés: le cas de Phnom Penh, Cambodge. *L'espace politique*, 29. Available at: espacepolitique.revues.org/3886.

Folke, C., Carpenter, S.R., Walker, B., Scheffer, M., Chapin, T. and Rockström, J. (2010). Resilience thinking: Integrating resilience, adaptability and transformability. *Ecology and Society*, 15(4), 20–28.

Forsyth, T. (2003). *Critical Political Ecology*. London: Routledge.

Ghertner, D.A. (2011). Green evictions: Environmental discourses of a "slum-free" Delhi. In R. Peet, P. Robbins and M. Watts (eds.), *Global Political Ecology*. New York: Routledge.

ING Holdings. (2015). *Overall Project Concept*. ING-Holdings.com (accessed April 1, 2019).

Jackson, W. and Cheang, S. (2014). The civil service's phantom workers. *Phnom Penh Post*, 17 October. Available at: www.phnompenhpost.com/post-weekend/civil-service%E2%80%99s-phantom-workers (accessed March 8, 2019).

JICA. (2009). *Spatial Distribution and Density of Population—Cambodia*. Available at: www.stat.go.jp/info/meetings/cambodia/pdf/a02_chap.pdf (accessed March 29, 2019).

Keo, P. (2018). *Discourses, Institutions, and Power: Political Ecology of Community-based Natural Resources Management in Cambodia*. PhD dissertation. Singapore: National University of Singapore.

Kijewski, L. and Chheng, N. (2018). Equitable Cambodia allowed to reopen. *Phnom Penh Post*, February 26. Available at: www.phnompenhpost.com/national/equitable-cambodia-allowed-reopen.

Landau, L.B. (2007). Power. In M. Bevir (ed.), *Encyclopedia of Governance*. Thousand Oaks: SAGE Publications.

Leach, M. (ed.). (2008). *Re-Framing Resilience: A Symposium Report*. STEPS Working Paper 13, Brighton. Available at: http://steps-centre.org/wp-content/uploads/Resilience.pdf (accessed March 25, 2019).

Leach, M., Mearns, R. and Scoones, I. (1999). Environmental entitlements: Dynamics and institutions in community-based natural resource management. *World Development*, 27(2), 225–247.

Mahanty, S. (2002). Conservation and development interventions as networks: The case of the India Ecodevelopment Project, Karnataka. *World Development*, 30(8), 1369–1386.

McSweeney, C., New, M. and Lizcano, G. (2008). *UNDP Climate Change Country Profile: Cambodia*. UNDP, 1–27.

Ministry of Environment. (2014). *Cambodia Climate Change Alliance*. Camclimate. org Available at: www.camclimate.org.kh/en/activities/cambodian-climate-change-alliance.html (accessed March 7, 2019).

National Institute of Statistics. (2016). *Cambodia Socio-Economic Survey 2016*. Available at: www.nis.gov.kh/nis/CSES/Final%20Report%20CSES%202016.pdf (accessed March 8, 2019).

Nishikawa, M. (2018). *JICA's Cooperation for Water Environment Improvement in Phnom Penh*. City for All. Royal University of Phnom Penh, Phnom Penh. November 29, 2018. Presentation.

Phnom Penh Capital Hall. (2019). *District*. Phnom Penh Capital Hall. Available at: http://phnompenh.gov.kh/en/maps/location/district/ (accessed March 25, 2019).

Royal Government of Cambodia. (2008). *Sub-decree 124 on the Boundaries of Cheung Ek Lake*. Issued 3 September 2008.

Royal Government of Cambodia. (2014). *Cambodia Climate Change Strategic Plan 2014–2023*. Available at: www.camclimate.org.kh/en/policies/nccc-news/197-cccsp-2014-2023-kh-en-final.html (accessed March 25, 2019).

Royal Government of Cambodia. (2018). *National Strategic Development Plan (2019–2023)*. Available at: www.mop.gov.kh/en-us/Home/Download/181.

Sahmakum Teang Tnaut (STT). (2016a). *Facts and Figures: Boeung Tompun Lake Communities*. Available at: http://teangtnaut.org/?lang=en (accessed March 25, 2019).

Sahmakum Teang Tnaut (STT). (2016b). *Sub-decree of Phnom Penh Master Plan*. Sahmakum Teang Tnaut. Available at: http://teangtnaut.org/sub-degree-phnom-penh-master-plan/?lang=en (accessed March 29, 2019).

Sahmakum Teang Tnaut (STT). (2019). *Map of Boeung Tumpon*. Unpublished Map.

Sasin, P., Pern, H., Dekkers, W., Flower, B., Grimsditch, M. and Ee, S. (2015). *Human Rights Based Spatial Planning in Cambodia—Guidelines*. Phnom Penh.

Sovann, C., Irvine, K.N., Suthipong, S., Kok, S. and Chea, E. (2015). Dynamic modelling to assess natural wetlands treatment of wastewater in dynamic modeling to assess natural wetlands treatment of wastewater in Phnom Penh, Cambodia : Towards an eco-city planning tool. *British Journal of Environment and Climate Change*, 5(2), 104–115.

Springer, S. (2011). Articulated neoliberalism: The specificity of patronage, kleptocracy, and violence in Cambodia's neoliberalization. *Environment and Planning A*, 43(11), 2554–2570.

Strategic Program for Climate Resilience. (2018). *About Us*. Spcrcambodia.org. Available at: http://spcrcambodia.org/en/about-us-en/ (accessed March 7, 2019).

Un, K. and So, S. (2011). Land rights in Cambodia: How neopatrimonial politics restricts land policy reform. *Pacific Affairs*, 84(2), 289–308.

UNESCO. (2010). *UNESCO National Education Support Strategy Cambodia 2010–2013*. Available at: https://unesdoc.unesco.org/ark:/48223/pf0000188018 (accessed March 8, 2019).

United Nations. (n.d.). *'Summary' Cambodia—UNTAC Background*. Available at: https://peacekeeping.un.org/mission/past/untacbackgr1.html (accessed March 8, 2019).

University of Notre Dame. (2017). *ND-GAIN: Notre Dame Global Adaptation Index*. Available at: www.gain.org/ (accessed March 25, 2019).

World Bank (WB). (2018). *Urban Development in Phnom Penh*. Available at: www.worldbank.org/en/country/cambodia/publication/urban-development-in-phnom-penh (accessed March 8, 2019).

Chapter 12

Are Children the Key to Designing Resilient Cities After a Disaster?

Robyn Mansfield

Figure 12.1 Children of San Jose de Chamanga, Ecuador.
Source: Robyn Mansfield (2017)

Introduction

The economic cost of disasters between the years 1998–2017 is estimated at USD 2,908 billion, of which 91 percent of events were attributed to climate change and affected approximately 4.4 billion people (UNDRR, 2019). 'Rapid and often risk-blind urbanization' is identified as one of the main culprits for the ongoing and widespread vulnerability of people (CRED and UNISDR, 2018: 24). The United Nations Office for Disaster Risk Reduction's (UNDRR) 'Global Assessment Report on Disaster Risk Reduction 2019', or 'GAR 2019', calls for a re-examination of how to deal with risk. UNDRR warns that 'surprise is the new normal', and urges governments and decision-makers to take action and incorporate a future-thinking and systemic approach to risk in policy development to reduce vulnerability and build resilience (UNDRR, 2019: iv). While the area of resilient urban development and design shows improvement in recent years in the assessment of UNDRR's Disaster Resilience Scorecards (UNDRR, 2019), rapid urbanisation and the increase of informal settlements in hazard-prone areas is growing faster than infrastructure development with low-income countries most affected. The GAR 2019 cautions against complacency, calling for increasing investment in disaster prevention, incorporating political and socioeconomic factors into developing the built environment, and adopting more creative approaches to building resilient cities (UNDRR, 2019).

Watson describes a resilient city as 'a sustainable network of physical systems and human communities', identifying the role of communities in developing resilient cities as decision-makers, and therefore needing to be recognised as an essential component for achieving resilience (Watson, 2016). Numerous frameworks exist for determining how to identify and develop city resilience. However, such frameworks generally tend to oversimplify the complexity and scale of the roles all individuals play in this artificially and human-developed construct (UNISDR, 2019; Kendra et al., 2018; ARUP, 2015; Pervin et al., 2013; Jha et al., 2013). Watson touches on the area of 'modularity', recognising that the individuality of smaller neighbourhoods and the subsequent different responses built on strong local identity may provide the potential for greater resilience in the face of disasters (Watson, 2016: 22). The potential for taking a neighbourhood approach to the development of resilient cities emphasises the human element of disasters; both in cause and prevention of future disasters with the hypothesis of a resilient city as a patchwork of connected neighbourhoods containing resilient communities.

The occurrence of a disaster provides a unique opportunity to build back a more resilient city using a stronger participatory response in a realm generally dominated by 'experts' and with top-down approaches. Rebuilding the physical environment after a disaster is generally politically reactive and driven by the urgency to return to a new state of normalcy, yet case studies that demonstrate meaningful participatory and locally led responses have been shown to produce sustainable and culturally appropriate urban responses and develop longer-term community resilience (Schilderman, 2016; Charlesworth and Ahmed, 2015; Venkatachalam, 2011; Shaw et al., 2010). When participatory processes are examined, however, 'community' is typically identified as a generic entity, rather than as a fragmented set of individuals with varied and often conflicting needs and capabilities that can increase vulnerability in both disaster risk reduction and rebuilding after a disaster (Wachtendorf et al., 2018; Leadbeater, 2013). Children in particular are greatly affected by disasters and there is a growing body of research that identifies how a physically changed environment after a disaster affects their well-being (Peek et al., 2018). Peek et al. also highlight that children have 'the time, energy, creativity, and capacity to contribute to disaster risk reduction' (p. 257), offering an exciting proposition for involving children in urban planning. Less understood is the long-term impact of children's participation on community resilience, or lack thereof, in the rebuilding process after a disaster, how to expand their participation to a city scale and how to take into consideration the different needs of children whether these are socioeconomic considerations, age, cultural roles in society, religious beliefs, gender, sexual preference, a combination of factors and so on.

This chapter brings literature on the role of children as active citizens into resilient cities discourse, and presents two case studies of settlements that were affected by disaster to demonstrate the ongoing impact of excluding children in the rebuilding process. The case studies were selected as an examination of resilience factors after a disaster at a neighbourhood scale and to highlight the impact on urban resilience of children's participation in rebuilding after a disaster. The biases and institutional barriers that prevented children's participation in decisions regarding reconstruction after a bushfire are examined in the first case study. The second case study is an exploration into the devastating impact of excluding children in the prioritisation of infrastructure projects after an earthquake.

Finally, this chapter calls for further research into children's participation in small settlements after a disaster to understand their significance as 'neighbourhood models' that could be scaled up to city neighbourhoods. The two settlements are in very different socioeconomic, cultural, and religious settings and affected by different types of disasters, but both identify critical points for further examination to identify whether children's participation is the missing link to developing more resilient cities.

Who Defines What a Resilient City Is?

In 2013, The Rockefeller Foundation pioneered the 100 Resilient Cities initiative in response to the increasing need to focus on a more systematic and strategic approach to dealing with the increasingly complicated risks and potential for large-scale disruption associated with rapid urbanisation (100 Resilient Cities, 2016). Judith Rodin, a pioneer in quantifying the economic impact of resilience, describes resilience as a series of characteristics that are required for any entity to prepare, recover, adapt, and grow from disruptions and notes that the responsibility to achieve resilience lies with everyone[1] (Rodin, 2015). The City Resilience Framework, developed as part of the 100 Resilient Cities initiative, attempts to consolidate the learning from literature, case studies and cities to articulate what a resilient city looks like, and to support and guide municipal authorities, 'resilient city' contributors and stakeholders (ARUP, 2015). The Framework lists the first goal for achieving a resilient city as 'minimal human vulnerability', with a strong human-focused theme throughout the subsequent 11 goals. Elements of empowerment, community identity, decision-making and engagement are acknowledgements that human intervention underpins all aspects of developing a resilient city. Too often, however, the focus after a disaster is less focused on the role of individuals' connection with the impacted physical place and their capacity to participate in the reconstruction process, and more targeted towards an injection of funds into rapid construction efforts that are tangible, highly visible and demonstrate political responsiveness (Leadbeater, 2013; Shaw et al., 2010; Birch and Wachter, 2006).

Inextricably linked to building resilient cities is the concept of 'building back better' after a disaster in order to prevent a return to the pre-disaster vulnerable state and strengthen community resilience. A key component to 'building back better' is the incorporation of disaster risk reduction into policy and investment to avoid increasing vulnerability in the recovery and rebuilding process. The Sendai Framework for Disaster Risk Reduction 2015–30 has been touted as a people-centred framework, and while it explicitly calls for the participation of community sub-sets such as women, children, youth and people with disabilities in developing disaster risk reduction plans, the indicators do not provide the impetus required to mainstream their participation in the context of reconstruction (UNISDR, 2015).

Research into children's views on what constitutes a resilient city highlights a far more complex understanding of resilience. Derr et al.'s research demonstrates children's multifaceted connection to place in not only the physical sense, but in terms of social perspectives, governance and ownership of space, negotiating access and use of space, relationships, and the impact of a range of factors such as noises, maintenance and cleanliness, and perceived projected risks in their feelings of safety. The case study emphasised that children are clear in their idea of resilience, but the incorporation of their views into city resilience planning presented challenges and they are largely excluded from these planning processes. The authors identify children's participation as essential to reducing inequalities and ensuring cities are resilient for everyone, and notes that 'for children's perspectives to be included, frameworks themselves are not adequate but also the belief among those in power that children's voices matter' (Derr et al., 2019: 15).

Children's Role After a Disaster

The Sendai Framework was developed as a voluntary agreement for states to reduce their susceptibility to risk, and emphasised the need for a people-centred preventative approach through participation in the design and implementation of disaster prevention policies and plans (UNDRR, 2019: 311, UNISDR, 2015, para.7). The GAR 2019 emphasises the recognition in a number of key agreements that local action is essential for developing urban resilience and notes that meaningful participation of the most vulnerable stakeholders is required in urban planning processes (UNDRR, 2019). Despite this, indicators and targets measure this type of participation as supporting information rather than as a target in its own right.

International research presents strong evidence that children[2] are disproportionately affected by disasters,[3] identifying them as particularly vulnerable (UNICEF, 2016b, Children in a Changing Climate, 2016). At the same time, it is becoming more widely recognised that children play a valuable role in decision-making in disaster risk reduction and that the health and resilience of communities after a disaster is positively impacted when children are included in the recovery process (UNICEF, 2016b; UNICEF, 2016a). Despite this recognition, there is a gap regarding guidance and mechanisms for meaningful participation of children in decision-making and their role in communities (Plan International et al., 2016). Globally adopted agreements and proposals for sustainable development also demonstrate a lack of strength in acknowledging the contribution infrastructure and urban development make in increasing vulnerability to disaster risk. The report *A View from 2016* (Children in a Changing Climate, 2016) provides an analysis of six major global agreements with a series of recommendations that support children in a decision-making capacity, partnerships between children and government, child-led monitoring and evaluation, and involvement in developing resilient infrastructure focused on the protection of people rather than an assets-based approach. It notes the impact of disasters on children includes increased threat to life, risk of disease and malnutrition, increase in inequity, lack of attendance at school, increase in displacement, descent into poverty and increase in threats such as abuse, exploitation, trafficking and child labour, all contributing to long-term negative impacts on the resilience of communities (Children in a Changing Climate, 2016).

Save the Children has identified the importance of children's participation in decision-making after a disaster and their capacity to engage in disaster risk-reduction strategies (Featherston, 2014: ix). *The Children's Charter— An Action Plan For Disaster Risk Reduction For Children By Children* explicitly identifies children's right to participate in measures to protect their communities and identifies the reconstruction process after a disaster as critical to their well-being (UNICEF, 2011). Involving children in disaster risk-reduction activities is becoming more also recognised as beneficial to both individual children's and their communities' resilience (Peek et al., 2018; Haynes and Tanner, 2015). The lack of involvement in the recovery and reconstruction process however can lead to a range of detrimental outcomes and there is a gap in longitudinal studies into the ongoing effects of trauma and psycho-social needs of children affected by a disaster (Peek et al., 2018; Shaw et al., 2010: 10). Peek et al. suggest that future studies are required in areas such as the increasing role of children in climate change activities, and in particular the not-yet realised role of young people as the first generation of 'digital natives' and how this may impact future involvement with disaster situations (Peek et al., 2018: 256).

There is emerging recognition of the role children play in developing resilient cities with the release of reports such as *Child-Centred Urban Resilience Framework* (Plan International et al., 2016), *Child-Centered Risk Reduction—Contributing to Resilient Development* (UNICEF, 2016), and *Towards the Resilient Future Children Want: A Review of Progress in Achieving the Children's Charter for Disaster Risk Reduction* (Bild and Ibrahim, 2013). There is a growing body of research into the benefits of community-led design in recovering from the trauma of a disaster. Some of these case studies highlight gaps where local cultures have been misunderstood or disregarded leading to a failure in delivery or appropriateness of design solutions (Charlesworth and Ahmed, 2015; Donovan, 2013). Given the complexity of the make-up of communities and the very different needs of children, it can be surmised that where children have not participated, their specific requirements have potentially been ignored, or at best interpreted by adults in the reconstruction process, thereby reducing their resilience and impacting the community in the longer term. There is scope to build on previous case studies for further examination into the role of children in the consultation processes and the impact on their communities.

The repeated calls for action and lack of documented evidence of meaningful consultation with children during the rebuilding and ongoing development of cities and towns after a disaster create an alarming gap. The United Nations *2030 Agenda for Sustainable Development* (UN General Assembly, 2015) identifies children as the necessary agents of change for a better world—a sentiment echoed in a number of global agreements identified in the report 'A View from 2016' that acknowledges children will inherit the choices made today and should therefore absolutely be involved in decisions that will affect them (Children in a Changing Climate, 2016).

The following two case studies identify ongoing research opportunities and call on decision-makers and designers to empower children in their decision-making processes.

Case Study One: Reconstruction After Bushfire, Australia

Several Victorian local government areas were greatly affected by the bushfires of 2009, in particular on February 9, known as Black Saturday.[4] Over 2,000 homes were lost and an estimated AUD$77 million loss and damage to public infrastructure including roads, parkland, schools and community infrastructure (Royal Commission into Victoria's Bushfires, 2009, Vol 1., App. A). There were 173 deaths as a result of the bushfires, including 23 children and an additional 20 children that lost one or both parents (Victorian Bushfire Reconstruction and Recovery Authority, 2009: 12).

A number of strategic economic and urban development plans have been developed since the fires for and by affected local government authorities. The consultation process for these documents varied and it is not clear what role and level of participation children played in those processes, if any at all. Using a modified version of the 'Child Friendly Cities Framework Governance Checklist' (UNICEF, 2011), the questionnaire 'A Child Friendly Community Self-Assessment Tool For Community Service Providers And Child Advocates' (UNICEF, 2011) and the 'Child-Centred Urban Resilience Framework' (Plan International et al., 2016),[5] local and state government employees[6] were interviewed[7] to glean an understanding of the barriers they perceived to consulting with children after the bushfires in the development of urban plans and what impact this may have had on their communities. While there were significant challenges in conducting the interviews,[8] the resulting information provided a strong indication of the need for further work.

The scale of the damage by the bushfires was so great that an alternative approach to recovery required additional capacity, resulting in the formation of the Victorian Bushfire Reconstruction and Recovery Authority (Victorian Bushfire Reconstruction and Recovery Authority, 2011). While this body provided much-needed capacity, there were a number of issues identified related to the top-down nature of the Authority that in a lot of cases excluded sections of communities and local government providers.

The interviews revealed that consultation with communities after the fires was inconsistent and beset by extreme challenges such as lack of resources, unrealistic timeframes and the complexity of working with highly traumatised people, supported by findings in the 2011 Legacy Report (Victorian Bushfire Reconstruction and Recovery Authority, 2011). There was general agreement that children were poorly consulted with and in some cases not at all. It was noted that children have different needs and understanding how to manage this was extremely challenging, compared with adults who were seen to be 'more predictable' in a highly stressful environment. When consultation occurred regarding child-centred infrastructure, adults generally provided the input into what they thought children needed. There were also few local children available during key consultation processes for local schools that had been destroyed. The redesign of one public park, focused on children and the incorporation of artwork involving children, was viewed by officers as joyful and a success.

All interviewees acknowledged the capacity of children and the under-utilisation of their capabilities, particularly in engagement and decision-making. One interviewee recounted the valuable role children played in assisting affected children in a bushfire relief centre, noting that they identified children's needs better than adults did. However, the recognition of children's value in providing input into the design of physical infrastructure was limited except in the case of playground design.

A number of barriers were identified that prevent or hinder the participation of children, particularly when it comes to involving children in municipal decision-making and especially after a traumatic disaster. These barriers can be simplified into general themes of leadership, unconscious bias and systems, and included:

- Lack of awareness and understanding of the role children play as active citizens, especially at leadership level;
- Lack of understanding in how and why to conduct meaningful engagement with children;
- Lack of understanding in how to listen and interpret engagement with children;
- Lack of resources and skill;
- Lack of commitment to elevating the role of children in decision-making.

Personal perceptions of validity were identified as an organisational barrier to engagement with children, regardless of the subject matter. While municipal authorities generally have community engagement policies and toolkits, officers are not necessarily required to monitor and evaluate the type, extent or success of the engagement. When, how and what value there is in children's input was not consistently understood and was reflected in the interviews conducted with state government officers.

Interviewees had access to community engagement policies along with a supporting toolkit at the time of the fires. Whilst the tools provided good resources for developing a community engagement plan, 'community' is identified as a generic entity without specific mention of children and no guidance on consulting them after a traumatic event which adds an additional layer of complexity. Interviewees spoke of the challenges in how to conduct meaningful and safe engagement with children and to ensure that their input is significant and not overridden by adults. This issue extended to how other organisations connect with Council officers, such as schools, and their ability to conduct meaningful conversations with their students when partnering in engagement activities. Conversely, there was also a perception that members of the community were unaware, unwilling, too busy or didn't know how to engage with the Council.

The lack of inclusion of children in infrastructure planning was seen as a barrier to good infrastructure outcomes. The first example involved consultation with adults regarding a recreation precinct and trail where community members provided self-interested responses rather than consideration of community needs. The second example involved the construction of a large sporting facility, of which the scale, design and governance of the facility is a barrier to use by young people as the centre is viewed as a clean, 'adult' environment, and did not reflect the recreational needs of the community. As a result, the existing buildings are underutilised and not financially viable to maintain. One interviewee stated that the use of a public facility is determined by 'personalities plus ownership plus control', which in this case was at odds with children's needs.

This case study highlighted the institutional barriers to children's participation, rendering them invisible during the reconstruction phase of disaster recovery. What it also demonstrated was an inherent bias against the belief in children's value in municipal decision-making processes, despite unanimous agreement in children's potential capacity. The unpredictability of a child-focused process and the resources required suggested that priorities were steered towards political outcomes rather than resilient community development and favoured a top-down approach.

Case Study Two: Reconstructing Chamanga, Ecuador

On 16 April 2016, a 7.8 degree Richter scale earthquake damaged 60–70 percent of houses in the Paroquia de Chamanga on the coast of Ecuador. In February 2017, an international collaboration between academic institutions and local practitioners[9] conducted a workshop to provide design assistance to build on the work being developed by local community, government and academic institutions. The areas of focus included public open space, urban fabric and socioeconomic place-making and built on pre-identified plans to contribute different thinking (Arroyo and Taller Internacionales con Participantes, 2017).

Social and planning issues faced by the community over many years were exacerbated after the earthquake. Reconstruction was slow to commence and focused on housing and water, leaving key public open spaces neglected and ineffectual. New housing areas and temporary settlements were constructed a kilometre away from the original township creating a segregated community and increasing distances for children to access schooling and public social and recreational spaces. Public infrastructure affected included the soccer ground and other sport facilities, town plaza, play equipment, access to the beach, the cultural centre, schools and the principal staircase which was a culturally significant gathering place for food, music and play. The earthquake also had a devastating impact on the local economy leading to drug addiction, dealing and trafficking.

Local government officials conducted tours with workshop members providing background to the slow reconstruction process and expressing hope that additional design work feeding into the urban plan would prompt a flow of much-needed funds.

While the task for the workshop members was to design for the whole of community, it was impossible to ignore the repeated topic of children entering the consultation. Community members expressed concern for their children, highlighting the use of children in the drug trade and a lack of constructive areas and activities for social interaction and recreation. Hand-painted informal signs scattered around the town encouraged children to say no to drugs and yes to education, with a belief that the neglect of rebuilding child-focused infrastructure immediately led to children being targeted by drug traffickers. Over 2,000 students attended local schools, but there were no footpaths and the unsealed roads had developed into quagmires. A temporary school had been erected while construction progressed on the permanent structure, but a lack of play facilities resulted in children playing in open drains, exposing them to water-borne diseases and mosquitoes. The staircase was no longer safe for children to play on. There was a desire to reactivate sports through a championship. Children were learning hip-hop and reggae dance but had nowhere to perform. It was clear that children were critical in our design-thinking and had to-date been largely ignored with dire consequences.

In addition to the design of public open spaces, the workshop provided resources to develop a joint small-scale urban action. The selected projects included the construction of a toilet block in the new village area and the clean-up, repair and beautification of the principal staircase in the original town. It was hoped that this would involve members of the community and contribute to Chamanga's reconstruction plan.

During the construction work, a small group of community members joined in or watched the workshop participants. What was noticeable

Figure 12.2 Hand-Painted Signs by Local Residents Were Erected Throughout the Town Encouraging Children to Focus on Education, Living and Happiness Rather Than Drugs, San Jose de Chamanga, Ecuador.

Source: Robyn Mansfield (2017)

however was the eagerness of a group of children to participate in the beautification component. The children were of primary school age and younger, and predominantly girls. Despite the language differences, the children were able to understand what the workshop participants were trying to do; they then learned each step of the process, offered us water, then ushered us out of the way so they could take over. The children worked tirelessly until the project was finished at the end of the day and demonstrated their ability and desire to be involved in the reconstruction process. They also demonstrated empathy towards workshop participants who were struggling in the intense heat; offering water, cooling spray and indicating that overheated people should rest while the children carried on with the project.

While the value of involving children in this reconstruction process is open to speculation, what is obvious is the impact of ignoring the role child-friendly infrastructure had on the social fabric of this community and the children's desire to be involved in their community. The loss of community open space for cultural activities, gatherings and play, the destruction of recreational facilities, fragmented access to key areas of town, and decline

Figure 12.3 Children Learning Mosaic Techniques in the Staircase Clean-Up Project, San Jose de Chamanga, Ecuador.

Source: Robyn Mansfield (2017)

of the economic market at best led to a fragmented community and at worst exposed children to dire and long-term health consequences associated with water-borne diseases, drugs, mental health problems and criminal activity. It essentially created a second disaster.

Children's Participation—Capability Versus Complexity

The Australian report *Don't Leave Me Alone* identifies that children are not passive citizens and that a disaster may actually have an empowering impact on children (Davie, 2013: 6), while Gibbs et al. note that children played a powerful decision-making role after the Victorian 2009 fires, terming them as 'competent survivors' (Gibbs et al., 2015: 199). Gibbs further identifies, in another study, that children can contribute and find benefit in contributing to the recovery and rebuilding process and identifies government infrastructure as having an impact on children (Gibbs et al., 2014: 21–22).

Understanding how to interpret children's input and translate it into meaningful outcomes that are not tokenistic is limited. This complexity has been grappled with extensively by Roger Hart, who developed the Ladder of Youth Participation (Figure 12.4), influenced by Arnstein's *A Ladder of Citizen Participation* (Arnstein, 1969) and used by UNICEF, which has generated debate as to the role and extent of children's participation (Hart, 2008). Hart identifies a key issue in the segregation of children from their communities, removing the ability to informally participate with adults and even with children of other age groups, thereby diminishing their community role (Hart, 2008: 20). While the ladder was not intended to provide levels of superiority in engagement, it has highlighted the gaps in children's participation and presents a critical perspective to instigate reflection.

UNICEF's report, *Promoting Children's Participation In Democratic Decision-Making,* identifies that there are widespread attitudes that adults know what is best for children and this has consistently failed children despite the articulation of the meaning of 'best interests of the child' in Article 4 of the Convention on the Rights of the Child (UN Committee on the Rights of the Child [CRC], 2013; Lansdown, 2001). General Comment No.14 acknowledges that children are easily manipulated by adults and that adults do not always act in the child's best interests, either intentionally or unconsciously (UN CRC, 2013). The United Nations Convention on the Rights of the Child underpins a range of international agreements that identify children's right to opinions and the right to express their views, and while these agreements are endorsed internationally, the embedded unconscious bias still remains as evidenced in studies such as *A View from 2016* (Children in a Changing Climate, 2016).

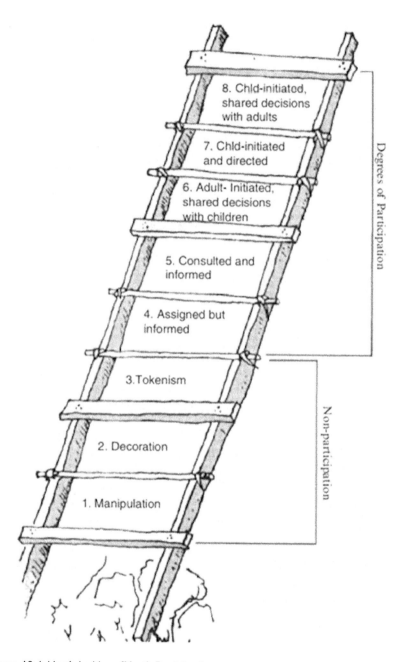

Figure 12.4 Hart's Ladder of Youth Participation.
Source: Hart (2008) Reprinted/adapted by permission from Springer Nature

UNICEF (United Nations International Children's Fund) has developed the 'Child Friendly Cities Framework', underpinned by the United Nations Convention on the Rights of the Child, as a framework and set of tools for government and citizens to work together to improve liveability, governance and the participation of all in decision-making in matters that affect people. While children's rights are a legal obligation, there is also demonstrated evidence that prioritising children and involving them in decision-making can break cycles of poverty and increase the overall health of communities (UNICEF, 2016b; UNICEF, 2004). Subsequent UNICEF documents provide additional guidance specific to working with children in emergency situations (UNICEF, 2016a; UNICEF, 2007). There is little evidence to suggest that these tools have been used to assess the levels of meaningful engagement of children post-disaster and whether they have potential to fulfil the gaps identified in 'A View from 2016'.

The *Handbook of Disaster Research identifies* that research into children and disasters has increased noticeably in the last decade as the vulnerability of children is increasingly understood (Peek et al., 2018). It is noted, however, that more attention should be given to children's capacities and strengths, acknowledging their contribution to their families and communities before, during and after a disaster. While research into children's attachment to place is noted, there appears to be a large gap in understanding the role children can play in the reconstruction process.

There is strong evidence to suggest that barriers to engagement with children in government are a sectoral issue and, based on the Ecuador case study, this may be an international issue rather than just confined to the Australian context. Children have great capacity and capability, but the approach to engagement during non-emergency times poses challenges that are greatly exacerbated after an emergency. Children's ability to influence the reconstruction process after a disaster through participation in strategic planning initiatives is largely unexplored, but presents opportunities for developing child-friendly approaches to post-disaster urban planning. Embedding children's participation in organisation and community culture will ensure their role is better understood and the barriers reduced or eliminated. Further research and policy improvement will ease challenges to engagement, and the development and strengthening of partnerships prior to disasters will ensure more trusting relationships between funding authorities and communities. Leadership and long-term commitment is required, but ultimately, the meaningful and ongoing engagement with children will improve communities' resilience and ability to recover from future emergency situations.

Conclusion

The complexity of these two case studies offers insight into an individual scale view of how rebuilding for resilience after a disaster requires neighbourhood-size 'bites' of a city. While a blanket approach to improving the physical infrastructure of a city after a disaster may be required, it ignores the essential component of the human resilience building required for developing a resilient city and should not exist in isolation. To operate at a city scale requires a top-down generic view of community, while approaching it from a neighbourhood scale provides the opportunity for a 'community acupuncture' approach—an alternative view of the commonly understood term 'urban acupuncture', an approach to urban improvement based on the medical idea of 'strategic punctual interventions' that will trigger expansive positive outcomes (Lerner, 2011), and one that sees every subset of local communities as essential for the health of all others. Critical to this approach is an understanding of the connection and overlap between neighbourhoods, which is perhaps easier to articulate between small settlements that again offer opportunities for examination to understand application at a city scale.

What is clear from these two cases studies is that children's participation in the reconstruction and ongoing governance processes after a disaster is complex and faces significant barriers. While children have been identified in these studies as an all-encompassing term for anyone under the age of 18, it highlights their invisibility in the processes and the devastating consequences. The long-term impact of the exclusion of children in these processes is yet to be understood, however there are clear indications that the resilience of these two townships has been compromised as a result. Given the contained size of the townships, the implications for transposing this at a city-scale situation raises deep concerns. These case studies demonstrate that localised specific risks can result in a major blow to the resilience of a place.

Further research is needed to better understand how to meaningfully consult with children who are likely to be suffering from significant trauma and risk after a disaster in order to better understand the long-term benefits for themselves and their communities, and also to challenge biases and barriers to empowering and involving children in what is generally seen as an 'adult domain'. Research should also seek to examine the impacts of factor such as age, disability, culture, socioeconomic factors, access to technology, religion and other factors to articulate the specific needs of subset groups of children. Viewing communities as a series of pressure points that are all inextricably linked to the resilience of the whole will perhaps provoke a far more inclusive and creative approach to developing resilient cities. Whilst we can only speculate on the intrinsic value children's participation may have had on the physical and social fabric of these two communities, by the very nature of their dependency, children are likely to be some of the most connected, capable, social and creative members of communities, and may well provide the key to developing resilient cities.

Notes

1. While Rodin identifies 'everyone' as being responsible for achieving resilience, the human face is hidden behind organisations and governments in *The Resilience Dividend*. This is perhaps inevitable when the impact of disasters is measured in economic terms and the drain of resources. The resulting discussion and case studies then tend to favour a top-down approach to resilience based on the injection of funds from government and non-government agencies and ignores the complexities that exist in subsets of communities and how to develop resilience in the face of delayed or reduced injections of funding.
2. For the purposes of this report, 'children' refers to persons up to the age of 18 as per the United Nations definition under the Convention on the Rights of the Child UNICEF. 2005. *Convention on the Rights of the Child Frequently Asked Questions* [Online]. UNICEF. Available: www.unicef.org/crc/index_30229.html [Accessed 9 April 2017].
3. The IFRC definition of 'disaster' is used in this report:

   "A disaster is a sudden, calamitous event that seriously disrupts the functioning of a community or society and causes human, material, and economic or environmental losses that exceed the community's or society's ability to cope using its own resources. Though often caused by nature, disasters can have human origins." International Federation of Red Cross and Red Crescent Societies (IFRC). 2019. *What is a Disaster?* [Online]. IFRC. Available: www.ifrc.org/en/what-we-do/disaster-management/about-disasters/what-is-a-disaster/ [Accessed 2019].

4. 'Black Saturday' refers to the day of greatest impact from bushfires that were burning across Victoria, Australia on 7 February 2009.
5. The 'Child Friendly Cities Governance Checklist' was used to form the basis of the interviews with council staff. These tools confirmed a known factor that children are absent from general decision-making, and especially in a post-disaster environment where they are often relegated to the sidelines while adults talk adult problems. The interviews were expanded to test the principles identified in the 'Child-Centred Urban Resilience Framework', and to understand the roles and level of understanding of the interviewees which uncovered key barriers that would need to be examined before a child-friendly approach could become embedded.
6. Between March and May in 2017, semi-structured interviews were conducted with five local government staff including three men and two women, and informal interviews with four neighbouring local government staff, two state government staff in emergency services and a senior state government officer who was seconded to the Victorian Bushfire Reconstruction and Recovery Authority (VBRRA) in 2009. Key local government officers were selected based on their roles in working with children, developing processes and strategic work relevant to reconstruction projects, planning for disaster risk reduction and response to future disasters. There has been turnover of staff since 2009, so the sample included both new staff to understand current and future engagement practices, and those who were present when key strategic plans were developed in response to the bushfires. Four senior officers from a neighbouring council were consulted with to test the findings against their experiences regarding consulting with children and post-Black Saturday consultation.

   Emergency Management Victoria was identified as a key driver of post disaster response and developing community resilience. Local Government Victoria was undertaking a review of the Local Government Act at the time of the research with a stronger focus on deliberative community engagement. These agencies were consulted with to provide input into recommendations resulting from this research.

7. Semi-structured interviews were used to understand existing processes and policies regarding engagement of children in municipal decision-making, identify barriers to participation of children and develop knowledge in levels of understanding regarding the rights of children in decision-making. The interviews were designed to elicit anecdotal analysis on the current participation of children in municipal engagement, the role of Council's staff in working through issues involving children and a deeper understanding of the engagement that occurred post-Black Saturday. The interview questions were designed using the 'Child Centred Urban Resilience Framework' Plan International, Australian Aid, Swedish Government and ARUP 2016 Child-Centred Urban Resilience Framework, The Rockefeller Foundation I Arup and 'The Child Friendly City Governance Checklist' as guides, applying a disaster and trauma lens to the checklist questions. This was to assist in determining barriers and opportunities to inform recommendations for future actions.

8. There were challenges in running an interview process. A structured format was challenging as participants were keen to reflect on their own experiences in response to the trauma they had experienced. Whilst there was strong support for the research, trauma was still evident with several current and previous staff members, with some choosing not to participate, and difficulty finding staff members who had since left the organisation. Anonymity was a key concern, not only for participants but for the Councils involved in the research. This served as a warning of the unpredictable nature of trauma and the sensitivity required when consulting with affected people.

9. The workshop was developed by Universidad de Catalunya, Barvcelona in partnership with local authorities in Ecuador, The Pontificia Universidad Catolica de Ecuador (PUCE), Royal Melbourne Institute of Technology (RMIT) and University of Tokyo. A publication was created to support work already being developed and explored place-making as a tool to address preexisting issues such as socioeconomic and planning issues. The workshop was underpinned by key reports on demographics, geological analysis and consultation with local authorities and residents throughout the workshop.

References

100 Resilient Cities. (2016). *100 Resilient Cities Official website* [online]. Available at: www.100resilientcities.org/#/-_/ (accessed November 17, 2016).

Arnstein, S. (1969). A ladder of citizen participation. *JAIP*, 35, 216–224.

Arroyo, C.M. and Taller Internacionales Con Participantes. (2017). *Reconstruyendo Chamanga*. Barcelona: UIC Barcelona.

Bild, E. and Ibrahim, M. (2013). *Towards the Resilient Future Children Want: A Review of Progress in Achieving the Children's Charter for Disaster Risk Reduction*. Milton Keynes: World Vision.

Birch, E.L. and Wachter, S.M. (2006). *Rebuilding Urban Places after Disaster Lessons from Hurricane Katrina*. Philadelphia: University of Pennsylvania Press.

Charlesworth, E.R. and Ahmed, I. (2015). *Sustainable Housing Reconstruction: Designing Resilient Housing after Natural Disasters*. Abingdon, Oxon and New York: Routledge.

Children in a Changing Climate. (2016). *A View from 2016, Child-centered Disaster Risk Reduction and Climate Change Adaptation in the 2030 Agenda for Sustainable Development.* London and New York: Children in a Changing Climate.

CRED and UNISDR. (2018). *Economic Losses, Poverty and Disasters (1998–2017)* [online]. Centre for Research on the Epidemiology of Disasters, CRED. Available at: www.emdat.be/publications (accessed June 14, 2019).

ARUP. (2015). *City Resilience Framework.* London: The Rockefeller Foundation and Arup.

Davie, S. (2013). *Don't Leave Me Alone, Protecting Children in Australian Disasters and Emergencies.* East Melbourne, Australia: Save the Children Australia.

Derr, V., Corona, Y. and Gülgönen, T. (2019). Children's perceptions of and engagement in urban resilience in the United States and Mexico. *Journal of Planning Education and Research*, 39, 7–17.

Donovan, J. (2013). *Designing to Heal.* Collingwood, Victoria: CSIRO.

Featherston, A. (2014). *Tsunami Ten Years On, Stories of Change.* London: Save the Children.

Gibbs, L., Block, K., Harms, L., Macdougall, C., Baker, E., Ireton, G., Forbes, D., Richardson, J. and Waters, E. (2015). Children and young people's wellbeing postdisaster: Safety and stability are critical. *International Journal of Disaster Risk Reduction*, 14(2), 195–201.

Gibbs, L., Di Petro, M., Ireton, G., Mordech, S., Roberts, M., Sinclair, J., Wraith, R. and Harris, A. (2014). Core principles for a community-based approach to supporting child disaster recovery. *The Australian Journal of Emergency Management*, 29, 17–24 [online].

Hart, R.A. (2008). Stepping back from 'the ladder': Reflections on a model of participatory work with children. In A. Reid, B.B. Jensen, J. Nikel and V. Simovska (eds.), *Participation and Learning: Developing Perspectives on Education and the Environment, Health and Sustainability.* Netherlands: Springer.

Haynes, K. and Tanner, T.M. (2015). Empowering young people and strengthening resilience: Youth-centred participatory video as a tool for climate change adaptation and disaster risk reduction. *Children's Geographies*, 13, 357–371.

International Federation of Red Cross and Red Crescent Societies (IFRC). (2019). *What is a Disaster?* [online]. IFRC. Available at: www.ifrc.org/en/what-we-do/disaster-management/about-disasters/what-is-a-disaster/ (accessed 2019).

Jha, A.K., Miner, T.W. and Stanton-Geddes, Z. (2013). *Building Urban Resilience, Principles, Tools, and Practice.* Washington, DC: The World Bank.

Kendra, J.M., Clay, L.A. and Gill, K.B. (2018). Resilience and disasters. In H. Rodrigues, W. Donner and E.J. Trainor (eds.), *Handbook of Disaster Research*, 2nd ed. Switzerland: Springer.

Lansdown, G. (2001). *Promoting Children's Participation in Democratic Decision-Making.* Florence, Italy: UNICEF.

Leadbeater, A. (2013). Community leadership in disaster recovery: A case study. *Australian Journal of Emergency Management*, 28, 41.

Lerner, J. (2011). Urban acupuncture. *Harvard Business Review*, April 18.

Peek, L., Abramson, D.M., Cox, R.S., Fothergill, A. and Tobin, J. (2018). Children and disasters. In H. Rodríguez, W. Donner and W.E.J. Trainor (eds.), *Handbook of Disaster Research*, 2nd ed. Switzerland: Springer.

Pervin, M., Sultana, S., Phirum, A., Camara, I.F., Nzau, V.M., Phonnasane, V., Khounsy, P., Kaur, N. and Anderson, S. (2013). *A Framework for Mainstreaming Climate Resilience into Development Planning*. London: International Institute for Environment and Development (IIED) Working Paper, Climate Change, November 2013.

Plan International, Australian Aid, Swedish Government and Arup. (2016). *Child-Centred Urban Resilience Framework*. London: The Rockefeller Foundation and Arup.

Reed, S.R. and Friend, R. (2016). *A View from 2016, Child-centered Disaster Risk Reduction and Climate Change Adaptation in the 2030 Agenda for Sustainable Development*. Available at Children in Climate Change website (CCC): www.childreninachangingclimate.org/uploads/6/3/1/1/63116409/a_view_from_2016_ccc.pdf.

Rodin, J. (2015). *The Resilience Dividend: Managing Disruption, Avoiding Disaster, and Growing Stronger in an Unpredictable World*. London: Profile Books Ltd.

Royal Commission into Victoria's Bushfires, McLeod, R.N., Pascoe, S.M. and Teague, B.G. (2009). Victorian Bushfires Royal Commission: Interim Report. Melbourne, Australia: Government Printer for the State of Victoria.

Schilderman, T. (2016). How does reconstruction after disaster affect long-term resilience? In T. Francis (ed.), *Urban Disaster Resilience, New Dimensions from International Practice in the Built Environment*. New York: Routledge.

Shaw, J., Mulligan, M., Nadarajah, Y., Mercer, D.A. and Ahmed, I. (2010). *Lessons From tsunami recovery in Sri Lanka and India* [online]. Melbourne, Australia: Monash University. Available at: http://artsonline.monash.edu.au/mai/files/2012/06/post-tsunami-1.pdf (accessed 2016).

UN Committee on the Rights of the Child (CRC). *General Comment No. 14 (2013) on the Right of the Child to Have His or Her Best Interests Taken as a Primary Consideration (art. 3, para. 1)*. UN Committee on the Rights of the Child, 62nd Session ed. Geneva: United Nations.

UNGA (United Nations General Assembly). (2015). *Resolution adopted by the General Assembly on 25 September 2015: 70/1: Transforming Our World: The 2030 Agenda for Sustainable Development*. A/RES/70/1. UN General Assembly.

United Nations Childrens Fund (UNICEF). (2004). *Building Child Friendly Cities: A Framework for Action*. Florence, Italy: Innocenti Publications.

United Nations Childrens Fund (UNICEF). (2005). *Convention on the Rights of the Child Frequently Asked Questions* [online]. UNICEF. Available at: www.unicef.org/crc/index_30229.html (accessed April 9, 2017).

United Nations Childrens Fund (UNICEF). (2007). *The Participation of Children and Young People in Emergencies*. Bangkok, Thailand: UNICEF.

United Nations Childrens Fund (UNICEF). (2011). *Final Toolkit 2011* [online]. UNICEF. Available at: http://childfriendlycities.org/research/final-toolkit-2011/ (accessed 2016).

United Nations Childrens Fund (UNICEF) (2016a). *Child-centered Disaster Risk Reduction, Contributing to Resilient Development*. UNICEF.

United Nations Childrens Fund (UNICEF). (2016b). *The State of the World's Children: A Fair Chance for Every Child*. New York: UNICEF.

United Nations Childrens Fund (UNICEF), Plan International, Save the Children and World Vision. (2011). *Children's Charter—An Action Plan for Disaster Risk*

Reduction for Children by Children. Available at: https://plan-international.org/publications/childrens-charter-disaster-risk-reduction.

United Nations International Strategy for Disaster Reduction (UNISDR). (2015). *Sendai Framework for Disaster Risk Reduction 2015–2030.* Geneva, Switzerland: UNISDR.

United Nations International Strategy for Disaster Reduction (UNISDR). (2019). *Disaster Resilience Scorecard for Cities* [online]. UNISDR. Available at: www.unisdr.org/campaign/resilientcities/toolkit/article/disaster-resilience-scorecard-for-cities (accessed June 14, 2019).

United Nations Office for Disaster Risk Reduction (UNDRR). (2019). *Global Assessment Report on Disaster Risk Reduction.* Geneva, Switzerland: UNDRR.

Venkatachalam, T. (2011). When people are involved. In M.J. Aquilino (ed.), *Beyond Shelter, Architecture for Crisis.* London: Thames and Hudson.

Victorian Bushfire Reconstruction And Recovery Authority. (2009). *Rebuilding Together: A Statewide Plan for Bushfire Reconstruction and Recovery.* Melbourne, Australia: Victorian Bushfire Reconstruction and Recovery Authority.

Victorian Bushfire Reconstruction and Recovery Authority. (2011). *Legacy Report.* Melbourne, Australia: State Government of Victoria.

Wachtendorf, T., Kendra, J.M. and Deyoung, S.E. (2018). Community innovation and disasters. In H. Rodríguez, W. Donner and E.J. Trainor (eds.), *Handbook of Disaster Research*, 2nd ed. Switzerland: Springer.

Watson, G.B. (2016). *Designing Resilient Cities and Neighbourhoods.* New York: Routledge.

Chapter 13

Identifying Resilience in Recovery—Complexity, Collaboration and Communication

David Sanderson

In recent years, efforts aimed at addressing disaster risk in urban areas have coalesced around enacting the concept of resilience. Resilience-related programming by aid agencies and others concerning naturally triggered disasters are often geared towards actions aimed at improved preparedness, mitigation and (if all goes well) prevention. Examples include improved forecasting and warning, better seismic design, and for existing buildings, the retrofitting of public buildings such as schools and hospitals. Flood-prevention measures include better site planning to avoid building on low-lying land. Good programmes have also focused on the behavioural and social aspects of building resilience (such as teaching children what to do when an earthquake strikes) as much as the physical aspects. Focusing on pre-disaster resilience through better mitigation and preparedness has had many successes. The IFRC *2016 World Disasters Report. Resilience: saving lives today, investing for tomorrow* discusses the benefits of improved preparedness, noting that 'many disasters have been reduced or even totally prevented' (IFRC, 2016: 13), citing examples from Bangladesh and elsewhere. More recently, in May 2019, India managed to avoid high-level losses of life in the State of Odisha when Cyclone Fani struck its coast. The government evacuated over one million people, leading to around 40 recorded deaths. This compares to the Super Cyclone of 1999 that struck the same area, killing over 20,000 people. The 2019 cyclone caused widespread damage that will take years to recover from—but the absence of a high death toll demonstrates the live-saving nature of preparedness.

While considerable attention has therefore been given to using the concept of resilience as a rallying cry to better prepare for disasters, much less attention has been given to thinking about how resilience can be built immediately after a disaster, while relief and subsequent recovery operations are underway. At this point it is worth noting that different definitions of resilience commonly span the 'before and after' of disasters. For instance, the IFRC provides the following definition:

> Resilience is the ability of individuals, communities, organizations or countries exposed to disasters and crises and underlying vulnerabilities

to anticipate, reduce the impact of, cope with, and recover from the effects of shocks and stresses without compromising their long-term prospects.

(IFRC, 2016)

In recent work undertaken by the author, an absence of an overt focus on the latter half of the definition, i.e., 'resilience in recovery' was apparent. The work concerned the production of a book, *Good Practice Review (GPR) in Urban Humanitarian Response* (Sanderson, 2019), that was released in July 2019. The book was commissioned by the UK's Overseas Development Institute (ODI) and the Active Learning Network for Accountability and Performance (ALNAP). The work reflects the recognition that humanitarian aid—itself derived mostly from rural experiences—needs to 'urbanise', that is, change and evolve its own approaches to be more effective in meeting the challenge of urban disasters.

The review looked at the practices of humanitarian aid organisations (mostly United Nations agencies, international and local NGOs, and members of the Red Cross Red Crescent Movement) in responding to crises in urban areas. As well as naturally triggered disasters (which are the subject of this chapter), crises included climate change, conflict, violence and the results of forced migration, leading to refugees and internally displaced persons (IDPs) living in cities. The work involved an extensive review a wide range of recent literature concerning urban humanitarian response, including agency reports, peer-reviewed papers and evaluations. Drafts of written sections were peer reviewed by between four and nine experts working in humanitarian response.

Throughout all the documents reviewed, an explicit link between how post-disaster recovery actions contribute to building resilience was hardly, if ever, made. This, of course, does not mean that recovery actions do not contribute to building resilience, but rather that these points are not being made explicitly—which it is argued here is needed to build the case that resilience can be a focus in recovery as well as in preparedness.

In order to contribute to this, the remainder of this chapter identifies and discusses three key post-disaster recovery actions that contribute towards building resilience. Before presenting this, however, it is perhaps necessary to ask, what does a resilient city look like? This is in order to give the subsequent discussion on how humanitarian recovery can contribute to 'something to aim at'. While extensive literature exists that discusses strategies and approaches for building more resilient communities[1]—not least in this book—this section reviews a small number of key initiatives.

What Does a Resilient City Look Like?

According to the Rockefeller Foundation's 100 Resilient Cities initiative, 'Building urban resilience requires looking at a city holistically: understanding the systems that make up the city and the interdependencies and risks they may face' (Rockefeller Foundation, 2019). Factors include unemployment, public transport, violence, and food and water availability. The UN International Strategy for Disaster Reduction's (UNISDR) *Making Cities Resilient* campaign identifies 'ten essentials' which include realistic, risk-compliant building regulations and land use planning principles, education and training programmes on community-based disaster risk reduction, and affected populations placed at the centre of reconstruction efforts (UNISDR, nd).

There are also plenty of agreements that in recent years have included resilience as a desired outcome, the best known of which are probably the United Nations' Sustainable Development Goal (SDG) 11, often referred to as 'the urban SDG', that aims to 'make cities inclusive, safe, resilient and sustainable', and SDG 9, that among other things concerns building resilient infrastructure. The New Urban Agenda, agreed in Quito at HABITAT III in 2016 (UN, 2016), emphasises the need a number of times over to build resilience to hazards, disasters and climate change. Concerning the Pacific in particular, the declaration emerging from the Fifth Pacific Urban Forum (PUF) held in July 2019 in Fiji's capital, Suva, refers to 'resilience' and 'resilient' ten times, relating for instance to infrastructure, housing and design principles[2] (UN-Habitat, 2019).

Despite some exceptions, there appears to be less literature in the humanitarian/development space on what a resilient city actually looks like. One such exception is extensive research undertaken by the engineering firm Arup for the Rockefeller Foundation which formed the basis for the City Resilience Index (CRI), which identifies 'eight functions of a resilient city'. These are that a city delivers basic needs; safeguards human life; protects, maintains and enhances assets (such as buildings and transport networks as well as natural systems, such as rivers and ground water); facilitates human relationships and identity; promotes knowledge, education and innovation; defends the rule of law, justice and equity; supports livelihoods; and stimulates economic prosperity (Arup, 2014).

At a community level, work undertaken by Twigg (2009) for the Interagency Group of UK NGOs concerned identifying (non-location specific, i.e., rural or urban) characteristics of disaster-resilient communities. Thematic areas of this diagnostic tool include governance, risk assessment, knowledge and education, risk management and vulnerability reduction, and disaster preparedness and response. Follow-on work undertaken as part of this initiative by the IFRC, 'characteristics of a disaster-resilient community' identified particular characteristics that such communities are knowledgeable and healthy, organised, have economic opportunities and are connected with external actors (IFRC, 2011).

Three Actions for Building Resilience in Recovery

With the previous section in view, the following section identifies three sets of actions that agencies are undertaking in recovery that contribute to some or all of the previous points, i.e., contributing towards resilient cities. The actions, which emerge from the GPR research discussed earlier, are: engaging in complexity, in particular using a systems view to interpret this; collaboration, recognising the wide range of actors within a city and the need to engage better; and, communication with affected populations, which is taken here to mean aid agencies listening better by using participatory assessment tools.

Engaging in Complexity

Cities are anything but simple—infrastructure, density, verticality, diversity, scale, commerce, culture, markets, inequality and entrepreneurship are just some of the words associated with 'urban'. Complexity is the first key point here, because traditional humanitarian aid has, on some levels, simplified its approaches to the point of abstraction from reality—a seemingly straightforward logistical exercise of delivering goods to people who have lost them (as exemplified by the Cluster approach, discussed later). This section suggests engaging with cities by seeing them first and foremost at two levels—the macro, systems level, and secondly, at a people-centred level.

Cities as Systems

Seeing cities as a series of systems helps to make the connections between different elements and functions of a city. Systems can be defined as 'an interconnected collection of things (for example people, institutions, infrastructure, societal norms, economy or ecosystems), organised in a pattern or structure that changes frequently' (Levine et al., 2017: 5). UN-Habitat identifies five attributes of urban systems, namely functions (such as governance and social processes), organisations (for example neighbourhood groups), space, physicality (infrastructure and buildings) and change over time (UN-Habitat, 2018). Given the immediacy of much humanitarian response, combined with tight timeframes and donor priorities that separate emergency response from long-term development, this last point is often forgotten in recovery operations. A systems view helps agencies decide where limited efforts go in post-disaster recovery. As is often highlighted in these discussions, in seeking to ensure a water supply, does an agency/collection of agencies seek to repair a whole water supply system (probably not, given the scale of the task, though they may have a role in advocating for the prioritisation of specific services, perhaps)?

A further example is health. The World Health Organisation (WHO) for instance 'emphasises the need to understand urban healthcare in terms of systems, comprising six inter-related sub-systems—governance, health financing, health workforce, service delivery, essential medicines and technology and health information systems' (WHO, 1993, cited in Sanderson, 2019: 227). Providing immediate and longer-term health provision post-disaster is often vital, but a risk for agencies is ignoring the existing health systems—hospitals, doctors, nurses, health centres—that already exist and who needs to be engaged with and not ignored.

The GPR found that good practice in health response

> includes prioritising working through, rebuilding or improving pre-existing healthcare systems as early as possible. Health interventions must be sustainable, and must not be seen purely as short-term life-saving measures built in parallel, as they then undercut existing systems. This can be as devastating as the disaster itself, taking years to recover.
>
> (Sanderson, 2019: 229)

People-Centred Approaches

If systems provide a helpful, macro-level perspective of the complexity of the city, then this view needs to also be balanced with a people-centred perspective—given that the focus of humanitarian action is especially about assisting those who are the most vulnerable. There is a wealth of literature and approaches on people-centred approaches, emerging in particular from developmental practice (see for example Chambers, 1995; Hamdi, 2010). Indeed, the chapter in this publication concerning 'endogenous resilience' speaks to this subject (see McEvoy et al.). The GPR uses one such approach that takes an assets/vulnerability approach (Carney, 1998; Anderson and Woodrow, 1989), wherein, simply put, the less assets people have, the more vulnerable they are. Assets include belongings, goods and cash, but also, importantly, social networks and friendships (usually called social capital) and skills (human capital).

There is plenty of evidence that social capital is a particularly powerful and important asset post-disaster (see for example Archer and Boonyabancha, 2011)—as the adage goes, *it's your neighbours that pull you out of the rubble*. In the absence of social capital, people are especially vulnerable. In urban areas, this often coincides with people who may be outcast or ostracised by 'mainstream' society. For example, in Bangladesh's capital city Dhaka, a World Bank study (2006) found that people living in some poorer neighbourhoods self-identified three levels of 'ill-being'—the social poor, the helpless poor and the hated poor. Quoting from a paper published by the author that summarised the study,

> The helpless poor are identifiable by their old clothes and pained faces. They can afford neither health care nor education for their children. In urban contexts, this group is referred to as the 'hard-core poor'. 'Most of them are widows, separated, or have husbands with ill health', say women. The women also say that the hard-core poor often beg, have no reliable income, and live in sublet rooms and tin shacks. Disabled

people are also among the hated poor. Members of these households often starve. Lacking land and other assets, they do not have access to loans, even from family or friends. In addition, they are not accepted as members of local organisations, and thus cannot benefit from group assistance as a last resort.

(Sanderson, 2012)

Effective humanitarian response aims to meet basic needs, but as the previously discussed health illustration demonstrates, stopping there is not enough. In humanitarian language, the parallel might be with providing relief alone, that while providing the essential task of saving lives does little to contribute to effective recovery. Urban response, however, needs to go further if resilience is to be strengthened (and existing services not undermined).

Cash

Arguably, an approach in humanitarian programming that is both system and people-focused cash transfer programming (CTP). The use of cash is growing rapidly. 'In 2016, cash transfers and vouchers were worth approximately $2.8 billion, a 40 per cent increase from 2015' (Development Initiatives, 2018). It has been argued that cash transfers should be the primary response in urban areas (Cross and Johnston, 2011). Cash is something of a 'no-brainer' in urban response—people live mostly by buying goods from markets which are plentiful in cities (including often after disasters). Cash gives agency to people to prioritise their own needs. It helps fuel urban systems such as local markets, supporting traders and commerce. It uses existing mechanisms—after the first of the Nepal earthquakes, a number of international NGOs partnered with local banks to distribute funds quickly (Sanderson et al., 2015).

There is evidence of CTP's effectiveness in Pacific cities, in both the short- and longer-term. According to Save the Children (2019), CTP has been used to support communities post-Tropical Cyclone Winston in Fiji and for people displaced from Ambae due to volcanic activity in Vanuatu, as well as during Tropical Cyclone Pam. 'For some areas of Fiji, CTP has been found to be feasible immediately after a disaster, while for others, it would be more appropriate in the longer term in order to help affected communities recover and rebuild'. Research by Oxfam in Vanuatu found that CTPs had wide application, particularly in urban areas where access to markets was stronger (Oxfam, 2019).

While CTP is not perfect (which sectoral approach is?), and there are a number of programming decisions to make, such as which modalities to use (such as vouchers or cash), and considerations to address for effective programming, the growing evidence is that CTP ought, as noted before,

Collaboration

The previous section outlined the scale and complexity of cities operating concurrently at two scales. A key element of complexity concerns the functions of cities, and those who live in them. The golden rule in humanitarian response is that organisations are doomed to fail if they work in isolation (though a good number still choose this route). Given the multitude of actors in a city, collaboration is vital. Cities are homes to all kinds of 'actors'—government authorities at all levels, in particular city government; civil society groups; businesses of all kinds—including both 'formal' entities (that pay tax) and informal businesses such as street vendors and faith groups. And then there are gangs, who can act as neighbourhood-level gatekeepers, often in poorer urban settlements. The GPR notes that,

> while most gangs are unsupervised teenage peer groups, many are institutionalised in ghettos, barrios and *favelas* across the world. Also, 'Gangs are "social actors" whose identities are formed by ethnic, racial and/or religious oppression [and] through participation in the underground economy' (Winton, 2014: 406).

> (Sanderson, 2019: 25)

The principle mechanism for humanitarian coordination, the cluster approach,[3] does not make much room for local actors—and certainly not for gangs. The setup is principally for international aid organisations, with local actors such as local authorities and local NGOs often feeling excluded. One study of the response of 13 INGOs following Typhoon Haiyan found that, across the track of the typhoon, local government was largely bypassed by aid agencies that worked directly at the community level (Sanderson and Delica Willison, 2014: 15).

While the evidence is that having clusters is far better than having no clusters at all (Humphries, 2013), the cluster system is increasingly recognised for not engaging sufficiently with the complexities of the city. The International Rescue Committee (IRC) has concluded,

> The traditional cluster system does not lend itself to the complexity of needs, services and systems across an urban landscape with humanitarian agencies struggling to deal with the complexity, density and built environment of towns and cities or [un]able to take full advantage of the potential a city has to offer.

> (IRC, 2015: 5)

The Inter-Agency Standing Committee (IASC) states,

> the current cluster system is structured around sectors of expertise and sectorial coordination, while in a context of urban crises there might be a need to identify and respond holistically to multi-sectorial needs in a given territory, requiring stronger inter-cluster linkages and coordination at city-level.
>
> (IASC, 2016: 1)

Collaboration, ranging from information exchange, negotiation, discussion and possible coordination, with a number of actors, despite the cluster approach, is obviously vital. Concerning gangs, who can be the gatekeepers to lower-income settlements that humanitarian agencies focus on, there is a growing body of research and experience on how to engage. ICRC notes that it is important to gain acceptance from gang leaders, that there needs to be a benefit accrued to gang leaders, and to avoid undermining the status and position of gangs in recovery and relief efforts (Ferris, 2012).

Area-Based Approaches

An approach in urban humanitarian recovery operations that is gaining increasing traction is area-based approaches (ABAs)—an approach drawn from urban planning. ABAs aim to strengthen local ownership in neighbourhood-based recovery. ABAs have struck a chord in particular with shelter and settlements practitioners, who have found post-disaster shelter recovery particularly difficult in urban areas using 'top-down' supply-based approaches (see for example Sanderson et al., 2014).

A review of 30 case studies of ABAs undertaken by the Global Shelter Cluster Working Group (2018)[4] identified a number of key commonalities, which include: engage with and build the capacity of local actors, work closely with local authorities, understand the context, and align humanitarian and developmental priorities. The review also found that engaging in complexity was especially apparent in a number of circumstances, in particular in relation to housing, land and property (HLP) rights, in scaling up activities beyond particular locations (a problem when it comes to the 'isolated project' conundrum), and, linked to the last point, the negative impact on neighbouring communities who may not be receiving assistance.

These experiences reflect engagement in the genuine difficulties of working in the city. In another study (Sanderson, 2017) that interviewed a number of ABA practitioners on the complexity of enacting ABAs, the outcome was one of difficulty. As one interviewee stated, 'If there was a simpler approach then we'd be doing it!' In relation to 'usual' humanitarian practice, another interviewee noted, 'the humanitarian aid system likes simplicity . . . urban life however is not [simple]!' Another interviewee

> described a failed urban ABA following 2013's Typhoon Haiyan in the Philippines: an INGO had designed an ABA programme working with local government to develop parcels of land for building medium-density housing with retail space, linked with livelihoods programming and WASH, and making use of a revolving fund. When there was a change in management, however, the programme was cancelled because, according to the [interviewee], the programme was considered 'too complicated' and the new leadership was insufficiently invested in the programme. As a result, recovery operations followed a traditional single-sector, input-driven approach.
>
> (Sanderson, 2017: 8)

In terms of what does work in enacting urban ABAs, the GPR cited ten principles that align to the broad project management cycle—assessment and design, implementation, and monitoring and evaluation. The principles include undertaking people-centred actions and the importance of collaboration. One principle identifies the need for realistic timeframes that match the reality of recovery, which are beyond the usual scope of tightly framed relief and recovery operations. Another one concerns using flexible project management tools such as adaptive management (Chambers and Ramalingam, 2016). A further principle is for better participatory assessments, which is discussed in the next section, communication.

Communication—Listening Effectively Through Assessments

While humanitarian response is by definition for a fixed time period, from the perspective of populations caught up in emergencies, such events are part of the continuum of the lives of cities and those who live in them. Time and again, post-disaster evaluations, and the testimony of people, point to a humanitarian approach that does not sufficiently communicate with affected populations. Communication here is two-way—taking care to communicate to affected people and taking the time to listen.

There are a number of initiatives by specialist organisations and networks that are seeking to improve communications, for instance OCHA's Communications with Communities (CwC) initiative, which 'is based on the principle that information and communications are critical forms of aid, without which disaster survivors cannot access services or make the best decisions for themselves and their communities' (OCHA, 2014). Another is the CDAC (Communicating with Disaster Affected Communities) Network, which aims to improve 'communities' ability to connect, access information and have a voice in humanitarian emergencies' (CDAC, 2019).

Identifying Resilience in Recovery   215

Despite such initiatives, however, communication—in the sense of generalist (i.e., non-communication specialised) humanitarian aid agencies listening well enough to the concerns, needs and abilities of affected populations—is still inadequate. Anderson et al.'s seminal work in this area, 'Time to Listen', found that, of the 6,000 people interviewed who were caught up in emergencies across the world, the overwhelming response was to slow down and listen better to what was actually needed (Anderson et al., 2012). In the first few months following the 2015 Nepal earthquakes, a response review undertaken of international NGO responses reported the following:

> The Inter-Agency Common Feedback Project's first Community Survey, produced by Ground Truth Solutions, makes for sobering reading. . . . The survey reports widespread dissatisfaction from communities with the response so far. Key issues include: a feeling that aid is not fairly distributed; that NGOs are not listening well enough (a finding states 'almost half of respondents feel they are not heard at all', while another states 'When women were asked if their particular problems are being addressed, a resounding 73 per cent said "very little" or "not at all"'); that 58 percent of respondents see little or no progress in the relief effort; that main problems are not being addressed (primarily permanent housing, as noted before); and a lack of information.
>
> (Sanderson et al., 2015: 5)

While this remains a problem, the GPR found positive efforts among agencies who are increasingly adopting a range of urban assessment approaches. These include context analysis (to get better understanding of a particular location outside of the emergency itself, such as an analysis of markets), participatory assessment approaches (where agencies and communities jointly gather and analyse information), response analysis, where (if done well) information is carefully reviewed for better and more informed actions, and targeting (in order to identify the most vulnerable).

The GPR also reported on the need to undertake multi-sectoral (as opposed to single sector) activities—in much the same way as ABAs, discussed earlier, are enacted—in undertaking assessments. A systematic review into urban targeting found that,

> Sector-based vulnerability analyses and targeting approaches are ill suited to complex urban crises, where needs are interrelated. A population's needs for shelter, WaSH [water, sanitation and hygeine], health, food security and livelihoods do not exist in isolation from one another. Rather, needs interact to shape vulnerability, and must thus be met with a multi-sectoral approach to guide targeting.
>
> (Patel et al., 2017: 31)

Conclusion

Arup's eight functions of a resilient city and Twigg's characteristics of a resilient community, presented earlier, respectively describe actions that go beyond meeting basic needs alone, to include systems and infrastructure, healthy populations, a good quality of life, equity, productive livelihoods and economic opportunity. Similarly, in order to build future resilience post-disaster, humanitarian aid also needs to go beyond meeting basic needs alone. Of the many different facets of urban humanitarian response, three actions in particular have been identified and discussed in this chapter. The first, engaging in complexity, means adapting tools and approaches that are cognisant both of the macro (systems) picture and also at the level of the individual. If both are considered concurrently in humanitarian programming and decision-making, then there may be less risk of enacting recovery programmes that may serve just one purpose while ignoring others.

Collaboration, as part of a wider discussion on coordination and engagement with the multitude of urban actors, presents one of the most fundamental challenges for urban engagement. The roots of too many well-intended yet ultimately unsuccessful projects lie in agencies not taking enough time to engage meaningfully with stakeholders, who will be present in a city long after the humanitarian 'circus' has left town. Good humanitarian action needs to contribute positively to local governance, and not to erode or undermine it. This point has been well acknowledged in wider discussions, not least the 2016 World Humanitarian Summit (WHS) that called for greater participation and ownership of local organisations (UN, 2016a).

Thirdly, communication—listening effectively to communities affected by disasters—needs to improve. This is not only a matter of greater programming efficiency, but also one of dignity: being heard is an essential factor aiding recovery. This chapter has taken the angle that listening takes place by agencies largely through the assessment tools they employ; while of course the field is wider than that, assessment approaches are a recognised part of the humanitarian toolkit that can always be improved on.

Building resilience therefore occurs not only in enacting efforts before a crisis, but can be contributed to after a disaster, through a number of humanitarian actions—three of which have been explored in this chapter. There are critics who argue that going beyond a relief-focused mandate alone is a form of 'mission creep' that overwhelmed and under-resourced aid cannot deal with. This chapter has sought to argue, however, that in urban response this is not an option, and that successful aid actions can combine both the meeting of immediate basic needs with actions that build longer-term resilience.

Notes

1. For an overview of resilience in humanitarian action, see for instance the IFRC's 2016 World Disasters Report that focuses on resilience, available at: https://media.ifrc.org/ifrc/publications/world-disasters-report-2016/
2. See also the Framework for Resilient Development in the Pacific, available at: http://tep-a.org/wp-content/uploads/2017/05/FRDP_2016_finalResilient_Dev_pacific.pdf
3. The Inter-Agency Standing Committee (IASC) 'describes key cluster functions as supporting service delivery, informing strategic decision-making, planning and strategy development, advocacy, monitoring and reporting on the implementation of the cluster strategy, contingency planning, preparedness and capacity-building, and integrating early recovery from the outset of the humanitarian response'—extract from GPR
4. Unfortunately, there are no case studies from the Pacific.

References

Anderson, M., Brown, D. and Isabella, J. (2012). *Time to Listen: Hearing People on the Receiving End of International Aid*. Cambridge, MA: CDA Collaborative Learning Projects.

Anderson, M. and Woodrow, P. (1989). *Rising from the Ashes: Development Strategies in Times of Disaster*. Boulder: Westview Press.

Archer, D. and Boonyabancha, S. (2011). Seeing a Disaster as an Opportunity—Harnessing the Energy of Disaster Survivors for Change. *Environment and Urbanization*, 23(2). London. Available at IIED: http://journals.sagepub.com/doi/full/10.1177/0956247811410011.

Arup. (2014). *City Resilience Index: Research Report Volume I: Desk Study*. Available at: https://www.arup.com/perspectives/city-resilience-index.

Carney, D. (1998). *Sustainable Rural Livelihoods: What Contributions Can We Make?* London: DFID.

Chambers, R. (1995). Poverty and livelihoods. Whose reality counts? *Environment and Urbanization*, 7(1). Available at: www.archidev.org/IMG/pdf/p173.pdf.

Chambers, R. and Ramalingam, B. (2016). *Adapting Aid: Lessons from Six Case Studies, IRC and Mercy Corps*. Available at: www.mercycorps.org/sites/default/files/Mercy_CorpsADAPT_Adapting_aid_report_with_case_studies.7.21.16.pdf.

CDAC. (2019). *CDAC Purpose*. Available at: www.cdacnetwork.org/who-we-are/vision-mission-strategy/ (accessed September 2019).

Cross, T. and Johnston, A. (2011). *Cash Transfer Programming in Urban Emergencies: A Toolkit for Practitioners*. CaLP. Available at: www.urban-response.org/resource/7056.

Development Initiatives. (2018). *Global Humanitarian Assistance Report 2018*. Bristol: Development Initiatives. Available at: http://devinit.org/wp-content/uploads/2018/06/GHA-Report-2018.pdf.

Ferris, E. (2012). *Urban Disasters, Conflict and Violence: Implications for Humanitarian Work*. Brookings Institution. Available at: www.brookings.edu/on-the-record/urban-disasters-conflict-and-violence-implications-for-humanitarian-work/.

Global Shelter Cluster. (2018). *Settlement Approaches in Urban Areas: Compendium of Case Studies*. Geneva: IFRC and UNHCR. Available at: www.shelterclu ster.org/sites/default/files/docs/urbansettlementcompendium_uswg_july2018.pdf.

Hamdi, N. (2010). *The Placemaker's Guide to Building Community*. London: Earthscan.

Humphries, V. (2013). *Improving Humanitarian Coordination: Common Challenges and Lessons Learned from the Cluster Approach*. Medford, MA: Tufts University.

IASC. (2016). *Guidance Note for Improving Coordination and Responses to Urban Crises in the Humanitarian Programme Cycle through the IASC and its Cluster System*. IASC Working Document.

IFRC. (2011). *Characteristics of a Safe and Resilient Community*. Community Based Disaster Risk Reduction Study. Available at: www.ifrc.org/PageFiles/96986/Final_ Characteristics_Report.pdf.

IFRC. (2016). *World Disasters Report. Resilience: Saving Lives Today, Investing for Tomorrow*. IFRC (Editors: Sanderson, D. and Sharma, A.). Available at: https:// media.ifrc.org/ifrc/publications/world-disasters-report-2016/.

Inter-Agency Common Feedback Project. (2015). *Community Survey*. Available at: www.humanitarianresponse.info/en/system/files/documents/files/community_ survey_r1_1.pdf.

IRC. (2015). *Humanitarian Crises in Urban Areas: Are Area-based Approaches to Programming and Coordination the Way Forward?* New York: IRC. Available at: www.syrialearning.org/resource/21830.

Levine, E., Vaughan, E. and Nicholson, D. (2017). *Strategic Resilience Assessment Guidelines* Portland, OR: Mercy Corps. Available at: https://reliefweb.int/report/ world/stress-strategic-resilience-assessment-guidelines-document.

OCHA. (2014). *Communications with Communities (CwC)*. Available at: https:// reliefweb.int/sites/reliefweb.int/files/resources/OOM-CommunicationwithCom munities_eng_311013.pdf.

Oxfam. (2019). *Vanuatu Cash Transfer Feasibility Assessment*. Available at: https:// resources.oxfam.org.au/pages/view.php?ref=1853&search=%3A2019%7C04&o ffset=0&order_by=relevance&sort=DESC&archive=0&k=&

Patel, et al. (2017). *What Practices are Used to Identify and Prioritize Vulnerable Populations Affected by Urban Humanitarian Emergencies? A Systematic Review*. Humanitarian Evidence Programme. Oxford: Oxfam GB. Available at: https://fic. tufts.edu/wp-content/uploads/Urban-Humanitarian-Action-Systematic-Review. pdf.

Rockefeller Foundation. (2019). Available at: www.100resilientcities.org›resilience.

Sanderson, D. (2012). Building livelihoods of the most marginalised in urban areas: Strategic approaches from Dhaka. *Environmental Hazards*, 11(2), January. Available at: www.tandfonline.com/doi/abs/10.1080/17477891.2011.609881.

Sanderson, D. (2017). Implementing Area-based Approaches (ABAs) in urban postdisaster contexts. *Environment and Urbanization*, 29(2), 349–364.

Sanderson, D. and Delica Willison, Z. (2014). *Philippines Typhoon Haiyan Response Review*. Available at: www.alnap.org/system/files/content/resource/files/main/dec-hc-haiyan-review-report-2014.pdf.

Sanderson, D., Rodericks, A. Shrestha, N. and Ramalingam, B. (2015). *Nepal Earthquake Emergency Response Review*. London and Ottawa: DEC and HC. Available at: www.dec.org.uk/sites/default/files/PDFS/dec_hc_nepal_response_review. pdf.

Sanderson, D., Sharma, A., Kennedy, J. and Burnell, J. (2014). Lost in transition: Principles, practice and lessons from Haiti for urban Post-Disaster Shelter Recovery Programs. *Asian Journal of Environment and Disaster Management (AJEDM)*, 6(2), 131–151.

Sanderson, D. (2019). *Urban Humanitarian Response Good Practice Review* No 12. London: ODI/ALNAP. Available at: https://goodpracticereview.org/12/.

Save the Children. (2019). *Cash Transfer Programming Improves Dignity of Beneficiaries in Fiji and Vanuatu*. Available at: www.savethechildren.org.au/media/media-releases/cash-transfer-report-fiji.

Twigg, J. (2009). *Characteristics of a Disaster Resilient Community*. London: UCL.

UN. (2016a). *The Grand Bargain: A Shared Commitment to Better Serve People in Need*. Available at: https://interagencystandingcommittee.org/system/files/grand_bargain_final_22_may_final-2_0.pdf.

UN. (2016b). *New Urban Agenda*. Available at: http://habitat3.org/the-new-urban-agenda/.

UN-Habitat. (2018). *City Resilience Profiling Tool*. Available at: http://urbanresiliencehub.org/wp-content/ uploads/2018/02/CRPT-Guide.pdf.

UN-Habitat. (2019). *Fifth Pacific Urban Forum Declaration*. Available at: www.fukuoka.unhabitat.org/info/news/puf.html.

UNISDR. (nd). *Making Cities Resilient Campaign*. Available at: www.unisdr.org/we/campaign/cities.

WHO. (1993). *The Urban Health Crisis: Strategies for Health for All in the Face of Rapid Urbanisation*. Geneva: WHO.

Winton, A. (2014). Gangs in global perspective. *Environment and Urbanization*, 26(2). Available at: https://journals.sagepub.com/doi/abs/10.1177/0956247814544572.

World Bank. (2006). *Dhaka: Improving Living Conditions for the Urban Poor*. Washington, DC: World Bank. Available at: http://documents.worldbank.org/curated/en/938981468013830990/Dhaka-Improving-living-conditions-for-the-urban-poor.

Index

Note: page numbers in *italic* indicate a figure on the corresponding page. Page numbers in **bold** indicate a table on the corresponding page. Page numbers with a 'n' plus a number indicate a chapter endnote on the corresponding page.

Academic-Practitioner Collaboration for Urban Settlements, South Pacific (APCUS-SP) 117
Aceh 153
Active Learning Network for Accountability and Performance (ALNAP) 117, 207
Adaptation Fund 54, 68, 69–71
adaptive capacity: assessment of 125; CCCI on 56; definition of 57; endogenous 65; Honiara Climate Change Vulnerability and Adaptation Assessment on 56; housing modifications and 154–155; HURCAP on 57–58, 63–65; of infrastructure 57; RAFT on 130; resilience and 3, 12, 126, 154; social capital and 57–58, 78, 81; SPC on 122; of technology 57; transformability and 154
adaptive management 214
Aekefo-Feraladoa 58, 67–68
affordable housing 8, 74, 100
Africa 11, 66, 141
AIDs 98–99
Ambae Island 31, 211
American Samoa *55, 123*
area-based approaches (ABAs) 31, 117–118, 213–214
Asia xi, 141–144; *see also specific countries*
Asian Development Bank (ADB): CCCA funding from 181; Climate Investment Fund 176; on

coastal flooding 142; on cultural characteristics of informal settlements 80; on development challenges 74; on informal economy 25; PCRAFI 42; on social accountability 98; SPCR 176, 181–182; on urbanisation 86, 89; on youth migration 24
assets, built 90, 94
ATMs 102–103
Australia 148, 188, 191–194, 197, 201n4, 201–202nn6–7

Bainimarama, Frank 27
Bamforth, Tom 107–118, 118n2
Bangkok 153
Bangladesh xi, 210
banking 102
Barth, Bernhard 53–71
Beckwith, Laura 171–183
Beijing 146
belonging: action plans and 60; citizenship and 115; clan and kinship connections and 85; governance and 116–117; humanitarian action and 30, 108, 113–118; identification and emotional attachment in 114; politics of 115; PUF5 on sustainable development and 133; as a social location 113; urban management, planning, and 127
Beverly Hills 111, 112
Blacksands 108–115, *110*, 118n2
'Blue Pacific' narrative 4
Boeung Kak 179

Boeung Tompun 171–174, *172, 173*, 179–180
'bonding' and 'bridging' social capital 86
Bruce, Laura 22–31, 74–87
'build back better' approach 35, 39, 43, 49, 187, 189
building codes and regulations 29, 82, 94, 112, 159, 208
built environment: built assets 90, 94; cluster approach and 212; components of 25, 90, *92*; in CRPT 90, *91*; economic growth and expansion of 25; on Fongafale Islet 25; natural environment embedded in 148, 150; 'net zero carbon' 144; in Port Vila 93–96; resilience of 96; self-help initiatives in 153–155; urban forms 25, 90, 93–94, 127; UNDRR on 187; *see also* housing; land tenure
Burns Peak 114
bushfire, in Australia (2009) 188, 191–194, 197, 201n4
businesses, formal 29–30, 212
businesses, informal 7, 25; *see also* markets, street; vendors, food and goods

C40 54
Cagayan de Oro 153–154, 159–167, *161, 164*
Cambodia 171–183
Cambodia Climate Change Alliance (CCCA) 175–176, 178, 181–182
Canberra 148
Cankiri Province 153
capitalism 37
carbon emissions: from Asia 141; CCCI on 56; FRDP on 29; 'net zero' 144, **147**, 148; reducing 26
Caribbean 4, 41
Carrasco, Sandra 152–168
cash-transfer programming (CTP) 31, 39, 211–212
catchment areas 15, **62**
censuses 14, 78, 117, 135n1
Charter for Change 36
'Child-Centred Urban Resilience Framework' (Plan International) 192
children 77, *84, 186*, 188–200, *195*, 201n2
China 141–142, 146

chupu 82
Cities and Climate Change Initiative (CCCI) *54, 56*
citizenship 6–8, 16, 115, 153
CITYNET 54
City Resilience Framework, The 188–189
City Resilience Index (CRI) 208
City Resilience Profiling Tool (CRPT) 90–91, *91, 92*, 104nn2–3
civil society organisations (CSOs): in Cambodia 179; Climate Resilient Honiara and 98; on development plans 49; in disaster response and recovery 29; humanitarian-development divide and 43, 45, 47; resilience and 7; social accountability and 98; urban identity and 116; in urban partnerships 126; *see also* community-based special interest groups
climate action implementation programme 28, 54
climate action plans: from Climate Resilient Honiara project 69–70; developing 54; HURCAP 58–66, **62**, **64**, 131; participatory approach to 65
climate change: blaming problems on 6; *The Lancet* on health risk of 143; mitigation of 26, 89; nexus of urbanisation and 28, 37, 141; planning for 54–56, 60, 141–150; rate of 26, 122
climate change adaptation: in Cambodia 174–176; CCCI emphasis on 54; challenges facing Asia 141; culture and kinship networks in 96; DRR and 13, 26; FRDP on 28–29; GLTN workshops on 67; hazard and risk mapping in 17; HURCAP on 60; as inadequate 4; by infrastructure 143–144; land tenure and 66–67; P4CA on 149; resilience and 71, 141; risk reduction through 96; strategic planning for 148; urbanisation in 26
Climate Investment Fund 176
Climate Resilient Honiara project 54, 68, 69–71
cluster approach: vs. ABAs 118; built environment and 212; definition of 49n2; fit-for-purpose subnational 30–31, 48–49; to humanitarian

222 Index

action 45–46, 48–49, 49n2, 209,
212–213, 217n3; risk integration
principles in 46
coastal erosion 37, **64**
coastal squeeze 3, 10
Committee on the Rights of the Child
(CRC) 197
communal title 68, 82
communes, population of 183n2
Communicating with Disaster Affected
Communities (CDAC) Network 214
Communications with Communities
(CwC) initiative 214
'community acupuncture' approach 200
community-based special interest
groups 81–85; *see also* civil society
organisations (CSOs)
community engagement plans 193,
202n6
community profiles 69
complexity, engaging in 209–213, 216
Connell, John 3–18
Constituency Development Funds 9
context analysis 215
Cook Islands, map of 55, *123*
Council for the Development of
Cambodia (CDC) 177
credit 41, 94
cultural and kinship groups 7, 58, 96;
see also gangs; *wantoks*
customary land 3, 8–9, 65–67, 112–113,
116, 125
customary land tenure 8, 79, 82–83,
87n4, 114, 134
cyclones 57; *see also* tropical cyclones;
individual storms

Dangol, Neeraj 152–168
Day, Jennifer 107–118
deforestation 5; *see also* logging
Delhi 141, 142, 146
development: ADB on challenges in
74; in Australia, after 2009 bushfires
192; cluster approach and 45–46;
of customary land 125; domestic
strategies for 4, 13; ethnic tensions
and 66; in Fiji 41–47, *44*; formal
regulations for 125; in hazard
zones 15; housing adaptations and
155, 167; HURCAP on 60–62, **62**;
integrated approach to 12, 142, 148;
limitations of models for 168; LRRD

models on 35; neo-colonial/neo-
liberal approaches to 15; pathways
for **147**; plans for 10, 31, 43–49, *44*;
PSUP and 63; RAFT and 129–132;
resilience and 4, 11, 76, 80; rural
bias in 41–42; sex work and 98–99;
vulnerability to disaster risk from
190, *wantoks* and 71; WUF on
145; *see also* nexus, humanitarian-
development; sustainable
development
disaster 199, 201n3
disaster preparedness and mitigation:
cluster approach to 49; in Fiji 47,
49; FRDP on 29–30; in HURCAP
62; Interagency Group of NGOs
diagnostic tool on 208; resilience and
134, 206; risk reduction through 96;
social capital and 81; urbanisation
discussed in 26
disaster response and recovery: ABAs
for 213; in Australia, after 2009
bushfires 188, 191–194, 197,
201–202n6; children's participation
in 188, 190–200; cluster approach
to 45–46, 48–49; 'community
acupuncture' approach to 200; CSOs
in 29; CTP in 31, 39, 211–212;
development plans and 45–46; in Fiji,
after TC Winston 39, 41–45, 47–48;
fit-for-purpose subnational cluster
for 30–31; FRDP on 29–30; health
services in 209–210; humanitarian-
development divide in 43, 45–49;
integrating at national, municipal,
and local levels 26; interviews during
and after 202n8; localisation of
47–48; LRRD models on 35; policies
on 42, 47–48; resilience in 206–217;
'right to housing' in 115–116;
rural bias in 30, 41–42; after San
Jose de Chamanga earthquake
194–197; Sendai Framework on
35; social capital and 81, 210; in
Solomon Islands, after flooding 42;
systems-based approach to 209–210;
technology in 29; in Vanuatu, after
TC Pam 48
disaster risk reduction (DRR): barriers
to 17; in 'build back better' approach
189; children's participation in 188,
190–191; climate change adaptation

and 13, 26; developing 3; factors affecting 16; FRDP on 28–29; GAR on 186–187, 189–190; government leadership of 152, 168; from hazard event planning 13; hazard mapping in 17; HURCAP on 60, **64**; Local Governments for Sustainability plans for 70; *Making Cities Resilient* on 208; neglect of 5; nexus of climate change, urbanisation, and 28, 37; through preparedness and mitigation 96; resilience action plans for 131; urban vs. rural 42; vulnerability in 187; WASH services and 10
disease, drought, and dust, IPCC on 142

earthquakes: children's participation in reconstruction after 188; corrupt building practices and collapse during xi; housing seismic performance studies 160, 162–163, 165–166; HURCAP on 60; in Nepal 211, 215; Port Vila's risk of 94; in San Jose de Chamanga 194
ecology *91*
Economic and Social Commission for Asia and the Pacific (ESCAP) 27, 29
economic growth: built environment expansion and 25; constraints on, in PICs 4; inequality and 18; land tenure and 8; policies on urban 26; in Port Vila 100; positive contributions of urban 42; PUMA, STUMP, and 28–29
economic structure 99–101, 104n4
economy: building a resilient 102; components of 90, *92*, 99–100; in CRPT 90, *91*; global, access to 24; monetised vs. subsistence 112; in Port Vila 99–103; rural, focus on 37, 76; after San Jose de Chamanga earthquake 194; *see also* informal economy
ecosystem services 131
Ecuador 54, *186*, 194–197, *195*, *196*, 199–200
education: access to, in urban areas 4, 24, 37, 76; Cambodian post-secondary 178; in Fiji, after TC Winston 39; housing and 118; PVMC responsibility for 101; resilience and

208; right to 98; after San Jose de Chamanga earthquake 194–195
Elang Etas and Elang Etas Community Association (EECA) 116
electricity: access to 5, 22; capacity for grid to adapt after disaster 14; diesel fuel for 93; easements for 24; in Fiji, after TC Winston 39; FTE leases and 67–68; in Honiara 57; in Lautoka 41; renewable 148; in Vanuatu 93, 101; vulnerability assessment of 57
emergency management plans 12
emergency shelters 39, **64**; *see also* relief centres
emergent groups 30
employment: access to, in urban areas 4, 24, 37, 76; ethnic tensions and 66; in informal businesses 25; land tenure and 8; as sex worker 98–99
energy consumption 141
environmental management 5, 26, 28–29, 94–95
Erakor 111
Eratap 111
Esmeraldas 54
European Union (EU) 176
evacuation centres 39
'evergreen clusters' 36, 46
exposure 57

Fani (Cyclone) xi, 206
Federated States of Micronesia (FSM) 55, **122**, *123*
Fifth Pacific Urban Forum (PUF5) 4, 26–27, 133, 208
Fiji: CTP in 31, 211; humanitarian-development nexus in 34, 36–37, 39–49, *44*, 49n1; Lautoka *23*, 38, *38*, 41; map of *38*, *55*, *123*; Nadi *23*, *38*; population of 37, **122**; street markets in 127; TC Winston and xi, 31, 34, 37–40, 43–45, 47–49; urban policy lag in 41–42; urban population 37–38, **122**; Vanu Levu Island 39; Women Markets for Change programme in 127; *see also* Suva
Filipino-Chinese Friendship Village 159, 163–166, *164*
financial services: access to 102; credit 41, 94; land tenure and 8, 41; in Port Vila 102–103; Women Markets for Change programme on 127

224 Index

Finnish Pacific Project (FINPAC) 82, 84, 87n6
fire 68, 142–143, 188, 191–194, 197, 201n4
fiscal stability and municipal finance 100, 101–102
fixed-term estate (FTE) leases 67–68, 82
flooding: adaptation initiatives 154; ADB on coastal 142; in Cagayan de Oro 160, 162–165, 167; causes of, in PICs 3; hazard risk mapping for **64**; Honiara Climate Change Vulnerability and Adaptation Assessment on 56; of informal settlements 60; IPCC on 142; in Kathmandu 154, 156–159, 166; of Mataniko River 5, 56; in Ontong Java 68; in Phnom Penh 171; preventive measures for 17, 206; of reclaimed swampland 25; TC Winston response and Solomon Islands 48
Fongafale Islet 25
food security: flooding and 3; in informal settlements 5; resilience and 208; shelter, WASH services, and 215; street markets and 7, 127; from subsistence activities 22
Foukona, Joseph 130–131
Framework for Resilient Development in the Pacific (FRDP) 13, 27–31, 36, 71, 129
French Polynesia, map of 55, *123*

gangs 30, 114, 212–213
Gero, Anna 34–49
Gilbert Camp 58
Gita (Tropical Cyclone) xi, 109–111
glacial melting 142
Global Alliance for Urban Crises (GAUC) 103, 117
Global Assessment Report on Disaster Risk Reduction (GAR) 186–187, 189–190
Global Land Tool Network (GLTN) 67
Global Shelter Cluster Working Group 213
Good Humanitarian Donorship initiative 35
Good Practice Review (GPR) in Urban Humanitarian Response (Sanderson) 207, 210, 212, 214–215, 217n3

governance: in Africa, lessons learned from 66; Bainimarama on 27; belonging and 116–117; CCCI on 56; cluster approach and 45–46, 48; decentralisation of 47; humanitarian action and 216; humanitarian-development nexus and 34, 36–37, 39 19, 44; in HURCAP 62, 65; Interagency Group of NGOs diagnostic tool on 208; kin-based 7; national urban policies on 26; Pacific Humanitarian Partnership on 36; PUF5 on systemic approach to 133; RAFT on 128–133; resilience capacity and 16, 65–66; rural focus of 111–113; social capital and 81; traditional leaders 7; transformation in 122, 125, 127, 133–134; types of 25; WUF on 145
government-owned land 8, 65, 112
'Grand Bargain' 36
Green Climate Fund 71
'green evictions' 179
grievance redress mechanism (GRM) 97
Guam, map of 55, *123*
Guangzhou 146

Haiyan (Typhoon) xi, 212, 214
Handbook of Disaster Research 199
Hanuabada 10–11
Hart, Roger 197
hazard maps 15, 17, **64**
health services: access to, in urban areas 24, 37; in disaster response and recovery 209–210; in Fiji, after TC Winston 39; GPR on 210; PVMC responsibility for 101; resilience action plans for 131; for sex workers 98–99; WHO on urban 209
heat: in Cambodia 171; housing adaptations for relief from 162, 165–166; infrastructure designed to reduce impact of 29; IPCC on 142; pollution and 143; population (2050) living in poverty with 23; sensitivity to 57; WHO on 143
HIV 98–99
Honiara: Aekefo-Feraladoa 58, 67–68; affordable housing in 8; CCCI in 56; census in 85; Climate Resilient Honiara project 54, 68–71; colonial-based land tenure in 79; early

warning systems in **64**, 82; emergency shelters in **64**; 'ethnic tensions' and armed conflict in 66; evictions in 6; flooding in 5, 56; FTEs for 67–68, 82; Gilbert Camp 58; hazard risk mapping for **64**; HURCAP on 58–66, **62, 64**, 131; Koa Hill 56, 58; Kukum 58, *59*, 67, 68; land area of 78; land disputes in 8, 79; map of 55, *59*, *75*, *123*; mobility in 85; official ISZs in 63, 78; Panatina Valley 131; PEBACC 63; percentage of population in informal settlements 10, 63, 74, 78; population of 78; priority issues for 60, *61*; Renlau 74, *75*, 78–79, 81–85, 87n4; resilience capacity in 65–66, 79; sea wall for 68; sense of belonging in 60, 85; TOLs for 66–67; upgrading informal settlements in 126; urban growth in 78; urban management, planning, and policies for 78; voting in 85; vulnerability assessment of 56–58, 60, 63–65; *wantoks* in 68, 79; WASH services in 11, 57, 60–63; water tank installation in 63; White River 58; zoning in *62*; *see also* Ontong Java

Honiara Climate Change Vulnerability and Adaptation Assessment 56

Honiara Urban Resilience and Climate Action Plan (HURCAP) 58–66, *62*, *64*, 131

housing: ABAs for 213; adaptations, self-built 152–168, *157*, *161*, *164*; affordable 8, 74, 100; building codes and regulations for 29, 82, 94, 112, 159, 208; community improvements to 125; density and location of 68; in Nepal, after 2015 earthquakes 215; objectives of research on 94; 'one-day' 109; in Philippines, wind and seismic performance studies 160, 162–163, 165–166; policies for 6; in Port Vila 100–101; as priority issue 60; progressive building of 167–168; PUF5 on 208; rehabilitation of, rural vs. urban 42; resilience action plans for 8, 131; 'right to adequate' 115–116; after San Jose de Chamanga earthquake 194; 'slumization' of 154; vulnerability assessment of 57; *see also* shelter

humanitarian action: ABAs for 31, 117–118, 213–214; Barber's critique of, after TC Pam 109; belonging and 30, 108, 113–118; cluster approach to 45–46, 48–49, 49n2, 209, 212–213, 217n3; collaboration in 212–214, 216; communications during 214–216; CTP in 31, 39, 211–212; customary land tenure and 114; equitable, responsibility for 115–116; governance and 216; GPR on 207, 210, 212, 214–215, 217n3; land tenure and 112–114; localisation of 36, 47, 49; LRRD models on 35; people-centred approaches to 210–211, 214; resilience in 216, 217n1; rural bias in 30, 41–42, 108, 109–112; simplified approaches to 209; Sphere Standards for 116; systems-based approach to 209–210; Urban Context Analysis Toolkit for 117; urban management and planning and 37; WHS on 47

identity, urban 108, 114–116, 212
income: access to guaranteed basic 96; Honiara new house prices and 8; inequality based on 100; from informal businesses 7, 25, 65; minimum, policy on 98; statistics on 14

India xi, 141–142, 146, 148, 206
Indonesia 142, 146, 152, 153
informal economy: ADB on 25; discouraged by government 7; gangs in 212; markets 7, 30, 127, 130, 211; PNG policy for 127; PUF5 on integrating 133; role of 25; vendors in 7, 127, *128*, 130

informal settlements: bulldozing of 6; data on 14–15; description of 80; eradication of 155; evictions from 6, 179; health, demographic, and socioeconomic surveys of 25; vs. official ISZs 63, 78; political will to support 152; upgrades to 9, 56, 126; *see also* low-income settlements; slums

Informal Settlement Zones (ISZs) 63, 78

infrastructure, urban: adaptive capacity of 57; blanket approach to, after

226 Index

disaster 200; children, impact on 194–197; climate change adaptation by 143–144; critical 14; in CRPT 91; designing to reduce 'heat islands' 29; FTE leases and 67; funds for 14; in HURCAP 62; 'living' 148; natural 171; PUF5 on 208; real-time data collection and evaluation of 14; retrofitting for energy efficiency 29; after San Jose de Chamanga earthquake 194–196; SDGs on 208; spatial analysis of 25; standard for 25; USDRR on 187; vulnerability to disaster risk from 190

institutions 175, 177

Inter-Agency Standing Committee (IASC) 213, 217n3

Intergovernmental Panel on Climate Change (IPCC) 22–23, 26, 142–144, 146, 175

International Committee of the Red Cross (ICRC) 213

International Covenant on Economic, Social and Cultural Rights (ICESCR) 115–116

International Federation of Red Cross and Red Crescent Societies (IFRC) 201n3, 206–208, 217n1

International Rescue Committee (IRC) 212

Jakarta 142, 146
Japan 141, 142, 146
Johnson, Olivia 89–103
Jones, Paul 121–135

Karachi 146
Kathmandu 153–159, 157, 166–167
Keen, Meg 3–18, 121–135
Keo, Piseth 171–183
Khmer Rouge 178
kin-based governance 7; see also wantoks
Kiribati 5, 55, 122, 123, 126
Koa Hill 56, 58
Kukum Fishing Village 58, 59, 67, 68
Kyoto 146

Ladder of Citizen Participation, A (Arnstein) 197
Ladder of Youth Participation (Hart) 197, 198

Lancet, The 143

land: ABAs for 213; customary 3, 8–9, 65–67, 112–113, 116, 125; exploitation of 95; government-owned 8, 65, 112; in HURCAP 62; marginalised 24; mobilisation of 9; RAFT on 129–131

land administration 94–95

landslides 64, 67–68, 163

land taxes 94, 101–102

land tenure: behavioural norms, institutional culture, and 96; for canoes 87n4; city boundaries and 41; classification statistics on 95; climate change adaptation and 66–67; colonial-based 25, 79; customary 8, 79, 82–83, 87n4, 114, 134; development plans, policies, and 10; employment and 8; financing and 8, 41; FTE and 67–68; GLTN workshops on 67; housing adaptations and 156–157; humanitarian action and 112–114; informal vs. insecure 79; institutional culture, behavioural norms, and 96; internecine violence over 8; mix of colonial and customary 25; objectives of research on 94; PUF5 on reforming 133; resilience and 8, 66–68, 83, 87; 'right to housing' and 115–116; social capital and 81–82; TOLs and 66–67; types of 8; upgrading informal settlements to gain 126; utility meter placement and 11; in vulnerability assessments 63, 66–67; WASH services and 8, 10–11, 41, 67–68, 179; see also title, land

land-use mapping 15

land-use planning: evidence-based 15; vs. human-centred approach 133; in HURCAP 62; for informal settlements 5; integrated approach to 12; P4CA on 149; resilience and 96, 208; Vanuatu's Land Sector Framework and 95–96

Lautoka 23, 38, 38, 41

Lewis, J. 167

'Linking Relief, Rehabilitation and Development' (LRRD) 35

Live and Learn's M-Wash initiative 63

Local Governments for Sustainability (ICLEI) 54, 64, 70

Index 227

localisation 47
logging 66; *see also* deforestation
Lord Howe settlement *see* Ontong Java
low-income settlements 23; *see also* informal settlements; slums

Mahogany Village 159–163, *161*
Majuro 5, 24, *123*
Malaita Province 55, 83
Manila 146
Manples 108–115, 118n2
Mansfield, Robyn 186–202
Mariana Islands, Northern 55, *123*
market connectivity 100, 102–103
markets, street 7, 30, 127, 130, 211; *see also* vendors, food and goods
Marshall, Leeanne 74–87
Marshall Islands 5, 55, **122**, *123*
McEvoy, Darryn 53–71
Mekong River 174
Melanesia: informal settlements in 24; map of 55, *123*; percentage of population in informal settlements 74; population of **122**; rural bias in politics 26; rural-urban migration in 5; urban informal safety nets in 7; WASH services in 10; *see also specific countries*
Metropolis 54
Micronesia 24, 55, **122**, *123*; *see also specific countries*
migration: ADB on youth 24; civil unrest disrupting 78; climate-induced 143; domestic development focus and 4; push-pull factors in 74–76; rates of 37; unemployment and 24; urban population growth from 3, 5; urban to rural 6–7; based on *wantoks* 68, 79; WUF on 145
Mitchell, David 53–71
mobile telephones 14
mobility 85, 90, *91*
Mumbai 146
municipal public services *91*; *see also* utilities

Nadi 23, *38*
Nauru 55, **122**, *123*
Nepal 153–159, *157*, 166–167, 211, 215
New Caledonia, map of 55, *123*
New Delhi 142

New Hebrides Trench 93
New Pacific Urban Agenda 80
New Urban Agenda (NUA): adoption of 141; assessment of 13, 145; climate change-urbanisation nexus and 141; CRPT and 104n2; FDRP and 28; implementation of 144; integrated approach to 142; on local involvement 152; on resilience 80, 208; SDGs and 141–142, 144; UNFCCC and 144; urban management and planning in 142
nexus, climate change-urbanisation 28, 37, 141
nexus, humanitarian-development 34, 36–37, 39–49, 44, 49n1
Niue, map of 55, *123*
non-governmental organisations (NGOs) 14; *see also individual organisations*
Norman, Barbara 141–150
Noumea, map of *123*

Ocean and Cryosphere in a Changing Climate, The (IPCC) 23
Ontong Java: classification of 78; communal title in 68; description of 68; flooding in 68; FTEs for 82; location of 74; longevity of 78; map of *75*; photos of 77, 84; social capital in 81–85; special interest groups in 82–85; vulnerability assessment of 58; *wantok* in 83; WASH services for 68, 82
Overseas Development Institute (ODI) 207

Pacific Catastrophe Risk Assessment and Financing Initiative (PCRAFI) 42
Pacific Community (SPC) 122
Pacific Ecosystem-based Adaptation to Climate Change (PEBACC) 63, 70
Pacific Humanitarian Partnership 36, 46
Pacific island countries (PICs): economic growth constraints in 4; IPCC on climate risks in 142–143, 146; map of 55; urban growth in 107, 112; urban identity in 108; urbanisation in xi, 22; *see also specific countries*
Pacific Islands Forum Secretariat (PIFS) 4, 36

228 Index

Pacific Urban Agenda (PUA) 13, 129
Pacific Urban Forum (PUF) 4, 26–27, 133, 208
Paga Point 6, 8–9
Pakistan 146
Palau 55, **122**, *123*
Pam (Tropical Cyclone) 30, 47–48, 66, 107–118, 121, 211
Panatina Valley 131
Pango 111
Papua New Guinea (PNG): map of 55, *123*; National Policy for the Informal Economy 127; population of **122**, 135n1; urban policies in 26; *see also* Port Moresby
participatory assessment approaches 215
Participatory Slum Upgrade Program (PSUP) 63
people-centred approaches 210–211, 214
Philippines: Cagayan de Oro 153–154, 159–167, *161*, *164*; Filipino-Chinese Friendship Village 159, 163–166, *164*; Mahogany Village 159–163, *161*; Manila 146; Minimum Design Standards and Requirements for Economic and Socialized Housing Projects 159; National Building Code 159; population in coastal zones 142; seismic performance and wind resistance studies of housing in 160; Sorsogon 54; Typhoon Haiyan and xi, 214; Typhoon Washi and 154, 159–160
Phnom Penh 171–175, *172*, *173*, 177–183
Pinheiro Principles 115–116
Plan International 190
Planners 4 Climate Action (P4CA) 149
Planning and Urban Management Agency (PUMA) 28–29
'Planning for Climate Change' guide 54, 58, 65, 69
political ecology 182
pollution 5, 143
Polynesia 55, **122**, *123*; *see also specific countries*
poor, levels of 210–211
Port Moresby 6, 8–11, 24, 30, 114, *123*, 126
Port Vila 6, 10, 90–103, 107–116, *110*, 118n2, *123*

Port Vila Municipal Council (PVMC) 101–102
Post Disaster Needs Assessment (PDNA) 109
power 175
prisons 30
property rights 94, 116, 124, 213
property taxes 94, 101–102
public transport 29, 148, 155, 208

real property value 100
relief centres 192; *see also* emergency shelters
religion 86
remittances 4, 7
renewable energy 144, **147**, 148
Renlau 74, 75, 78–79, 81–85, 87n4
Rennell and Bellona Province 55, 83, 87n9
Research for Development Impact Network (RDI Network) 74
resilience: action plans for 131; adaptive capacity and 3, 12, 126, 154; barriers to 17; blanket approach to disaster response and 200; 'Blue Pacific' narrative and 4; building codes and regulations and 208; of built environment 96; Cambodian policies on 174–176; children's idea of 189; climate change adaptation and 71, 141; cluster approach and 46; 'community acupuncture' approach to 200; community-based special interest groups and 85; concept of 76; CRI on 208; CSOs and 7; definition of 11, 80, 104n1, 124, 206–207; development and 4, 11, 76, 80; development plans and 49; disaster preparedness and mitigation and 134, 206; in disaster response and recovery 206–217; diversity and 83; education and 208; endogenous 58, 63–66, 71, 80, 210; equitable 70; factors affecting 15–17; FINPAC and 82; food security and 208; housing adaptations and 154, 167–168; in humanitarian action 216, 217n1; HURCAP on 60, **64**, 65; IFRC on 206–207; implementation and sustainability of 63; land administration and 95; land tenure and 8, 66–68, 83, 87; land-use planning and 96, 208;

Making Cities Resilient on 208; as a mobilising metaphor 125; NUA on 80, 208; policies and 7, 12, 124–127; political economy of urbanisation and 12, 124; as process 80, 167; public transport and 208; in RAFT 122, 127–135; reflective learning and 178; Rockefeller Foundation on 11, 124, 152; Rodin's description of 188; in SDGs xii, 76, 80, 208; social capital and 79, 81–82, 85–86; social dimensions of 125–126, 128, 134; social inclusion and protection and 96–97, 134; socio-ecological origins of 80; SPC on 122; spontaneous 152, 167; subsistence activities and 134; sustainability and 80, 104n1, 124–125, 133–134; sustainable development and 4, 11, 124; systems-based approach to 89, 125; thematic areas for 60–62; top-down approach to 201n1; unemployment and 208; urban management and planning and 125–127, 134; urban partnerships for 126; vulnerability and 167; *wantoks* and 16, 66, 71; WASH services and 5; water availability and 208; Watson on urban 187

Resilience Dividend, The (Rodin) 201n1

resource allocation 30, 108, 114

response analysis 215

Responsiveness, Adaptation, Facilitation and Transformation (RAFT) 122, 127–135

Risk Mapping and Planning for Urban Preparedness (Beca & NIWA) 94

Rockefeller Foundation: *100 Resilient Cities* programme 28, 134, 188, 207–208; CRI 208; on resilience 11, 124, 152

Rodin, Judith 188, 201n1

roofing 23, 57

Samoa 26, 28–29, 55, 112, **122**, *123*

Sanderson, David 22–31, 206–217

sangkat 177–178, 183n2

San Jose de Chamanga *186*, 194–197, *195, 196*, 199–200

Save the Children 190, 211

sea level rise 37, 57, 146

sea walls 68, *132*

Secretariat of the Pacific Regional Environment Programme (SPREP) 63, 70

sector-based vulnerability analyses and targeting approaches 215

Sendai Framework for Disaster Risk Reduction 35, 141, 152, 168, 189

Senegal, Saint Louis 54

sensitivity 57

Seoul 146

sex workers 98–99

'shallow politics' 13

Shanghai 141, 142, 146

Shantinagar area 155–159, *157*

Sharif, Maimunah 142

shelter: ABAs for 117–118, 213; access to adequate 141; 'build back safer' emphasis on 39; emergency 39, **64**; from emergent groups 30; food security, WASH services, and 215; Sphere Standards for 116; *wantoks* and 66; *see also* housing

Shelter Cluster 107, 109–112, 114, 115, 160

Singapore 148

Sitko, Pamela 22–31, 89–103

slums 63, 142, 153–155; *see also* informal settlements; low-income settlements

Small Island Developing States (SIDS) 53

social accountability 96–97

social capital 57–58, 78–79, 81–86, 210

social inclusion and protection: centralisation of service provision and 101; components of 90, *92*; in CRPT 90, *91*, 104n3; facilitating 134; indigenous forms of 7; need for greater 89; in Port Vila 96–99, 101; resilience and 96–97, 134

social learning 125

social protection floor 98

soil salination 37

Solomon Islands: disaster response policies in 42; flooding in 5, 48, 56; Malaita Province *55*, 83; map of *55, 123*; National Meteorological and Hydrological Services 87n6; National Urban Policy 56, 71, 72n4; Nation Urban Conference 8; NDMO 82; population of **122**, 135n1; Rennell and Bellona Province *55*, 83, 87n9; UN-Habitat's partnerships in 56; urban policies in 26; urban population growth in 67, 77, **122**; Women Markets for Change programme in 127; *see also* Honiara

Solomon Islands Home Finance Limited 8

Solomon Islands Red Cross Society (SIRCS) 82

Sopoaga, Enele 16

Sorsogon 54

South Korea 146

South Tarawa 5, 24, 28–29, *132*

South Tarawa Urban Management Plan (STUMP) 28–29

spatial analysis 25

Sphere Standards 116

STI risk 99

storm surges **64**

Strategic Program for Climate Resilience (SPCR) 176, 181–182

'strategic punctual interventions' 200

subsidiarity 11

subsistence activities 22, 25, 37, 65–66, 134

supply chain and logistics *91*

Surabaya 152

sustainable development: agreements on 190; factors affecting 15; IPCC on 144, 150; pathways for *147*, 148; PUF5 on belonging and 133; realistic and feasible 5; resilience and 4, 11, 124; technology and 148; transformation for 127, 133; urbanisation and 121; urban partnerships for 126

Sustainable Development Goals (SDGs): assessment of 17; on climate change-urbanisation nexus 141; humanitarian-development nexus and 35; on inclusive and participative approaches 152; on infrastructure 208; integrated approach to 142; NUA and 141–142, 144; RAFT and 129; resilience in xii, 76, 80, 208

Sustainable Pathways for our Cities and Regions (Norman) 146–148, **147**

Suva: land dispute-resolution processes on 9; map of *38, 123*; photos of informal settlements in *23*; population of 38; upgrading informal settlements in 9, 126; WASH services in 11

Sweden 176

systems-based approach 27, 89–103, 125, 133, 143, 209–210

taxes 94, 101–102

technology: access to, in urban areas 24, 76; adaptive capacity of 57; in disaster response and recovery 29; open data initiatives 14; sustainable development and 148; WUF on 145

'Temporary Occupancy Licenses' (TOLs) 66–67

Thailand 153

'Time to Listen' (Anderson et al.) 215

title, land 8, 68, 82

Tokelau *123*

Tokyo 141, 142, 146

Toma, Walker 89–103

Tonga xi, 23, *55*, 109–111, **122**, *123*

traditional leaders 7; *see also* kin-based governance; *wantoks*

Transparency International Vanuatu 97–98

tropical cyclones 26; *see also individual storms*

Trundle, Alexei 53–71

tsunamis 60, **64**

Turkey 153

Tuvalu 25, *55*, **122**, *123*

typhoons *see individual storms*

Uganda, Kampala 54

unemployment 24, 98–99, 208

United Cities and Local Governments (UCLG) 54

United Kingdom (UK) 207, 208

United Nations (UN): *2030 Agenda for Sustainable Development* 191; Agenda for Humanity 35–36; CRC 197; on disaster-prone countries 23; ESCAP 27, 29; *Guiding Principles on Internal Displacement* 116; in Pacific Humanitarian Partnership 36; Women Markets for Change programme 7, 127; *see also* Sustainable Development Goals (SDGs)

United Nations Development Programme (UNDP) 167, 176, 181

United Nations Economic and Social Council 115–116

United Nations Economic Commission for Europe (UNECE) 94
United Nations Framework Convention on Climate Change (UNFCCC) 54, 68–71, 144, 181
United Nations Human Settlement Programme (UN-Habitat): on Asian urbanisation 141; CCCI 54, 56; city vulnerability assessments by 131; CRPT 90–91, *91*, *92*, 104nn2–3; GLTN 67; 'High-Level Forum' report 142; on land administration 95; P4CA 149; 'Planning for Climate Change' guide 54, 58, 65, 69; PSUP 63; on resilience 80, 104n1; Solomon Islands partnerships 56; on urban systems 209; WUF 142, 145–146; *see also* New Urban Agenda (NUA)
United Nations International Children's Fund (UNICEF): *Child-Centered Risk Reduction* 191; 'Child Friendly Cities Framework' 199; 'Child Friendly Cities Framework Governance Checklist' 192, 201n5, 202n7; 'A Child Friendly Community Self-Assessment Tool For Community Service Providers And Child Advocates' 192; children, definition of 201n2; *The Children's Charter* 190; Convention on the Rights of the Child 197–199, 201n2; Fiji's WASH cluster and 46; *Promoting Children's Participation In Democratic Decision-Making* 197; on working with children in emergency situations 199
United Nations International Strategy for Disaster Reduction (UNISDR): *Making Cities Resilient* 208; Resilience Toolkit from **64**; Sendai Framework for Disaster Risk Reduction 35, 141, 152, 168, 189
United Nations Office for Disaster Risk Reduction (UNDRR) 186–187, 189–190
United Nations Office for the Coordination of Humanitarian Affairs (UNOCHA) 36, 214
United Nations Office of the High Commissioner (OCHR) 98, 115–116
University of the South Pacific 15
'urban acupuncture' approach 200
urban consciousness 114

Urban Context Analysis Toolkit 117
urban forms 25, 90, 93–94, 127
urbanisation: ADB on 86, 89; context, challenges, and costs of 5–6; efficient 25; 'failed' xii; FRDP on 27–28; 'nature-based solutions' to 27, 29; new approaches to 18; nexus of climate change and 28, 37, 141; opposition to 3, 15; plans for 26; resilience in political economy of 12, 124; sex work and 98; sustainable development and 121; USDRR on 186–187
urban management and planning: belonging and 127; CCCI on 56; children's participation in 188, 199; climate change and 6; effective masterplan for 71; factors affecting 15; GAR on participation in 189–190; humanitarian action and 37, 41–42; in HURCAP 60–62, **62**; limitations of models in 168; for low carbon emissions 29; NUA on 142, 145; 'ocean cities' approach to 27; P4CA on 149; pathways for 146–148, **147**; 'Planning for Climate Change' guide for 54; political representation and 113; political will for 121; PSUP and 63; PUF5 on processes for 133; RAFT and 128–133; resilience and 125–127, 134; risk reduction through 96; rural bias in 25–26, 41; social capital and 86; SPCR on 176; systems-based approach to 27, 89–90, 133, 143; Town and Country Planning Act on 78; training in 14, 24; UN-Habitat 'High-Level Forum' report on 142; WUF on 145–146
urban policies: assessment of past & present 5–7, 9; developing 37; enacting, challenges in 25–26, 121; factors affecting 13–14; FRDP on 129; limitations of 168; PUF5 on integrating 133; RAFT on 122, 128–129, 131, 133–135; resilience and 7, 12, 124–127; rural bias in 41, 129; SPCR on 176; WUF on 146
Urban Response Community of Practice 117
Urban Risk Management Strategy (Beca & NIWA) 95–96

232 Index

urban systems 209
utilities 101, 125, 143, 144; *see also* municipal public services; *specific services*

Vanuatu: AIDs and HIV prevention and treatment programmes in 99; Ambae Island 31, 211; Constitution on land in 112; CTP in, after volcanic activity 31, 211; description of 107; disaster response policies in 48; electricity in 93; Erakor and Eratap 111; HIV-positive cases in 98; Land Sector Framework 95–96; Land Use Planning Policy 95; map of 55, 123; National Integrity System Assessment 97; NIWA 94–96; Ombudsman, Office of the 97; PDNA of 109; population of 107, **122**; Port Vila 6, 10, 90–103, 107–116, *110*, 118n2, *123*; as a risk-prone country 4, 23; as tax haven 93; urban population growth in **122**; vulnerability to climate change xi; Women Markets for Change programme in 127
Vanu Levu Island 39
vendors, food and goods 7, 127, *128*, 130; *see also* markets, street
View from 2016, A (Children in a Changing Climate) 190–191, 197, 199
volcanic activity 31, 211
voting 85, 113
vulnerability assessments 54, 56–58

Wallis and Futuna, map of *123*
wantoks: community-based special interest groups and 83; definition of 79; migration based on 68, 79; overcrowding, sprawl, and 71; resilience capacity and 16, 66, 71; social accountability and 98; social capital and 83, 86; social safety nets through 7; during TC Pam 66
Washi, Typhoon 154, 159–165
water: EECA on 116; from emergent groups 30; in HURCAP **62**; IPCC

on 146; from natural springs 65; organising to obtain 16; polluted 5; real-time data collection and evaluation of 14; resilience and availability 208; reticulated, access to 10; after San Jose de Chamanga earthquake 194
water, sanitation and hygiene (WASH) services: access to 5, 10–11, 141; action plans for 131; benefits of 10; communal title and 68; DRR and 10; in Fiji 46; FTE leases and 67–68; in Honiara 11, 57, 60–63; land tenure and 8, 10–11, 41, 67–68, 179; in Lautoka 41; lessons learned from Africa 11; planning and policies for 28; in Port Vila 101; resilience and 5; standard for 25; vulnerability assessment of 57
water tanks 63, 65
Watson, G.B. 187
White River 58
wind 94, 160, 162–163, 165–166
Winston (Tropical Cyclone) 31, 38–39, 41–45, 47–49, 109, 211
Winterford, Keren 34–49
Women Markets for Change programme 7, 127
women's savings groups 65
workshop after San Jose de Chamanga earthquake 194–196, 202n9
World Bank 42, 97, 109, 177, 210
World Health Organization (WHO) 46, 98–99, 143, 209
World Humanitarian Summit (WHS) 35–36, 47, 216
World Mayors Council on Climate Change (WMCCC) 54
World Urban Forum (WUF) 142, 145–146
World Vision 14, 63, 84

Yuval-Davis, N. 113–115

zoning of landslide and flood-prone areas **62**

www.ingramcontent.com/pod-product-compliance
Ingram Content Group UK Ltd.
Pitfield, Milton Keynes, MK11 3LW, UK
UKHW021828190125
453847UK00019B/185